S0-ADP-645

WISE COUNSEL

A HISTORY *of* TILLEKE & GIBBINS

THAILAND'S OLDEST LAW FIRM

WISE COUNSEL

A HISTORY *of* TILLEKE & GIBBINS
THAILAND'S OLDEST LAW FIRM

by JOHN HOSKIN

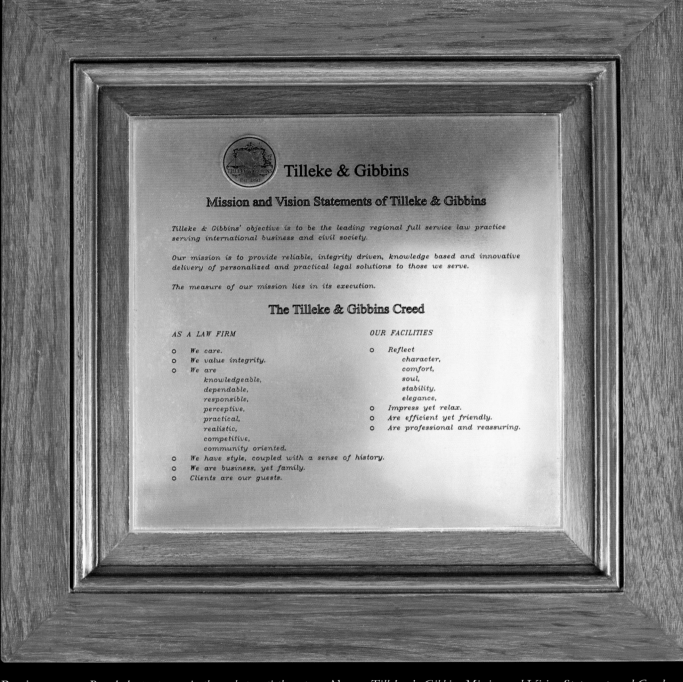

Tilleke & Gibbins

Mission and Vision Statements of Tilleke & Gibbins

Tilleke & Gibbins' objective is to be the leading regional full service law practice serving international business and civil society.

Our mission is to provide reliable, integrity driven, knowledge based and innovative delivery of personalized and practical legal solutions to those we serve.

The measure of our mission lies in its execution.

The Tilleke & Gibbins Creed

AS A LAW FIRM

- *We care.*
- *We value integrity.*
- *We are*
  knowledgeable,
  dependable,
  responsible,
  perceptive,
  practical,
  realistic,
  competitive,
  community oriented.
- *We have style, coupled with a sense of history.*
- *We are business, yet family.*
- *Clients are our guests.*

OUR FACILITIES

- *Reflect*
  character,
  comfort,
  soul,
  stability,
  elegance,
- *Impress yet relax.*
- *Are efficient yet friendly.*
- *Are professional and reassuring.*

Previous pages: *Bangkok street scene in the early twentieth century.* Above: *Tilleke & Gibbins Mission and Vision Statements and Creed written by David Lyman and displayed in the firm's offices.*

Wise Counsel *is dedicated to all present and future members of the T&G family. Here is a record of your heritage and professional cultural identity. Treasure this insight into the roots and endeavours of members of the T&G family in days gone by. Let your actions surpass them. Be extraordinary. Be inspiring. Make your forebears proud of you and of your achievements yet to come as you add to the fabric and history of this great law firm.*

Contents

Bas-relief portrait of William Alfred Goone Tilleke (left) *and court
scene of the 1893 Phra Yod trial, as displayed in the firm's offices.*

BAS-RELIEF PANEL ON MR. WILLIAM ALFRED TILLEKE

During the reign of King Rama V, in the year 1888, a Frenchman named Pavee came to the district of Muang Kammual in Siam and claimed that Muang Kammual belonged to Vietnam, then a colony of France. Thereafter, France sent in Monsieur Grossgurin with Vietnamese and French soldiers to force Phra Yod Muang Kwang ("Phra Yod"), a Siamese Border Commissioner in charge of Muang Kammual, to surrender Muang Kammual to France. Muang Kammual was invaded by French troops, and Phra Yod was arrested and taken together with other hostages to U-Tane Port. During the journey to the Port, Somewhere near Kang Jek, Phra Yod escaped. When he tried to assist in the escape of another hostage, Luang Anuruk, a fight ensued and Monsiuer Grossgurin was killed.

The French, angered, sent two additional warships, the *"Commet"* and *"Angcoston"*, to reinforce the *"Lutin"* stationed in the Chao Phraya River opposite the site of the French Embassy. The French, by gunboat diplomacy, attempted to force the following concessions from the Siamese Government.

• Admission that Muang Kammual was part of Vietnam.

• Withdrawal of Siamese troops and weapons from the left bank of the Mekong River.

• Compensation for all damages and losses incurred during the border hostilities and for damages incurred by a French vessel.

• Punishment for Phra Yod.

• Immediate payment of two million French in reparation.

The Siamese Government was forced to pay the two million French francs and to prosecute Phra Yod.

The case against Phra Yod was heard by seven judges. There were four prosecutors and four defense attorneys. The translation of the proceedings was done by Mr. Morerand. Mr. Tilleke (later known as Maha Ammart Tho Phraya Attakarn Prasiddhi) was the leading defense attorney. On March 17, 1893, the defendant was acquitted.

SCENE DEPICTED IN THE BAS-RELIEF:

LEFT — *William Alfred Tilleke* in his regalia as *Maha Ammart Tho Phraya Attakarn Prasiddhi* sometime between 1911-1919.

TOP — Three warships dispatched by France to be stationed in front of the French Embassy and the famous Oriental Hotel.

MIDDLE — Scene in the courtroom, Sansathityuthitham, during the first trial in special criminal court held on February 24, 1893.

RIGHT CORNER — Seated: three other defense attorneys *Mr. Pet, Mr. Mee* and *Mr. Ked. Mr. Tilleke (Maha Ammart Tho Phraya Attakarn Prasiddhi)* is seen standing in front of the judges with *Mr. Morerand* (translator) standing behind him.

LEFT CORNER — Prosecutors: *Luang Soonthornkosa, Mr. Hussabumruet, Monsieur Dudo* and *Monsieur Hadudin.*

PHRA YOD — Standing in the witness box in front of the Court Registrar.

Sculpted by CHANNARONG KHONGPHOKHAR
November 1987 (B.E. 2530)

Introduction

More than thirty years in the making from conception to delivery, this book on the history of Tilleke & Gibbins ('T&G') is the attainment of one of my dreams. An institution of the age, breadth and variety of experiences, which is the home and workplace of a cast of fascinating and interesting persons, being the repository of thousands of stories and case files that capture the life and times of Siam and Thailand and its people and businesses and governments and organizations and, and, and . . . over the past 120 years, has an obligation to record for posterity, and for the past and future members of the T&G family and our clients and friends, some of the events which have created and sustained us.

What is recorded in these pages of *Wise Counsel* is but a tiny sampling of the varied and myriad cases and files, trials and events, personalities and places to which our lawyers and staff over five generations have committed themselves.

My father Albert Lyman, who along with my mother Freda Ring Lyman purchased T&G in 1951 from its then surviving partner Victor Jaques, was a student of history and a voracious reader. At the insistence of his father he absorbed Tacitus and Plutarch's *Lives* in his early youth, and in turn prodded my sister Lucy and myself to read, read, read. He succeeded more with her than with me. My mother's influence got me started on her whodunit fiction (crime mysteries), my first foray into literature. *Classic Comics* introduced me to history.

With that conditioning I believe it was actually stamp collecting as a boy that sparked my interest in the history of the last century or so. Some of the Thai stamps I pull from letters in old T&G files. The conclusion, which took its time to evolve in my head, was that if the stamps were worth saving, so were the letters and documents from whence they came. By the time I was able to initiate a tangible appreciation for the history of T&G through its files, all of the remaining pre-World War II files had been devoured by white ants in my father's garage. The few other surviving T&G records and documents from prior to 1946 are mentioned in the text of this book.

Despite the absence of what I had expected would be

widespread enthusiasm in the firm for my T&G history project, I and other like-minded souls persisted in gathering every scrap of information we could find on the firm and its partners and luminaries served in the days of yore. Thanks to them we now have a special room dedicated to the storage of our archives. As to be expected, there was a paucity of information about the early days and a deluge of information from modern times, all of which had to be read, researched and catalogued.

I would like to extend my eternal gratitude to all the people who have contributed in countless small and large ways to gathering in the details of T&G and its people from times long past. Of immense help have been the families of Messrs Tilleke, Gibbins, Brighouse, Atkinson, Jaques and Jorgensen, who have dug through their personal memorabilia and memories to provide colour and character to the people and their lifestyles as told here. Anthony Hunt, ex-T&G staff and a retired British Foreign Service officer recorded the voices and stories in England of many of these families.

David Gibbins, grandnephew of Ralph Gibbins and also a solicitor in the UK, fortuitously approached us one day and he and his wife, Frances, generously tried to reassemble personal information about their ancestor; as did a grandniece in Australia, Margaret Machin, who contacted us just last year for information as she is doing her own family history. I then introduced the two cousins who never knew of the other's existence.

The war diary of Eric Deane, who recorded daily life in the Allied civilian internment camp in Bangkok from 1941 to 1945, as well as an unfinished autobiography by Samuel Brighouse, gave us in-depth insights into the lives and work of these men and those surrounding them in Siam.

Bonnie Davis is a treasure trove of information on the personalities and events in Siam in the late nineteenth and early twentieth centuries. I cannot thank her enough for her guidance and contributions to the contents of this history. Rosemary Whitcraft and her Thai researcher colleague Sunida Boonyanon

scoured the National Archives, the Public Prosecutor's office and museum, and other sources for information on the old partners.

Former and present T&G staff contributed their memories to our archives. Ina Jorgensen, the Danish secretary who looked after the interests of the firm during the war years and thereafter headed her own intellectual property law firm, shared her remembrances with us; as did her nephew Carl Zeytoon, who found the original agreement under which Mr Tilleke sold the firm to Messrs Brighouse and Atkinson.

David Hallmark, now the doyen of the solicitors' bar in Worcester, England has an encyclopaedic recollection of his days with the firm in the 1960s. Jack Hanlon, who retired from his second career as our COO and whose first career was 37 years with Goodyear International, made many contributions of the tales and people who influenced us and our growth. Khun Jeerwan ('Ead') was chief of our filing department for many years and allowed us to tap into her virtually photographic memory of our cases.

Karen Bunyaratarvej, then the curator of the Tilleke & Gibbins Textile Collection, with her sense of organization and appreciation of books and history, was the first person to try to bring order to the masses of papers and books and articles and things we had accumulated on T&G's glorious past. Most recently, my former secretary Khun Mayuree ('Mam') devoted many hours of her time to sorting photographs and historical documents to facilitate the research tasks of this book's writer.

After a false start with Paterson and Partners as writers and publishers, David Knapp, a Thai scholar, undertook the first real stab at creating this history book. The task of writing T&G's history passed through successive writers but it was my old friend John Hoskin and his cohort publisher Mark Standen who stayed the course and reduced the 120 years of the firm's activities to the pages before you. Absent their dedication, creativity, persistence and endless patience, my long-time dream of publishing this history book would have remained just a dream. Thank you, all.

David Lyman (aka 'DL')
Chairman and Chief Values Officer
Tilleke & Gibbins, Bangkok, Thailand

October 2009

Electric trams and power cables indicating Bangkok's increasing modernization in the late nineteenth century.

Carpe Diem
1890–1911

William Alfred Goone Tilleke.

When the young barrister William Alfred Goone Tilleke came to Siam in 1890 his future was delicately poised. Already highly accomplished, the 31-year-old Singhalese had left behind security and prestige enjoyed in his native Ceylon to seek his fortune in Siam, Southeast Asia's last surviving independent state. Unknowing but doubtless expectant, he stepped ashore at Bangkok to enter into a life that held not just promise but also the chance, if firmly grasped, to play a significant role in the development of modern Siam.

Just a few months before Tilleke's arrival, *The Bangkok Times* had written of what it thought was the 'excellent opening that exists in Bangkok for a really capable English barrister'. The weekly journal's claim was prompted by its reporting of a law suit brought by a young Englishman who had injured his foot falling off a tram. For *The Bangkok Times*, the pros and cons of the matter were less interesting than the fact that the winner of the suit ran up a bill of 795 ticals in a case lasting from 11 am to 4 pm, with a one-hour interval for lunch. ('Tical' is the old word for the baht, and in the 1890s 795 ticals would have been worth a little under 100 pounds sterling — approximately 5,000 pounds in today's money.)

Then, as today, the topic of exorbitant legal fees is best left to cocktail-hour conversations. *The Bangkok Times* was correct, however, in its assumption of the opportunities awaiting young lawyers, if not for precisely the right reason. Chance lay not so much in financial gain, but rather in the historical moment.

King Chulalongkorn pictured in a lawyer's gown.

Siam in the late 1800s was well set on a path to modernization that would lead it successfully into the twentieth century. King Chulalongkorn, Rama V (1868–1910), was then at the height of a glorious reign in which he brilliantly consolidated and expanded the enlightened policies initiated by his predecessor and father King Mongkut, Rama IV (1851–1868).

Prompted equally by a desire to open Siam to the outside world and by a need to parry the territorial ambitions of the Western imperial powers, especially Britain and France, King Mongkut had signed treaties with powerful European nations, as well as with the United States. These granted not only generous trade concessions, but also certain extraterritorial rights. The latter effectively excluded foreigners from Siamese jurisdiction and so gave rise to consular courts. These were basically foreign courts, separate from the Siamese judicial system, in which cases involving an Englishman or a Frenchman, for example, could only be tried by those countries' consular officials. This inevitably confused Siam's legal system, at the same time creating

The Bowring Treaty

Negotiated by Sir John Bowring, envoy of Britain's Queen Victoria, the Bowring Treaty of 1855 was the first of the historic agreements between Siam and the Western powers that granted generous trade concessions, as well as extraterritorial rights. The lifting of the tariff and monopoly restrictions that Bowring secured heralded a new age of commerce and international relations, but although the negotiations had

been amicable Britain backed its claims with a scarcely veiled threat of force should the talks break down. It is difficult not to read with a cynical eye Bowring's report on the conclusion of the treaty. 'We took departure', he wrote, 'from a country the recollections of which are associated in our minds with nothing but grateful recollections and hopeful anticipations.'

A courtroom scene that would have been familiar to the young Tilleke.

unprecedented opportunities for foreign lawyers.

Extraterritoriality, more than any other concession to the West, became a spur to judicial reform in Siam and, in 1892, two years after Tilleke's arrival, the Ministry of Justice was founded as one of the radical reforms introduced by King Chulalongkorn as part of his ambitious measures to build on his father's achievements in the modernization of Siam.

According to the *Royal Gazette* of 10 April 1892 the ministry was founded to deal with a rapid surge in lawsuits being brought before the courts. 'People are becoming increasingly engaged in trading,' the paper noted, 'thus business dealings among them have intensified.'

Before 1892 there were various types of traditional courts presided over by different ministries. It was an inefficient system that dispensed uneven justice, largely because it relied upon documentary evidence rather than direct examination. With the founding of the Ministry of Justice the judicial system was brought more into line with European practice.

By 1894 new criminal and civil courts had been set up in Bangkok

The introduction of consular courts in the latter half of the nineteenth century provided a stimulus for Siam to reform a legal system that was so archaic and so complex as to defy any foreign effort at comprehension. British lawyers, it appeared, could make it all so simple. In his charming reminiscence Consul in Paradise, *W.A.R. Wood, who joined the British Legation in 1896, notes: 'One of my former colleagues — a barrister — once remarked on the bench: "Law and common sense are synonymous terms." He was, of course, quite wrong. Law and common sense are not synonymous terms, though law and tripe very often are. Justice and common sense are synonymous terms, and any man possessing a little common sense can administer good justice, though he may sometimes need to get round the law in order to do so.'*

(and later in the provinces). Although the jury system was not adopted, there were three judges, the accused was deemed innocent until proven guilty, and there was a Court of Appeal. As described by HRH Prince Chula Chakrabongse, 'The procedure in court was similar to English practices and most of the earlier modern barristers had been called to the English Bar.'

Tilleke, if not English, was a British subject. He was also a thoroughly capable lawyer not inclined to obscurity, much less passivity. His arrival in Siam may not have been better timed for an aspiring young barrister, but he brought with him experience and qualities that were as advantageous as the historical moment.

The eldest of five sons, Tilleke was born on 21 August 1860 in the town of Mahapur in the Kandy territory of central Ceylon. The country, later renamed Sri Lanka, was then under British rule. Although colonial subjects, the family was an illustrious and wealthy one, its patriarchs prominent nobles at the court of Kandy. Tilleke's father, M. Goonetilleke, held the rank of Raja Vasala Mudiliyar, or Royal Gate Chief, the highest title that

Map showing Kandy in Sri Lanka (previously known as Ceylon).

the governor of Ceylon could bestow, and was one of only twelve Singhalese justices of the peace under the British administration. Two of his uncles were eminent scholars of Sanskrit and Pali.

Tilleke himself was to prove a worthy scion of such a family and even as a young student at St Thomas's College in Colombo he distinguished himself as a scholar, editor of the college magazine, and a leading figure in the debating society. After obtaining his college diploma, which made him a member of Calcutta University, he commenced his legal studies in Colombo. Four years later, in 1883,

he was one of only two students from a group of nineteen to pass the two-day test paper set by Chief Justice Burnside, which Tilleke later described as 'one of the severest examinations for admission into the legal profession that had been known up to that time'.

Having been called to the Bar, Tilleke returned to Kandy, a charming town picturesquely perched amid green hills, and immediately set up his own law practice. Within two years he had so established his mark as to be elected a municipal councillor and a magistrate. Yet such early success seems to have brought Tilleke little sense of fulfilment, and the ambitious young lawyer became convinced that his true career must lay elsewhere.

Accordingly, in 1887, at the age of 27, he left Ceylon, going first to India and then moving on to Burma and later to the Straits Settlements (comprised of what are now Malaysia and Singapore). Although we know little of his experiences in these British colonies, Tilleke clearly did not find the opportunity to capitalize on his legal knowledge, nor presumably did he feel he could flourish under British domination, as he finally sought refuge in the only country in South and Southeast Asia that remained free and independent.

Siam was indeed proudly independent. The sense of freedom — more deeply rooted than mere avoidance of colonialism — that is quintessential to the Siamese character would immediately have impressed any new arrival. Tilleke must have felt he could, figuratively, breathe more easily in what was to become his adopted country, but would he have been equally taken by what he saw physically? Most probably, yes. Bangkok, at that time a city of some 400,000 inhabitants, had undergone considerable change during the decade before Tilleke took up residence.

'Ten years ago', reads *The Directory for Bangkok and Siam 1894*, 'Bangkok was made up (in the minds of most persons) of a few mercantile houses in the lower part of the town, the Palace and the Hotel [presumably the Oriental, which officially opened in 1876]. What a change has of late come over this scene! One must remain a month in Bangkok, and steam up her noble river, the Meinam [which means simply 'river' but was long used by foreigners instead of the proper name, Chao Phraya River], before being brought to understand what a beautiful and thriving place it is.'

SIAM, BANGKOK.

Old postcard trumpeting the arrival of the steam train.

Adding convenience to the beauty, the *Directory* points out, was 'the establishment of the Telephone, the Parcel Post, the Electric Light, Electric Tramways, Railways etc., which in the history of any country are events of no ordinary interest'.

But rapid development did not detract from the image of Bangkok as the 'Venice of the East'. The city was dominated by the Chao Phraya River, both banks of which were lined with houseboats two or three rows deep, and a network of canals that spread out from it to form the main communication links. Dominating the cityscape were the tiered orange roofs and gilded spires of countless temples. Just as for today's visitors, the scene would have captivated Tilleke. Although he was himself from an Asian Buddhist country, such is the distinction of Siamese classical architecture that it cannot but have appeared exotic to him.

Yet Tilleke was nothing if not astute, and it is unlikely he would have been dazzled by these scenes beyond a lively first impression. He would have been familiar with both the grandeur and the poverty of British India, and while his Asian eyes may have softened his views, he would most probably have seen the two sides of the picture Bangkok presented, as did turn-of-the-century Belgian traveller Charles Buls:

'From the royal quarter', Buls wrote, 'rise the triple roofs and

Clockwise from top left: *Old postcard and postage stamp of the Rama V era; early view of Bangkok's General Post Office; postcard once commonly used for sending messages locally.*

An early twentieth-century land deed with the necessary stamps to make it a legal document.

Dear Sir,

The undermentioned goods have arrived

per steamer

ex

Goods ex Glamorganshire have arrived to
S.S. Nuen Tung today

१९३४८/११/४० ८८ ८८
९६९६

of which please hand us the through Bill of
Lading in exchange for our Delivery order
and take prompt delivery of same.

The Borneo Company, Limited.

Bangkok ......16...... 1910

Bangkok, located on the banks of the Chao Phraya River, was — and still is —Thailand's main port, and in the days prior to commercial air services it was the major point of entry for both visitors and goods.

triple arrows, golden, sparkling, flaming, characteristic elements of the Siamese architecture. Then, surrounding them, there is a forest of white, golden or enamel spires, flanking numerous temples. The effect is overwhelming for the newcomer. This is the Indies of which one dreams with its fantastic palaces, its golden minarets, its perfumed gardens, concealing in their pavilions, that are inlaid with mother-of-pearl and precious stones, the mysteries of the harem. Later, the mirage will disperse and a more attentive examination will reveal the poverty of all this oriental toy-shop.'

Buls clearly dipped his pen in purple ink, and countered the grandeur with the harsh description of 'toy-shop'. Even so, Bangkok was, and remains, a paradox, wondrous and woeful by turns. Nonetheless it was, in the late nineteenth century, a city on the move, and signs of dynamism would have struck the ambitious Tilleke more than tourist sights or scenes of poverty that can be found in any of the world's capitals. In the bustle of shipping on the Chao Phraya River, in sawmills, rice mills, the packed godowns along the riverbank, and in the commercial district's

imposing offices of the big European trading houses such as the Borneo Company (opened in 1856) and Windsor & Co. (founded in 1873), Tilleke would have seen a city of relentless commercial activity.

Indeed, as *The Directory for Bangkok and Siam 1894* reported, 'The trade of Bangkok has increased enormously within the last few years and now employs, to their fullest capacity, the steamers of the established lines. . . . The year 1893 has been an exceptionally good one with regard to rice and teak exports, probably the best on record . . . there is no doubt that Siam is attracting attention in the outside world as a market, due, in a great measure, to the fact of her steady development.'

Siam was, more than ever before, a land of opportunity and Tilleke joined a lively and expanding community of expatriates keen to make a career for themselves, either in commerce with one of the big trading houses, in developing such alien-sounding businesses as the Oriental Bakery and the Aerated Water Manufactory, or in the service of the Siamese Crown, which then employed

The Oriental

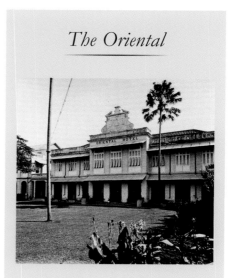

In Tilleke's day, and still now for many travellers, the Oriental was the place — if not quite the only place — to stay in Bangkok. An advertisement for the hotel in The Directory for Bangkok and Siam 1891, *the year after Tilleke's arrival, boldly declared: 'Largest and best appointed hotel in Siam . . . Magnificent view of the Meinam . . . A steam launch conveys passengers and their baggage to and from all Mail Steamers. . . . The splendid new Bar, together with the Billiard Saloon, Reading and Smoking rooms, Ladies Room &c., is fitted with every convenience. The Bedrooms are lofty, well ventilated, and open on to large verandas, with bathrooms.'*

Expatriates at work.

some 200 foreign advisers and experts in fields such as engineering, mining, surveying and finance. All were naturally in need of the professions, not least the legal profession.

Tilleke did not waste time, and eighteen months after his arrival he is named in *The Directory for Bangkok and Siam* as 'solicitor and conveyancer', one of less than a dozen entries in the directory's listing of lawyers. Not only did he quickly set up in practice, he rapidly began to earn a reputation as a legal lion. 'The Cingalese [sic] solicitor seems to be the champion in the local legal lists,' said a July 1892 press report on a case concerning rights to several hundred teak logs in which Tilleke 'had the felicity of securing judgement for Ticals 150 and costs against the clients of Messrs Mitchel and de Souza, barristers-at-law'.

That Tilleke should so quickly establish himself among the elite of Bangkok's legal profession must owe in part to his wealthy family background, his scholastic prowess and his boundless energy. But what thoroughly set him apart was a natural gift for oratory that few of his colleagues and rivals could match. It was this that so impressed the Siamese and which boosted his popularity among all classes as a gifted and resourceful advocate. It must also have helped remove any stigma that in those days might have attached to him as a British Asiatic subject; he appeared frequently before the magistrates of Her Britannic Majesty's Consular Court with the same status as — and commonly with greater effect than — his English and American colleagues.

There was certainly no shortage of work for him at the British Consular Court. The 187-strong British community then resident in Bangkok tended to be litigious, particularly in its habit of starting and dissolving companies with surprising frequency. At the same time the 7,000 or so registered British Asiatic subjects often found themselves in court over altercations with their Siamese neighbours. Whereas his fellow practitioners — puffed up by that sense of elitism so typical of the Western expatriate — frequently distinguished themselves through haughtiness rather than diligence, Tilleke succeeded through exceptional competence and was often retained by British clients in preference to his British-born competitors.

At the same time as Tilleke was building a name for himself in the consular courts, events in the wider arena were taking a turn that would result in the young lawyer being catapulted to fame and national prominence. For some years before his arrival in Siam, the French colonial authorities in Vietnam had been working ceaselessly to realize territorial gains in Laos, control over which had long been contested by Vietnam and Siam, with the latter in the late nineteenth century holding the more effective suzerainty. As historian David K. Wyatt points out, the French were inspired equally by a belief in the economic value of the Mekong valley and by a determination 'to match the growth of the British Empire in Burma with one of their own in Indochina'. France justified its ambitions by claiming that as the 'protector' of the Vietnamese Empire they should succeed to Vietnam's supposed former suzerainty over Laos.

The Gallic claims were, in the words of Wyatt, 'in defiance of historical reality and manufactured for the purpose of imperial aggrandizement', though that made them no less rigidly advocated, and by 1892 the French had begun making armed incursions into areas of Laos not effectively protected by any significant representation from Bangkok. Siam responded by strengthening the powers of its royal commissioners in the border areas of Nong Khai, Ubon and Champasak and beefing up its military defences. This, in turn, was inexplicably viewed by France as unlawful, and its representative in Bangkok, Auguste Pavie, formerly French consul in Luang Prabang, was ordered to express grave concern to the Siamese authorities.

Matters came to a head in early 1893. While Tilleke pursued such legal matters as the case of one Mrs Me Yah, a resident in the vicinity of the Customs House, who was assaulted with murderous intent by three relatives living with her, France announced it had determined that the entire eastern bank of the Mekong rightfully belonged to its Annamese protectorate. Then, when Siamese forces resisted French troops sent into Laos and a French officer by the name of Grosgurin was shot and killed by the Siamese commander, Phra Yod Muang Khwang, France had

The British Consular Court.

Remington, with offices on New Road (left), was the favoured maker of typewriters used in the courts of the past, while fans (below) kept courtrooms cool.

A mock-up in the Court Museum shows how the Attorney General's Office looked at the turn of the twentieth century. An old-style courtroom telephone (right).

its long-sought excuse to force its claim. French gunboats were dispatched to blockade the Chao Phraya River and, contrary to orders from Paris that the boats should stay outside the bar at the mouth of the river, they proceeded up to Paknam, resulting in a short engagement with the Siamese forts guarding the river — what popularly became known as the 'Paknam Incident'.

A witness to the confrontation, H. Warington Smyth, the English director of mines, bluntly pointed out the dilemma in which Siam found itself. 'I doubt if those responsible for the defences', Smyth wrote, 'ever considered what would happen if they succeeded in sinking a French ship. The whole French nation would have risen with a shout, and vengeance could not have stopped short of the conquest of the country.'

Powerless to resist, the Siamese made a bold attempt to defuse the situation by sending Prince Devawongse, head of the Ministry of Foreign Affairs, to congratulate the French on their success in passing the forts at Paknam and to agree to an immediate withdrawal of Siamese troops from the east bank of the Mekong. France,

notwithstanding the flimsiest of grounds for its gunboat diplomacy, pushed home its advantage and outrageously demanded the cession of the whole of Laos east of the Mekong, payment of an indemnity and, interestingly, the punishment of Siamese officers, including

Cover of a popular book at the time of the Phra Yod trial.

Phra Yod, responsible for French casualties in Laos. Siam had little option but to accept and a treaty was signed in October 1893.

This shabby episode in the history of European colonialism in Asia did, ironically, have its bright side for Tilleke, for whom it brought, unbidden, opportunities

to boost his distinction as a lawyer. In their pursuit to gain control over Laos the French worked not only on the military and diplomatic fronts but also more scurrilously by libellous attacks on Gustave Rolin-Jaequemyns, a former Belgian Minister of the Interior who was appointed as general adviser to King Chulalongkorn in 1892 and was much involved in the Franco–Siamese crisis of 1893.

The main vehicle for the attacks was the French-sponsored journal *Siam Free Press*, set up in 1891 as a rival to *The Bangkok Times* by a Mr. J.J. Lillie, described by Virginia Thompson in *Thailand: The New Siam* as 'an Irish rebel and journalistic genius'. Genius maybe, but the Irish rebel in his character came to the fore in one of his most stinging personal attacks on Rolin-Jaequemyns, in which he accused the Belgian of being an agent for England, and heaped scorn on him with terms such as 'treachery', reptile' and 'filthy and wretched trash'. Given the irreconcilable rivalries among Chulalongkorn's brothers and half-brothers, along with a natural Siamese suspicion of Westerners, the accusations inhibited the effectiveness of

Gustave Rolin-Jaequemyns

It was through the support of Gustave Rolin-Jaequemyns, King Chulalongkorn's general adviser, that Tilleke's career was effectively propelled on its meteoric rise. The Belgian's voluminous writings, all of great value in understanding Siam in the 1890s, repeatedly make clear that he demanded, above all else, intelligence and frankness in his associates, which accounts for the favour he showed Tilleke. Himself a man of formidable intelligence — he held honorary degrees from Oxford, Cambridge and Edinburgh in addition to a doctorate of law from his native city of Ghent — Rolin-Jaequemyns remarked on Tilleke's acumen after their first meeting. He also shared the Singhalese lawyer's passion to defend a just cause and a dislike of the might-makes-right spirit that was too often characteristic of the age. In his loyal service to King Chulalongkorn, for which he received a salary of 3,000 pounds a year, he played an outstanding role in the Siamese monarch's programme of reforms, including elaborating a Provisional Code of Criminal Investigation, a Civil Procedure and a Law on Evidence.

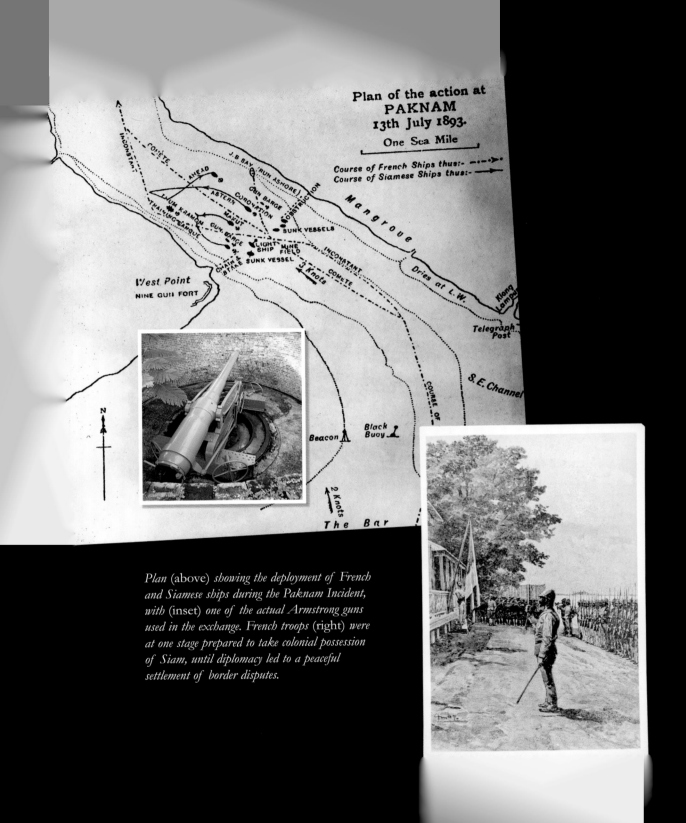

Plan of the action at PAKNAM 13th July 1893.

One Sea Mile

Course of French Ships thus:- ·—·—·—➤
Course of Siamese Ships thus:- ———➤

INCONSTANT

COMÈTE

J.B SAY (RUN ASHORE)

AHEAD

ASTERN

CORONATION

GUN BARGE

OBSTRUCTION

INUM KRAMOM

TRAINING BARQUE

GUN BARGE

MAKUT

SUNK VESSELS

LIGHT SHIP

MINE FIELD

CHAIN &
STAKE   SUNK VESSEL

INCONSTANT

COMÈTE

3 Knots

Mangrove

Dries at L.W.

Klong Lampou

Telegraph Post

S.E. Channel

West Point
NINE GUN FORT

N

COURSE OF

Beacon

Black Buoy

2 Knots

The Bar

Plan (above) showing the deployment of French and Siamese ships during the Paknam Incident, with (inset) one of the actual Armstrong guns used in the exchange. French troops (right) were at one stage prepared to take colonial possession of Siam, until diplomacy led to a peaceful settlement of border disputes.

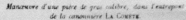

Les Marins et des canons-revolvers Hotchkiss dans la hune de l'aviso INCONSTANT au passage de la Barre du Meinam défendue par les forts de Pac-Nam

Manœuvre d'une pièce de gros calibre, dans l'entrepont de la canonnière LA COMÈTE.

L'INSPECTEUR GROSGURIN
de la Milice Annamite

CONTRE-AMIRAL HUMANN
Commandant en chef la division navale de l'Extrême-Orient

M. PAVIE
Consul Général de France à Bangkok

France's militant stance towards Siam during the Paknam Incident is well illustrated in the coverage of the conflict in a French journal of the day.

Rolin-Jaequemyns and caused him to spend much time writing refutations in *The Bangkok Times.*

Such libels in the *Siam Free Press* would eventually bring the general adviser to Tilleke as a client. Not that the young lawyer had been idle while France and Siam were confronting each other; throughout 1893 he was furthering both his professional career and his social standing in the community. In May he had won a judgement of 240 ticals in the French Consular Court for a woman whose mother had been killed by an 'extraterritorial' cow. In another case, Tilleke appeared with an English barrister in the defence of one Lal Bai, a British Asiatic subject accused of murder, and won an acquittal when no prosecution witnesses responded to summons.

Law, however, was not Tilleke's only professional interest at this time, and with public attention — and apprehension — focused on the French blockade, he busied himself in establishing his own newspaper,

The Siam Observer, in partnership with an American journalist G.W. Ward who served, according to Rolin-Jaequemyns, as editor, writer,

Tilleke (inset) *was a founding partner of* The Siam Observer.

typesetter, printer, proofreader and manager. Although Tilleke's time was soon taken up entirely with legal work, forcing him to sell his share in the *The Siam Observer* to his brother A.F.G. Tilleke, he

had created journalistic history in founding Siam's very first daily, a newspaper that was to flourish until the 1930s.

On Bangkok's select social scene, Tilleke cut a striking figure. A handsome man with a fine head of hair and waxed moustaches, a strong chin showing a determined character, and dark piercing eyes holding a glint of arrogance, he possessed that imposing air of authority and confidence still found in many a British barrister today. Without being cynical, it is clear that Tilleke's personal attributes were greatly enhanced by his inherited wealth. Bangkok's developing British community in the late nineteenth century was elitist and remained so well into the twentieth century. The English old-school-tie mentality prevailed and it is to be wondered if Tilleke, as a British Asiatic — even one with his recognized professional eminence — would have won acceptance in the highest social circles without his financial standing.

That, it scarcely needs saying, is a reflection not on Tilleke but on the British themselves. But wealth alone would have accounted for little without the aristocratic pedigree that Tilleke, as surviving portraits so clearly show, carried with pride. Proof of the social status he had won after just a brief period in Bangkok is evident in the guest list for a public dinner at the Oriental Hotel in honour of the marriage on 6 July 1893 of His Royal Highness the Duke of York to Princess May of Teck (the future King George V and Queen Mary), where Tilleke held ninth place among the 28 named 'British subjects present'.

Tilleke was, however, such an active man with wide-ranging interests that his social prominence came to be based on far more than that of merely being a regular guest at official functions and society dinner parties. Within a year of his arrival in Bangkok, he had acquired a string of horses that made him a leading figure in the city's growing racing set. Outside of his professional work, horse racing remained Tilleke's great passion throughout his life and he was to play such a leading role in the sport's development that he has been

Tilleke, pictured on the left, had a lifelong passion for horse racing.
(Courtesy of The Royal Bangkok Sports Club)

dubbed 'the father of horse racing in Thailand'.

In the late 1800s Bangkok's major venue for horse races was Sanam Luang (or the Pramane Ground, as foreigners generally referred to it), exotically set against the gilded spires and tiered roofs of the Grand Palace and Wat Phra Keo. Officially the site of royal cremations and traditional regal ceremonies, Sanam Luang was also, as it remains today, an area for public recreation and sporting activities, the city otherwise lacking wide-open spaces. Football, golf, even cricket were played here in the latter years of the nineteenth century, and it was here that horse racing first drew aficionados of the turf.

Given the lack of purpose-built facilities, sports at Sanam Luang were rather rough-and-ready events. Golf, for example, was described by W.A.R. Wood, who became British consul in Chiang Mai, as 'quite a ticklish affair on account of the large number of people walking about blithely oblivious to flying golf balls until hit by one'. So, before the nineteenth century drew to an end, moves were afoot to develop venues better suited to the sports that were becoming increasingly popular among

The Royal Bangkok Sports Club, which Tilleke helped found in 1901.
(Courtesy of The Royal Bangkok Sports Club)

The Royal Bangkok Sports Club

(Courtesy of The Royal Bangkok Sports Club)

'The Royal Bangkok Sports Club is an offshoot of the Bangkok Gymkhana Club. It holds a royal charter and the fine racecourse it possesses is held from the Siamese Crown at a peppercorn rental. Race meetings are usually held twice a year, with an occasional sky meeting thrown in. Racing is generally confined to Siamese ponies and it is wonderful how game these little animals run and what times they make.'

J. Antonio,
The 1904 Traveller's Guide to
Bangkok and Siam.

a growing number of Thais and expatriates.

The big breakthrough came in 1901 with the opening of The Royal Bangkok Sports Club (RBSC), which quickly established itself as not only the city's leading sporting venue with, among other facilities, its own racetrack, but also the most elite of social institutions. As a good sportsman and lover of horse racing, Tilleke was one of the prime movers in the founding of The RBSC — as he was also of the Royal Turf Club of Thailand — and served for seven years as clerk of the course. It was this eminence in the sporting world that helped foster a close and lasting friendship between Tilleke and the then crown prince, later King Vajiravudh, Rama VI.

A man to whom accumulation of wealth meant little, but who liked to spend lavishly, Tilleke indulged his love of racing by keeping his own stables — his racing colours were red with a white sash — and even having his own racetrack laid out in the grounds of his home, whimsically named Sans Souci, in the Tungmahamek district. It was here, as family legend has it, that he would encourage his children to place bets on training races.

Nearly matching the sporting fame of the man himself were Tilleke's horses which, according to the 1908 publication *Twentieth Century Impressions of Siam*, 'always

Title page of the informative Twentieth Century Impressions of Siam.

carry off a good proportion of the events at local race meetings'. Most famously, in 1903, Tilleke's runners set a record by winning all seven events in one meet.

Prestige as a sportsman is a mark of the man, illustrative of Tilleke's energy and joie de vivre, and so great was it that it could easily have come to overshadow his memory if it weren't for his even more outstanding reputation as a lawyer.

In September 1893 Tilleke was retained by Rolin-Jaequemyns through the recommendation of the British minister-resident, Captain Henry Jones. The libels against the Belgian in the *Siam Free Press* had continued — in spite of Lillie, the paper's editor, having been attacked in the street and badly beaten by some outraged young Siamese — and could no longer be ignored. As recorded in his diary, Rolin-Jaequemyns decided to sue: 'Because I have to do with a journalist who is sold to France and who makes a profession of personally attacking everybody who is not seen with a good eye by the French legation, it appears that there is some kind of public duty in tearing off their mask'.

The case came to court in November and the ruling was in favour of Tilleke's client. Rolin-Jaequemyns was enough impressed with his solicitor's performance that he made a special visit to convey personally his thanks two days after the trial. The outcome of the libel suit for Tilleke was to thrust him onto an even bigger stage. In the following

weeks, as Rolin-Jaequemyns drafted a royal proclamation creating a special court to try the unfortunate Phra Yod — whose prosecution for killing a French officer was demanded by the recently signed Franco–Siamese treaty — the Belgian decided that his own legal champion should play a key role in the defence. It was

Popular Thai graphic books told the Phra Yod story.

this impending exposure to the international limelight that was to launch Tilleke on a career of outstanding service to Siam.

The trial opened on 24 February 1894 at the Court of Appeal, where the Ministry of Justice remained until the end of the twentieth century when it was moved to its present site on Chaengwattana Road in the north of Bangkok.

For an idea of the setting, in *Siamese Sketches* Charles Buls described a typical Siamese criminal court at the turn of the century: 'The courts are installed in a vast edifice, in classical style, washed with yellow, in front of the square of the Royal Palace. The interior divisions are modelled on those of Western courts. It is a large rectangular room. At one of the extremities there is a platform for the Court. On the left, the bench of the accused and their defence. On the right, the Prosecution, a police officer and the lawyers of the Civil Prosecution. In the centre, the benches of the witnesses, at the back of which are a table for press reporters and benches for the public. . . . On the wall, there are two altars in front of which the witness must take the oath, one group before the Buddha, the other before a Chinese god. This oath is very long and contains a host of religious threats against false testimony. The Court is composed of a president and three judges.'

Buls added that the president he saw wore a black robe on top of his Siamese costume and 'seems to be rather hot under this double cover'.

The special court convened to try Phra Yod had seven, not three, judges, but otherwise it would have been similarly configured. However, what made this case different from any ordinary criminal proceedings was the intense public interest it aroused. Crowded within and without the courtroom were 'ministers, consuls, government officials, gentlefolk and common people', in the words of Sujarit Thavornsuk, who published an account of the Phra Yod story. It wasn't simply the international ramifications of the case that stirred interest (it was obvious that a Siamese court would be inclined to acquit, and that justice was overwhelmingly on Phra Yod's side), and the question that provided the suspense was whether Tilleke and the rest of the defence counsel (which also included an English barrister and two Siamese lawyers) could argue so convincingly that France would accept a verdict of Not Guilty.

Tilleke photographed at the time of the Phra Yod trial.

Tilleke came to the fore when he began his cross-examination of principal prosecution witness Bun Chan, the Cambodian interpreter of the slain French officer Grosgurin, in which he succeeded in establishing a pattern that became clearer and clearer as the trial proceeded: Bun Chan's account had a persistent tendency to change with repetition.

The result of the lengthy cross-examination, which was gruelling for both parties — with Bun Chan granted a rest period in between due to illness and Tilleke retiring at the end of it with a fever — was that Bun Chan's testimony, believed damning by the French, sounded hopelessly unconvincing.

The trial continued with the defence calling Phra Yod to the stand. His testimony, together with that of defence witnesses called later, differed from Bun Chan's most importantly on the question of whether the French forces of Grosgurin or the Siamese under Phra Yod opened fire first.

Finally, on 17 March 1894 the judges reached their verdict. It was read by the chief justice, His Royal Highness Prince Bijit Prijakorn, who prefaced the court's judgement with an expression of thanks to the contending counsel and to the recorder for their good work in a historic case 'whose effects on the future we are unable to foretell'. Prince Bijit further asked the French government representative 'to be understanding and sympathetic, realizing and recognizing that we have all tried to adhere to justice and honesty in our work at all times'. The verdict: a unanimous Not Guilty.

It came as no surprise that Prince Bijit's plea to the French representative fell on deaf ears. France wanted a conviction and, holding the upper hand in their relations with Siam, they would settle for no less. A second trial was held in June 1894 at the French Legation with a mixed court of three French and two Siamese judges, while for good measure a French gunboat was moored on the river outside the legation. As the court insisted all questioning be in French, Tilleke's role was that of advisor to the defence attorney, M. Duval. That Duval put up a spirited defence was to no avail, and the French judges listened only perfunctorily

Ralph Henry Bryan Gibbins.

before bringing in a verdict of Guilty. Phra Yod was sentenced to twenty years imprisonment although, hailed as a national hero, he served only four years before being granted a pardon.

The trials of Phra Yod are likely to be deemed infamous in the annals of jurisprudence as they served not the ends of justice, but merely the gratification of a vengeful Gallic colonial mentality.

In a way, however, a certain good, if not justice, did result: the trials brought sympathy for Siam in Britain and much of Europe, and prompted King Chulalongkorn to accelerate reforms that would help safeguard his country's sovereignty and further its prosperity. Tilleke also benefited, being propelled into further prominence that secured his own personal prosperity, as well as affording him a role in shaping the reforms of the nation.

While high public office would later be bestowed on Tilleke, the immediate impact of the Phra Yod trials was an enormous boost to his private law practice as commemorated today in the bas-relief at the firm's present offices. An augmented list of clients now more than justified a partnership. However, it was not until early in the new century that Ralph Henry Bryan Gibbins joined Tilleke and so brought into being what was, and which remains today, the most illustrious name in Thailand's list of law firms. Strangely, given the fame and longevity of the company, the partnership was remarkably short- lived.

Ralph Gibbins is something of a mystery, as family researches shed little light on his background and early life. It is known that he was born in 1873 at Havant in Hampshire, England, the eldest of eleven children, and it is safe to assume he had an upbringing typical of the upper middle class of his day. His name next surfaces at Middle Temple, the London Inn of Court, where he was registered as a student in 1898. His record there tells that he was 'late of the 4th Dragoon Guards', and so presumably, at the age of 25, he had abandoned a military career to take up law. In this he proved successful,

Gibbins in Dragoon Guards uniform.
(Courtesy of Margaret Machin)

being called to the Bar on 18 November 1901.

The reference to Gibbins having been in the Dragoon Guards is intriguing, since it is just

possible that his military service may have taken him to Siam where, as a visiting British officer in what was a small expatriate community, he could well have met Tilleke at some social or consular function. That, however, is merely speculation, although it is one way of accounting for why Gibbins decided to try his luck in Bangkok almost as soon as he had qualified. That Gibbins did quickly travel East is substantiated by a letter dated 3 May 1902 from Tilleke to the Siamese Minister of Justice, HRH Prince Rajburi concerning the hiring of a European assistant to help with work in the consular courts.

In the letter, Tilleke informed the minister that the 'steadily increasing' volume of government

A Growing Profession

'The [Bangkok] law school was started in 1897, and the average number of students has been annually increasing. The number on the books last year was 375, and the previous year 292, so that is evident that the judicial career and practice in the Siamese courts is becoming more attractive.'

A. Cecil Carter, ed.,
The Kingdom of Siam 1904.

His Royal Highness Prince Rajburi, Minister of Justice at the time when Gibbins joined the firm.

work in the various consular courts was such that 'it often happens that cases are so that I have to be at the same hour in two different courts'. To solve the obvious difficulty, Tilleke proposed 'that Mr. Gibbins be appointed a Crown Advocate with a small salary, say Ticals 240 a month, to help me generally in Government prosecutions in the Consular Courts'.

As a testimonial for Gibbins, Tilleke noted that 'he has already appeared in two jury cases for the Police Department, and has also appeared in three or four nationality enquiries, and I can testify to his general capabilities and careful work.'

The letter further notes that Tilleke had already 'engaged' Gibbins 'to assist me in my private practice'. So in the absence of any other surviving relevant record, it is reasonable to assume that the Tilleke and Gibbins partnership dates from 1902, although the firm may not have been officially incorporated until 1903 (the date given by future partner Victor Jaques when he sold the practice to Albert Lyman

The Ministry of Justice.

AGREEMENT made on the 30 day of March, 1909 between His Royal Highness Prince Rajburi Direk-rit, Minister of Justice, acting on behalf of His Siamese Majesty's Government for himself and his successors in Office,(hereafter called the Minister) of the one part and Ralph B. H. Gibbins, Barrister-at-Law, of the other part.

It is hereby mutually agreed by the said parties as follows :-

1. The said Ralph B. H. Gibbins shall enter the service of the Ministry of Justice as Assistant Legal Adviser for the term of five years and thereafter for an indefinite period. He shall devote the whole of his time to the said service, shall refrain from engaging in any other employment, profession or calling shall perform such duties as may be reasonably expected of him by virtue of his appointment to the best of his ability and power, and shall conform to and be bound by the general rules and practice of the Siamese Government on all points not specifically mentioned in this Agreement.

2. The said Ralph B. H. Gibbins shall receive from the first day of April 1909 a salary of Ticals five hundred (Tics.500) per month rising by annual increments of Ticals eighty (Tics.80) per month to a maximum salary of Ticals twelve hundred (Tics.1,200) per month.

The first two increments shall not become due

Agreement of Gibbins' appointment as Assistant Legal Adviser to the Ministry of Justice.

in 1951). One definite date is 3 December 1903, when Gibbins married Louisa Mary Davy in Singapore.

As to Gibbins' professional partnership, no hard evidence survives on which to base a judgement, although it is known that the firm was involved in several famous cases in the early 1900s. For example, in 1906 Tilleke & Gibbins was engaged in a long trial concerning settlement of the estate of the famous Admiral John Bush, founder of the Bangkok Dock Company and former harbourmaster.

Such important cases do suggest a successful partnership, and this is supported by the company name's survival. If the partnership had not been a success, Tilleke would scarcely have retained joint names when Gibbins left the firm, nor indeed would he have stipulated the company name be unchanged when he later sold the business.

The successes Gibbins must have enjoyed in private practice ended when he opted to further his legal career by entering government service.

Samuel Brighouse (top) *and
Reginald Douglas Atkinson* (above).

On 1 April 1909 the partnership was dissolved 'by mutual consent', with the business continuing 'to be carried on in the name of Tilleke & Gibbins as heretofore by W.A.G. Tilleke alone,' while Gibbins took up the post of Assistant Legal Adviser in the Siamese Ministry of Justice, posted initially in Chiang Mai and later in Bangkok.

Gibbins was clearly enamoured with Siam. In 1916 he became an adviser to, and judge of, the International Court in Bangkok (a court where the consul of an accused foreign national was allowed to sit as adviser), and a decade later was awarded a similar position in the Court of Appeal. He finally left Siam in 1931, the year before the bloodless revolution that changed the nation's form of government from an absolute to a constitutional monarchy. Although there is no direct proof, it is possible that Gibbins may have been aware of the coming revolution and, uncertain as to how it would affect his status, opted to secure his pension and take retirement. He died in England in 1944 at the age of 71.

Tilleke carried on his firm's business for only two years after Gibbins left the partnership before he, too, chose to devote his career to

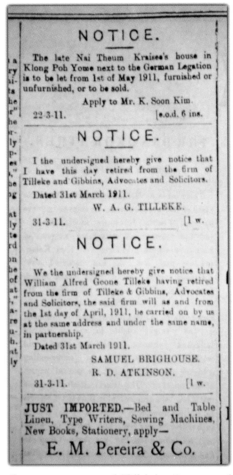

*Press announcement of Tilleke's retirement and
the establishment of a new partnership.*

government service, albeit at a more illustrious level than that of his former partner. So, in 1911, he sold the firm to two of his foreign associates, Samuel Brighouse and Reginald Douglas Atkinson. It is often a matter of amusement, if not bewilderment, that law firms tend to keep company titles bearing

THIS AGREEMENT entered into at Bangkok on the 1st day of March 1911 Between WILLIAM ALFRED GOONE TILLEKE of Bangkok (herein - after called the party of the first part) of the first part, SAMUEL BRIGHOUSE also of Bangkok of the second part and REGINALD DOUGLAS ATKINSON also of Bangkok of the third part. WITNESSETH that the said party of the first part who has for the past twenty years carried on business in Bangkok as Solicitor and Advocate first in his own name, and later in the name and style of Tilleke & Gibbins takes into partnership the said Samuel Brighouse and Reginald Douglas Atkinson preparatory to a sale of the whole business to them.

It is mutually agreed as follows :-

1.   That all sums of money due as fees to the firm up to the 31st December 1910 shall belong solely to the party of the first part and all sums of money due by the firm of Tilleke & Gibbins to clients and others up to such date shall be paid solely by the said party of the first part.

2.   That all money due to the firm from the 1st day of January 1911 to the 31st day of March 1911 shall belong to the party of the first part, to Samuel Brighouse and to Reginald Douglas Atkinson in the proportions of one third each and all moneys due by the firm from the date to the 31st March 1911 shall also be payable by them in the same proportions.

3.   In the matter of work undertaken before the 1st of January 1911 and not completed by that time a statement shall be made out showing how much shall be allocated for work done previous to and subsequent to the said date and a similar statement shall be made regarding work undertaken after the

them shall prior to so leaving make
of the first part for the payment
s or for the transfer of the payment
they become due and on failure to
party of the first part shall be
lance due on the said Promissory
diatley due and payable.

rniture and law books save and except
add party of the first part and the
all account books after the year
erty of the said Samuel Brighouse
son. The said W.A.G.Tilleke however
ver necessary to refer to any of
hours and if need be to take any

the first part undertakes not to
way the Promissory Notes given by the
Reginald Douglas Atkinson until the
fteen days after their due date and
intention to discount or pledge.
of the said parties have hereunto set
the day, month and year first above

In presence of

The original Sale of Business Agreement between Mr Tilleke the seller, and Messrs Atkinson and Brighouse, the buyers, complete with their signatures.

Shooting The Goat

THE BANGKOK TIMES
WEEKLY MAIL.

Selected from the daily issues of the "Bangkok Times" for the use of readers in Europe Australia, America, and Ch——

Vol. X., No. 8.]　　FRIDAY,　FEBRUARY 23, 1906.

YOU NEED A PAIR OF

HENA BOOTS

They are just what you were looking for—

Comfortable, Durable, and Smart.

Made (both Ladies' and Gentlemen's) in every description of Leather to either Button or Lace, and in so many shapes, sizes, and fittings that there is **NO FOOT WE CANNOT CLOTHE WITH COMFORT.**

PRICE: **16/6 & 21/-.**　CARRIAGE PAID TO ANY PART OF THE BRITISH EMPIRE.

When ordering send size or outline of foot (standing) on paper.

HENRY W. HALL & Co., LTD., 42, OLD BROAD STREET, LONDON.

—————

HE BANGKOK TIMES.

FRIDAY, 16TH FEBRUARY, 1906.

Mr. Balfour has yielded at last, and the onist Party is definitely committed to policy of a general tariff. He had I told very bluntly that if he didn't ept Mr. Chamberlain's policy his dership of a united party was at an d. In his latest pronouncement Mr. amberlain himself insisted that the rty must meet and settle its future icy. If the majority were in favour of pping fiscal reform, he wrote, a new organisation would be formed to work for that reform, since he, for one, would have nothing more to do with a policy of inaction or mystification in regard to the main object of his political life. Before the meeting, however, Mr. Balfour managed, in the old phrase, to "find salvation." He makes the well-worn excuse to himself that if he has to accept a general tariff it is to be quite a small one. Such a tariff is to Mr. Balfour unobjectionable in principle; to Mr. Chamberlain it is eminently desirable. But Mr. Chamberlain is not quibbling about unimportant details. His policy is now the policy of the Party; Unionist free traders will have to get out, for Mr. Balfour will no longer be able to juggle with words so that both sections can claim him as their leader. It is true the country has pronounced with remarkable emphasis against fiscal reform, but the country can change its mind, and now that the Unionist Party knows its own mind it should have a much better chance of success when next a general election comes round.

REUTER'S TELEGR——

BALFOUR AND CHAMBERL——
AGREEMENT REACHE——

London, February 16th—Mr. —— four, the ex-Premier, writing —— Chamberlain, says he holds th—— reform must remain the first con—— work of the Unionist Party.

He considers a moderate gene—— on manufactured goods and —— duty on foreign corn unobject—— principle.

Mr. Chamberlain, in his repl—— agrees, gladly accepts the po—— places his services entirely —— Balfour's disposal.

THE UNIONIST PART——

The meeting of the Unionist —— unanimously passed a vote of —— in Mr. Balfour.

Mr. Chamberlain cordially —— this.

But the Duke of Devonshire —— to agree with the fiscal policy —— shortly summon a meeting of —— Free Traders.

[Despatched to subscribers to —— service at 2 P. M.[February 16.]

SPECIAL GERMAN SE——
(The " Ostasiatischer Lloyd[" ——

THE MOROCCO CONFER——

Berlin, February 15th—— received a confidential memo—— taining proposals, supported —— of the Powers, regardi—— the Bank questions in —— The Conference has furthe—— Customs question.

M. Rouvier, in a comm—— Prince von Radolin, has exp—— gret at the anti-German polemics of the (French) Press.

—————

SHOOTING THE GOAT.

——o——

Mr. **J. R.** Bell lives somewhere up Citywards, and he has a compound wherein he cultivates flowers and shrubs. Now, he has, aforetime, been annoyed by the incursions of divers goats, fowls and other domestic pets belonging to certain natives of India who live adjacent. He had also had some dispute with the Indians about the erection on their part of a small wooden building next to his fence, which was an offence; so much so that he notified the Sanitary Department, which had the building removed. Thereupon the invasion of this goat occurred. The other morning he saw the goat browsing on the choicest results of his horticulture. This spectacle constituted the last straw, so he took up an air gun and fired two pellets at the goat. The goat went on browsing, but was presently removed by its owners.

This, however, was not the end of it, for Mr. Bell soon after received a document from the British Court for Siam " to show cause" etc. So he duly appeared before his Honour Judge Skinner Turner this morning. Mr. Beddard appeared for the goat's owners, Messrs. Gibbins and Saye for Mr. Bell. Mr. Gibbins pleaded guilty to the shooting on behalf of his client, but urged extenuating circumstances.

His Honour fined Mr. Bell five shillings and fifty shillings costs, for which sum Mr. Bell might, one would think, have bought the goat (with something to spare) and enjoyed mutt n chops for several days.

The Bangkok Times Weekly Mail, *23 February 1906.*

names of long-demised partners, with new partners being generally added to the list. Tilleke & Gibbins, however, has always been just that in spite of, as will be noted later, several outstanding partners in its later history. Of course, Tilleke was an historic figure — as well as a larger-than-life character — and it seems only just that his name should live on in the company he founded.

That Tilleke should culminate his career at the Siamese Ministry of Justice is not surprising considering his involvement with government service dating back almost to the beginnings of his private practice in Bangkok. Two years after the Phra Yod trials of 1894, Tilleke was made a public prosecutor, and

HM King Vajiravudh in legal attire.

a year later was promoted to Acting Attorney General, serving in this capacity until he was appointed Attorney General in 1902 by the royal command of King Chulalongkorn. His government contracts permitted him to continue in private practice, although Tilleke must have increasingly delegated more and more of the company's work to his juniors long before he decided to sell out.

The last years of his life were marked by ever-greater honours, though for such an energetic man there was no resting on laurels. The year 1910 was publicly momentous for Siam and personally so for Tilleke. In that year King Chulalongkorn died and was succeeded by King Vajiravudh,

In Jail

'The Siamese seem to attach little importance to individual liberty. Also, one uses and abuses imprisonment with an almost amusing ease. . . . Is one afraid an important witness will be missed at the rendezvous? He will stay in jail until the case is closed. The plaintiff himself is sometimes locked up to ensure that he will not disappear and thereby ridicule the court. Sometimes it happens that in a particular case everyone is in jail, except for the judges and the lawyers.'

Mr and Mrs Emile Jottrand,
In Siam: The Diary of a Legal Adviser of King Chulongkorn's Government, *1905.*

William Tilleke's wife Khuny[...] (above) with their four childr[en ...] the left) Sawang, Pitswong, [... (later Air Chief Marshal) and Prase[...] Tilleke's funeral in Bangkok [...] (Courtesy of Thipvibha Guna-T[...]

Pictured in Ceylon circa 1940[...] is Tilleke's youngest sister Eth[el ... right of centre) with her hu[sband ...] Edward; behind them their da[ughter] Ethel Jnr stands next to her [...] Guy Wikramanayake (centr[e ...]

Rama VI, while around this time Tilleke became a Siamese subject by naturalization.

Friendship between Tilleke and King Vajiravudh, resulting from a mutual interest in horse racing when the latter was still crown prince, continued to flourish after he acceded the throne and in 1912 the high esteem in which King Vajiravudh held the lawyer was made official when he bestowed upon him the title Phra Attakarn Prasit, making Tilleke the first foreigner so to be honoured.

Also during this reign it became the custom for surnames to be royally bestowed, and King Vajiravudh duly confirmed Tilleke's family name as Gunatilaka. In a certificate of confirmation His Majesty wrote: 'I see that the current surname of yours is fit and suitable . . . the word Guna, which forms an integral part of your original surname, considerably satisfies me. For, that word, when added to Tilaka, has a well meaning, sweet to the ear and so blessed a name. . . . May the surname Gunatilaka be blessed with perpetual prosperity, happiness and existence in the Kingdom of Siam.'

Titles and royal honours continued to be bestowed, and so numerous were they that it will

suffice to mention just the last two: in 1915 Tilleke was appointed a privy councillor and in 1917 he was awarded the most prestigious title of Maha Ammart Tho.

On 7 March 1917, a few days after suffering a heart attack, Gunatilaka, Phra Attakarn Prasit, but best known to posterity simply as Mr Tilleke, died at his Sans Souci home. He was 58. That evening, King Vajiravudh, who was away from Bangkok, telegrammed Tilleke's brother, Phraya Singhalasakhon: 'Much grieved to learn of the death of your brother whereby I have lost a valued official and a valued friend.'

During his life, Tilleke clearly had an eye for the ladies, and fathered thirteen children from numerous wives (polygamy being the norm for the Siamese aristocracy of the time). This perhaps accounts for the fact that he built more than ten houses in the lane that still bears his name, Soi Attakarn Prasit, which leads off the top of South Sathon Road.

One of the most charming stories of Tilleke's amorous life is told by Khun Sarirusm Bulpakdi Chunhakasikarn, a young lawyer who joined the firm in 1999. Knowing of no family relationship

William Tilleke's house, 'Sans Souci', where he died on 7 March 1917. Still today, the street bears his name.

to Tilleke when she applied for the job, she recognized some names when given a piece of company history as a translation test, and this prompted her to probe more deeply into her ancestors' background.

Khun Sarirusm discovered that her great grandmother, Khun Wad, was the sister of Luang Ram Kosa, at one time treasurer of Lop Buri,

Successful Siblings

All of Tilleke's four brothers followed his example and made successful careers overseas. In Siam, he was joined by his first and third younger brothers, both of whom distinguished themselves and became Siamese citizens. The elder, A.F. Tilleke, was for many years Deputy Director-General of the Harbour Department, attaining the title of Phraya Singhalasakhon, while the younger, Dr R.E. Tilleke, was head of Vajira Hospital and was made Phra Virachvejjakij. Tilleke's second younger brother, E.W. Goonetilleke, was manager of the P & O docks and warehouse in Singapore, and the youngest, E.R. Goonetilleke, was an electrical engineer in London.

whose daughters were renowned for their culinary skills. It so happened that Tilleke accompanied King Chulalongkorn on a visit to Lop Buri, for which Luang Ram Kosa's daughters prepared a banquet. Tilleke apparently savoured the beauty of the daughters as much as the taste of their cooking.

He later found an excuse to return to Lop Buri and wooed ardently one of the daughters, Lady Pua. Luang Ram Kosa was at first reluctant to give his daughter's hand in marriage to a dark-skinned foreigner. Eventually, however, he was won over by Tilleke's persistence and the marriage duly took place. Lady Pua, one of her sisters and Khun Wad then moved into Tilleke's burgeoning Bangkok household. Khun Wad eventually left when she found her own true love, but her and her niece's association with Tilleke means that one of the company's lawyers today can claim a relationship by marriage, albeit many times removed, to the firm's founder.

In addition to what must have been a charmed personal, social, and professional life lived to the full, Tilleke also played a

Offices of The Siam Electricity Co. Ltd.

significant role in the commercial and industrial development of his adopted country. At one time or another he was chairman of the Bagan Rubber Company, a director of the Bangkok Manufacturing Company, and was on the boards of the Siam Tramways Company and the Paknam Railway Company, among others. He further assisted in the formation of Siam Cement, becoming the first chairman of what is today one of Thailand's leading companies.

Ultimately, however, the founder of Tilleke & Gibbins should most fittingly be remembered as serving on the drafting committees for Penal Law, the Constitution of the Courts of Justice and Civil Procedure, and the Civil and Commercial Code. He not only practised law, he helped reform it.

William Alfred Goone Tilleke, Phra Attakarn Prasit, in ceremonial attire.

Samuel Brighouse was a stickler for proper form and social niceties. Even his casual dress had a formal look to it.

A Golden Era
1911–1941

On 1 April 1911 Samuel Brighouse and Reginald Douglas Atkinson became the new owners of Tilleke & Gibbins. The purchase fee was 'a substantial sum in those days', as Mr Atkinson's widow recalled in a 1987 interview, and the agreement was that it should be paid over a six-year period. In one of life's sad ironies, the final instalment was made in 1917, the year of Mr Tilleke's death.

At the time of sale, Brighouse had already been with the firm for four years, while Atkinson had joined the company in 1910, and the transition to new partners caused no ripples in the smooth running of the practice. Indeed, this was the dawning of a golden era.

In the first half of the twentieth century, Siam, renamed Thailand in

Atkinson in tropical white suit.

1939, saw the heyday of expatriate life. Foreign businesses flourished, especially the big trading houses such as the Borneo Company and the East Asiatic Company; their bosses, the 'Number Ones,' ruling the roost in a highly structured colonial environment. The fact that Siam, unlike all of its immediate neighbours, had never been colonized did not stop the British, European and American communities from pursuing with considerable success an imperial lifestyle, at least amongst themselves. Hospitable as always, the Siamese accommodated the situation without sacrificing their own integrity.

Under Brighouse and Atkinson, both of whom were British, Tilleke & Gibbins was well attuned to the ethos of the age and maintained the role its founder had established. As Atkinson's widow later described the company, it represented 'most of the leading firms in Bangkok at the time and many of the very important people in those days'. The former included the Bombay Burma

Trading Corporation, and the East Asiatic, Anglo–Thai and Borneo companies, while the latter ranged from royalty to a certain Mr Yee Ko Hong, a Chinese who ran 'all the gambling dens and lotteries up and down the country' until such activities were outlawed in 1917.

Not only in its practice did the firm keep the prestige of the past; in its personality it also reflected something of the colourful presence of Tilleke himself. This was an age when companies were still effectively stamped by the characters of their owners, and Brighouse and Atkinson, especially the former, were certainly 'characters', fully men of their times.

In spite of youthfully claiming he wanted to be a cattle auctioneer and admitting that he 'never had the slightest inclination towards law', Samuel Brighouse seemed destined from birth for a legal career. Born on 11 July 1881 at Ormskirk in the English county of Lancashire, Brighouse was the youngest of three sons (there were also six daughters, two of whom died at an early age). His father was an eminent solicitor

in the area, also a coroner of repute and an influential figure in local politics, and he was determined that his sons should succeed him in his practice. Sam went along with the paternal expectations, but his was a forceful and fiercely independent personality, and it was clear from the first that his life would be led on his own terms.

Pre-World War II offices of the Borneo Company, one of Bangkok's leading trading firms.

'I never took to school life; I hate having to do anything by the bell and I didn't like being persuaded by anyone to work,' he wrote in a fragment of unpublished memoirs. This probably accounts for his earliest memory of school, in which he recalled 'standing on a desk with a dunce's cap on my head'. Yet he was no fool and he excelled and took enormous personal pride in

any subject he truly liked. At school this was carpentry, and in his memoirs he describes making a tool box that was 'perfect' and of which he was 'very proud'. So proud that later in life he tried in vain to buy it back from the joiner to whom he had sold it when he needed money for his passage to Siam.

Otherwise, he viewed his school career at Bloxham, near Banbury in Oxfordshire, with cynicism. 'Religion seemed to be the main object of the school and there was chapel three or four times a day, he wrote. 'Since leaving I've hardly attended a church service except for weddings and funerals.' As for the masters, he said that all he learned from them was 'human nature and how awful and shallow it is'.

It would be a mistake to conclude that Brighouse was a gloomy man. Blunt and honest, perhaps, not suffering fools gladly, but also a man who delighted in the pleasures of life that appealed to him. When articled to one of his father's partners and studying for his law exams, he indulged with sheer enjoyment, as he makes clear in his memoirs, the sports of pheasant shooting and golf. Then, when the Boer War broke out at the close of the nineteenth century, Brighouse showed himself a man of action. In 1900 he joined the Lancashire Hussars, swearing that he was twenty years old when in fact he was still only nineteen. He served in Africa for the last eighteen months of the war, saw action, and was awarded the Queen's Medal with five clasps.

On his return to England, Brighouse completed his final law exams only to find that his father's office could not fulfil its promise; there was not even a partnership available for his eldest brother. After a few weeks of working as a junior in the family firm he spotted an advertisement in *The Times*: 'Wanted: Assistant Legal Adviser to His Siamese Majesty's Government.' The job was offering a salary of 375 English pounds a year plus an unfurnished house.

School Report

'I'm afraid the world has not much use for your class of boys.'

Brighouse's headmaster's words of farewell on his leaving school.

Brighouse duly applied and was called to what turned out to be a somewhat bizarre interview in London. He was asked if he was musical, which he wasn't, and was told that that was a pity as Siamese is a tonal language. More illogically, he was asked if he could ride a bicycle, to which he answered 'backwards'. In spite of these unpromising replies, Brighouse was offered the job and accepted. Announcing this to his father, the elder solicitor retorted, 'You must be a damn fool, and where the hell is Siam?' Undeterred, the young man sailed for the East in early 1907 aboard the SS *Gamba Maru*.

Brighouse's ship docked at Singapore from where, as was the usual routing in those days, he took a coaster, the *Nuen Tong*, a regular mail packet, for the last leg of the journey to Bangkok. Like other new arrivals at the time, Brighouse was recommended to stay initially at the Oriental, where he discovered the charms of this illustrious hotel were more than its brochures advertised. There', he recalled, 'I met the proprietor named Madame Toni. I think she had the biggest bust of any woman I have met, and I found afterwards that she was quite a local character.' (It seems that

A scene from the Boer War, in which Brighouse saw action.

in this instance Brighouse's memory was at fault: Madame Toni was the proprietor of the Hotel de la Paix, not the Oriental.)

The attractions of Brighouse's first accommodation in Bangkok were not, however, matched in any way by his post at the Ministry of Justice. Taking up his position of Assistant Legal Adviser, he firstly discovered he wasn't expected, and then found that he had 'absolutely nothing to do there except collect my salary at the end of the month'. He lasted in government service only three months before joining

Shipboard Romance

Shipboard romances between girls travelling to the East to join their fiancés and young men returning from home leave were common on the long voyages from England to Asia. The affairs were usually disastrous. Brighouse told the story of a friend, named Hall, who worked for the Borneo Company in Chiang Mai and built a lovely house in anticipation of receiving his bride-to-be. But when he went to Penang to meet her ship, his fiancée told him she intended to remain on board and marry a fellow passenger when they reached Hong Kong. Resigned, Hall returned to his empty house in Chiang Mai. However, it happened that when the ship reached Hong Kong the young lady's newfound beau announced he wouldn't marry her after all. So the girl telegraphed Hall in Chiang Mai saying she was now prepared to marry him. His telegraphed reply was, 'Go to Hell'.

Tilleke & Gibbins as a junior. His career as a lawyer in Bangkok now began in earnest, and in 1908 Brighouse and Tilleke appeared for Wang Lee & Co. in a case concerning the collision of lighters on the Chao Phraya River. Later in the same year Brighouse actually represented his employer in a dispute over the sale of a racehorse, which was heard in the British Consular Court.

Partners in court, Tilleke and Brighouse seemed equally partners in sport. As well as having a passion for golf, Brighouse was also a lover of horse racing and quickly established himself, probably with Tilleke's help, as a prominent member of The Royal Bangkok Sports Club and The British Club. As early as 1908 he was on the committee of The RBSC and later, in 1931, served a term as chairman. From 1911 onwards he was the club's lawyer, a professional role that was not to be eclipsed by his sporting activities, which included twice winning The RBSC's golf championship. On the horse racing scene he served at various times as starter and as steward of the course.

In 1909 it became clear that Tilleke, under pressure from increasing government work, was thinking of selling the firm,

Siam's first golf course, the Royal Hua Hin.

and so Brighouse set about looking for a potential new partner. One of his advertisements in the Hong Kong press brought a response from Reginald Douglas Atkinson, whom he interviewed in the British colony. Of the same age, the two men liked each other on first meeting and Atkinson was duly hired, moving to Bangkok the following year.

Born in 1881 into a well-to-do doctor's family in Kent, England, Atkinson served five years as an articled clerk before being admitted as a solicitor in 1904. Although the circumstances are not recorded, he followed the example of his partner-to-be by travelling East as soon as he had passed his professional exams. He settled in Hong Kong, became a proctor of the Supreme Court of Hong Kong, and entered the practice of Deacon, Luker

Atkinson and friend; always a popular man.
(Courtesy of Joan Atkinson)

Royal pass badge used on vehicles, 1930s.

& Deacon, where he worked for nearly six years until joining Tilleke & Gibbins.

Known to his friends as a fast-mover (a partner in his own law firm by the age of thirty), popular, patriotic and brave, Atkinson was equally a man of note as Brighouse, and the two men were to move Tilleke & Gibbins into a high gear while at the same time maintaining the good professional relations that Tilleke had so carefully fostered from the beginning.

The growth, expansion, and increased prosperity of foreign businesses in Bangkok during the early decades of the twentieth century bolstered both the workload and the esteem of Tilleke & Gibbins, consolidating its position as one of Bangkok's largest and leading law firms. Moreover, the royal connection, with which Tilleke was honoured on a personal level was, between 1911 and 1932, given professional standing as Tilleke & Gibbins was retained by the Privy Purse to assist in managing the private financial affairs of the king and the royal family. To conduct this business, Brighouse made a weekly visit to the Privy Purse and, with his car emblazoned with a large crest in the shape of a bull's head that served as an entry pass to the royal offices, he became a familiar sight in Bangkok's burgeoning traffic.

The winds of change were nonetheless beginning to blow and although these would scarcely ruffle the pages of the documents that piled up in the Tilleke & Gibbins' offices, effects on Siam itself were to be fundamental and far-reaching. The death in 1910 of the deeply revered King Chulalongkorn, whose long reign had made a profound impact on the country's politics, administration and culture, marked in many respects the end of an era. His son and successor, King Vajiravudh, Rama VI, although a worthy monarch, had a different style of rule and faced different problems.

Vajiravudh was the first Siamese monarch to be educated overseas (in England, at Sandhurst and Oxford, reading history and law at the latter), and

The Competition

Before 1940 there was little if any impediment to foreign lawyers practising in Siam. Tilleke & Gibbins' main competition in the first half of the twentieth century was from the firms of Wright & Gulley, Baguley & Tooth, and Naylor & Skinner. The name of the latter, a leading company in the pre-World War I era, gave rise to the popular notion that 'first they nailed you and then they skinned you'.

THE SIAM OBSERVER, SATURDAY, JANUARY 2, 1931.   11

WHITEAWAYS SCORE AGAIN!!

FOR

BIGGER . . . . .

. . . BETTER . . . . .

. . . . BARGAINS.

Men's Cotton Hose

252 pairs only
MEN'S GOLF HOSE
All cotton fancy turnover
top Golf Hose. Plain Fawn
and Grey shade legs.
Sizes 9 to 11½.
Usual Price Tcs. 2.25 per pr.

Sale Price
Tcs. 1.25
to clear.

MEN'S ... only
MEN'S ALL WOOL
V NECK SLIPOVERS
Made of nice quality all wool.
Plain Grey body with smart
contrasting V neck and border.

A Great Bargain
for the Cool Season!
Stocked in Small, Medium
and Large sizes

Sale Price
Tcs. 3.95 to
clear.

OUR ANNUAL STOCKTAKING

— SALE —

WILL COMMENCE ON

Monday, January 4th
and continue until
Saturday, February 6th.

During this Sale the whole of our
large and well assorted stock will be
offered at Reductions varying from

10 TO 50 Per Cent.

of our ordinary Low Selling Prices.

**A Unique Opportunity To Assist
You To Balance Your Budget.**

FOR

BIGGER . . . . .

. . . BETTER . . . .

. . . . BARGAINS.

372 only
MEN'S TENNIS SHIRTS
Hardwearing white mercerised
white twill tennis shirts with
polo collar attached. Stocked
with long and short sleeves.
Sizes 13½ to 17½.
Usual Price Tcs. 2.95 to 3.25 es.

Sale Price
Tcs. 1.95 to
clear.

**24 only BOYS V N...
PULLOVERS**
Made of nice quality...
wool. Very smart...
design. Good patte...
stock and fancy...
Colours Fawn a...
Grey etc.
Now in...

Sale Pri...
Tcs. 3.5...
to clear

54 only
THREE-PART BEDSTEADS
Well made bedsteads with strong wire
mattress. Reliable English make.
Finished in Black. Size 6 ft. 6 ins. x 3 ft.
Usual Price Tcs. 15.50 each.

Sale Price Tcs. 9.95
to clear.

**24 only
TABLE LAMPS**
All brass table
lamps complete
with wick and
chimney.
Exact as sketch.

Usual Price
Tcs. 3.95 each.
SALE PRICE
Tcs. 2.50
to clear.

SPECIAL !!

300 yards of Fancy Coloured Voiles.
Width 38 ins. Guaranteed fast colours, in a
fine range of large and small designs suitable
for Ladie's Jumpers and Dresses, also
children's wear.

A Great Bargain which can never be repeated!

Usual Price . . . . Tcs. 1.25 per yard.

Sale Price **Stgs. 60**
per yard

**20 only
SYNTAX
TABLE LAMPS**
Reliable brass
lamps complete
with globe, as
sketch.

Usual Price
Tcs. 3.95 each.

Sale Price
Tcs. 3.95
to clear.

**36 only
BROWN FIBRE SUIT...**
A Great Bargain in S...
Made of extra stout fibre...
strong locks and handle...
in perfect condition. Size...

SALE PR...
Tcs. 4.50...
to clear

**50 only
BATH TOWELS**
Absorbent and hard
wearing Brown Fibre
Bath Towels.
Size 25 x 55 ins.
Usual Price
Tcs. 3.95 each.
Sale Price
Tcs. 2.50
to clear.

**22 only
ENAMELLED TOILET SETS**
Neat and attractive toilet sets
containing five pieces as
sketch. Well made & finished.
Usual Price Tcs. 6.50 per set.

Sale Price
Tcs. 4.50 to
clear.

A GREAT CLEARANCE OF MEN'S GENUINE

SAXONE FOOTWEAR

152 Pairs only   Must Be Sold!
This genuine and unprecedented footwear
offer is only made possible by our desire
to clear out these Saxone Shoes to
make room for new stocks.

This Money Saving Opportunity
the greatest in our history, will
never occur again.

Worth Tcs. 25.50 & 27.50 per pr.

**To Be Cleared at . . .
. . . . ONE PRICE.**

NOW
Tcs. 10.00
Per Pair.

NOW
Tcs. 10.00
Per Pair.

TOBRALC...
THE TENNIS FAVO...

**84 yards only
TOBRALCO**
Hardwearing and washing fabric
for Ladie's and Children's wear
Stocked in Plain colours and...
Width 27 inches
Usual Price Tcs. 1.25 per yard.

Sale Price
Stgs. 90 to clear.

Very good...
Size 27 x 41...
and 31 x 51...
Usual Pric...

Sale Pric...
Tcs. 2.25
to clear

WHITEAWAY LAIDLAW & Co., Ltd., New Road, Bangkok.

AUCTION SALE.

: o :

ON THE INSTRUCTIONS OF

Messrs TILLEKE & GIBBINS

A large quantity of Glass Framed
Show Almirahs, Show Cases,
Shop Fittings and other effects,
Will be sold at the Auction Rooms at
Unakorn Road, Opposite S.A.B., City.

On Saturday, 15th May, 1920.
Commencing at 2 p. m.

BENJAMIN A. PERIERA,
Auctioneer.

12-5-20.]   12, 14. [2 ins.

MERRYWEATHERS.

PATENT

"MIDLAND"

STEAM PUMP.

Specially
designed for
Boiler
Feeding

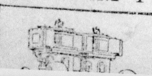

adjoi...

Bang...

betw...

M...

Bus...

U

*A catalogue of foreign goods (left) available
at Whiteaway Laidlaw in 1931, which occupied
the same address as Tilleke & Gibbins at
1169 New Road from 1951–1960.
Newspaper notice (above) of a 1920 auction
handled by Tilleke & Gibbins.*

Czechoslovakia & Middle Europe
Agencies.
Frant. Killinger—Director
Karel Vrabec— do.
Motor Accessories Dept :
L. K. Kang.
C. K. Tan.
Consultant Accountant and
Secretary—William Hwatt,
C. P. A., LL.B., etc.

Tilleke and Gibbins.

Advocates and Solicitors.

Partners :—
Samuel Brighouse, Solicitor.
R. D. Atkinson, Solicitor.
V. H. Jaques—Barrister-at-Law.
Miss Jørgensen—Stenographer.
Miss J. Jørgensen— do.
Nai Pheng Kim } Interpreters.
Nai Lek
Nai Kim Cheng } Clerks.
Nai Thien

Telephone No. 173.

Telegraphic Address : " Brigson "

Codes, A. B C. 6th Edition, Bentleys.

S. Tisseman & Co.

New Road, opposite Chartered
Bank Lane.
Watchmakers, Jewellers, Man-
ufacturing Goldsmiths and Silver-
smiths, Commission Agents, and
Dealers in Precious Stones.

Tel. Add : " Tisseman " Bangkok.

Telephone No. 1176

BY APPOINTMENT TO   H. M. THE KING.

THE
ORIENTAL STORES
LIMITED.
IMPORTERS OF :
PROVISIONS, WINES AND SPIRITS,
TOBACCOS, CIGARETTES AND CIGARS
SMOKERS' OUTFITTING.

Gentlemen's Outfitting, Silver and Electroplated
Ware, Art Porcelain, Perfumery, Soaps
and Toilet Preparations.

THE
DIRECTORY for BANGKOK and SIAM
1927.

Glassware, Porcelain & Cutlery, Household Utensils,
Stoves, Bedsteads & Bedding, Carpets,
Runners & Rugs, Filters, Safes.
Stationery, Books and Novels, Sporting Goods,
Travelling Implements, Camp Outfits,
Also Shipchandler's Stores.
etc.   etc.

ALWAYS FRESH STOCKS.

PRICES MODERATE : PROMPT DELIVERY.
WHOLESALE.

Telephones No. 179 and 647.

United Plantati
(INCORPORATE

Called to the Bar

(Courtesy of The British Club, Bangkok)

The British Club, which began in 2003, epitomized in its early days the colonialist, sexist and elitist mentality of Bangkok's expatriate community. Located on Suriwongse Road in the heart of the city's European quarter (the present clubhouse is pictured (above) in 1915), it lacked the recreational facilities of The Royal Bangkok Sports Club, having only tennis courts, and consequently established itself as a gentlemen's drinking club. Women were not eligible to become members: 'Ladies belonging to the family of [The British Club] members are entitled to the use of such rooms in the club as the committee may from time to time declare open to ladies,' noted a 1908 British publication. The bar was the club's focal point and here a strict hierarchy prevailed, with company bosses taking precedence over their juniors. In what amounted to an unwritten rule, seniors had the right to sit at the garden end of the bar, and rank descended down and around the rest of the bar. No one said anything, it just happened that way, and one moved up the bar as one's placing in the community rose.

was a lifelong, although not uncritical, anglophile — an attitude that found its most obvious expression in his promotion of football and other team sports in Siam. He also possessed literary talent and a love of the theatre, and employed his artistic gifts in an attempt to propagate a vision of a better world. This vision was allied to a strong sense of nationalism based on the triad of nation-religion-monarch, a clarion call that Vajiravudh was the first to popularize. It was also symbolized in the new (and current) national flag that he had designed as a tricolour in which red stands for nation, white for religion, and blue for monarchy.

Nationalism became the leitmotif of the reign. But others had their own concept of this and in 1912 a group of junior army officers was discovered plotting a coup. This aborted affair passed off quietly and Vajiravudh continued to pursue his own idea of nationalism, yet it was one that envisaged no significant change of institutions. The king tended to be introspective and he surrounded himself with coteries, which did little to foster true nationalism. This was to have serious repercussions, although they were not to become manifest until the following reign.

A keen promoter of sports, HM King Vajiravudh poses with a local football team.

Detracting from domestic politics was the outbreak in Europe in 1914 of World War I. Brighouse and Atkinson, equally courageous and patriotic, both wished to fight for their country, but one of them would have to stay and take care of the business in Bangkok. It is generally thought that, as the junior partner, Atkinson was the one chosen to go off to war, although the family history has it that the two lawyers drew lots, Atkinson being the winner or loser depending on your point of view.

Atkinson joined the Welsh Cavalry as a lieutenant and was packed off to the front lines in France. Wounded on one occasion, he survived to serve out the war with distinction, finishing with the rank of major. Following the armistice of 1918 he lost no time in returning to Bangkok.

Siam, too, made its contribution to the war effort. At first adhering to a policy of strict neutrality, the royal government eventually declared war on the Central Powers in 1917, and in the following year King Vajiravudh dispatched a 1,300-man expeditionary force comprising an ambulance section, drivers, mechanics and a flying squadron. Although this move was made towards the end of hostilities and the Siamese contingent did not see action, Siam's support of Britain and its allies was crucial for the country itself in that it led to participation in the Versailles

Peace Conference. This gave the Siamese delegation the opportunity to lobby the US, Britain and others for bilateral treaties more fair than those signed in the nineteenth century by King Mongkut.

The diplomatic effort eventually bore fruit and, beginning with the US in 1920, important new treaties were signed by the major Western powers. For Tilleke & Gibbins and the whole of Siam's legal fraternity, the greatest significance of these agreements was the ending of extraterritorial rights and thus the restoration of judicial autonomy. Gradually, throughout the 1920s, the consular courts — in which Mr Tilleke had figured so prominently — were abolished and

Period cigarette card showing a World War I Thai military uniform.
(Courtesy of The Royal Bangkok Sports Club)

foreigners now came under the jurisdiction of the Siamese courts and laws.

For Tilleke & Gibbins the 1920s was a period of growth and expansion. In 1924 the offices were moved to new premises at 719 Hongkong Bank Lane, just across New Road from the original location on Si Phaya Road. The upper floor of the two-storey building was sufficient for the firm's needs and the ground floor was sublet to Holland Siam Co. Ltd.

Office hours began at 8.30 am, then at noon everyone would go home for lunch. The working day ended at 4 pm, when it was the norm for the men to go to 'the club' (The Royal Bangkok

Black Tiger

The partners of Tilleke & Gibbins, like other expatriate professionals and businessmen, learnt to speak Siamese, some rather better than others. Mr Atkinson became quite fluent in the language but he never quite mastered the correct accent. This, as many foreigners have discovered, leads to problems in a language that is tonal. On one memorable occasion Atkinson had travelled to the court at Nakhon Pathom, just outside Bangkok, to defend a Siamese prince charged with killing a man. On his arrival he found that he had forgotten to bring his black lawyer's gown. There was nothing he could do except apologize to the court, which he did. As soon as he finished speaking, however, laughter burst out in the courtroom. Atkinson was perplexed at this and later asked his clerk what it was all about. 'Well, sir,' replied the clerk, 'you didn't say you'd forgotten your black gown; what you actually said was that you'd forgotten your black tiger.' The general word in Thai for 'dress' is 'suea', which has the same sound as the word for 'tiger' but is differentiated by the tone in which it is pronounced.

Clockwise from top: *Siamese troops on their way to Europe after Siam declared war on the Central Powers in 1917; Siamese and foreign officers; and part of Siam's expeditionary force on parade in Belgium.*

Bangkok Nursing Home

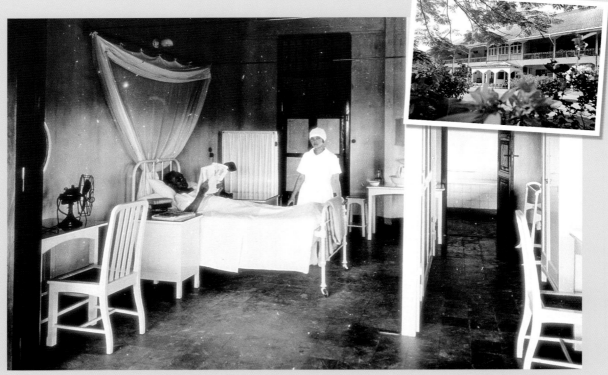

(Courtesy of BNH Hospital)

Among the many positions Brighouse held at various times in the foreign community, a role that did much to enhance the firm's good name, was chairman of the Bangkok Nursing Home. This venerable institution, founded in 1898 to serve the physical wellbeing of the expatriate community, was first located on Phya Decho Road but was moved to a site on Convent Road at the turn of the century. Housed in a charming two-storey colonial-style building with open verandas (this original structure can still be seen behind the large modern BNH Hospital that has today superseded it) it was described in the early twentieth century as being situated in the healthiest part of town', and was supported by 'all large firms, irrespective of nationality'. Staff included a matron and three European nurses. In the absence of resident physicians, patients were 'attended by their respective medical advisers'.

Sports Club) and indulge in 'sporting activities'. Social life tended to be on the formal side; there were no office parties and the idea of 'meeting the locals' was 'not on'.

At this time the staff of Tilleke & Gibbins consisted of, in addition to the two partners, a Thai lawyer Khun Rachasap; an accountant Mr Heggy, a Scotsman known to be fond of his country's finest product; an articled clerk Khun Luangsit, who became a Minister of Foreign Affairs after World War II; and one other clerk. Business was good to the extent that Brighouse could

The firm's offices in Hongkong Bank Lane.

afford to indulge his reputation for being a 'character', as expatriate businessman Eric W. Deane well remembered.

In 1922 Mr Deane's company, along with two other European firms, had engaged Tilleke & Gibbins in a bankruptcy case. Legal costs amounted to 270 ticals, which was billed a third each to the three parties. Deane wrote to Brighouse suggesting it would be fairer to split costs proportionally to the amount each claimant was owed by the defendant. To this Brighouse replied, 'We note your refusal to pay our professional fees and we have written you off as a bad debt.' Such generous, cavalier gestures were typical and led Brighouse to be fondly regarded, in Deane's words, as 'a fine chap'.

Brighouse also had a crusty side to his character and was known as something of a stickler in regards to correct social form. At The British Club, for example, it was customary for everyone to stand up when he entered the bar, and he would order home any young man whose hair he considered too long. He also had a reputation for resigning — and later withdrawing

Eric W. Deane.
(Courtesy of The Royal Bangkok Sports Club)

his resignation — from more committees than anyone else in Bangkok. Notably, as Deane recalled, Brighouse resigned from The British Club three times, on one occasion simply because he considered a footrail that had been added to the bar as 'undignified'.

At a Royal Bangkok Sports Club committee meeting, however, Brighouse once found himself gently pilloried. During a debate on whether or not to construct a swimming pool, Brighouse commented on the withdrawal of a proposed amendment as 'very satisfactory',

Dora Brighouse (top) *and her husband* (above) *sporting the sola topees, or pith helmets, that were much part of the dress of the day for men and women.*

Carrie Jorgensen 1920
The Prom Photo Studio
Bangkok Siam

Mr and Mrs Brighouse relaxing with friends
(left) (courtesy of Ann Sorensen); *Carrie, née
Jorgensen* (above) *worked at Tilleke&Gibbins
as a shorthand typist before marrying Reginald
Atkinson in 1929. She is pictured here* (top)
*on the balcony of the firm's offices in Hongkong
Bank Lane.* (Courtesy of Joan Atkinson)

whereupon the club's chairman addressed the committee at large, saying, 'Gentlemen, you've been listening to history: Mr Brighouse finds something satisfactory'.

On the domestic front, in 1912 Brighouse married Dora Berry — an old schoolfriend of his sister Elsie — whom he had met in England. They had three daughters, Mary, Ann and Jane, born respectively in 1917, 1922 and 1926. The future Mrs Carrie Atkinson, née Jorgensen, joined the firm as a shorthand typist in 1921. She married Atkinson, twenty years her senior, in 1929 and in so doing established an interesting family link as her sister Ina, who joined the firm in 1930 as a secretary, eventually became office manager and was to act as a caretaker of Tilleke & Gibbins during World War II.

In fact, the Jorgensen sisters were, in their own right, ladies of some note. Born in Bangkok and educated there and in Penang, both added footnotes to the social history of the foreign community. Mrs Carrie Atkinson was only the third female secretary to be employed in the city (the other two were a Miss Kemp, who was with the firm Lee, Cooper & Johnson, and Miss Sarah, who worked for the Borneo Company), while her sister had the distinction of being the first woman to drive a car in Bangkok.

Brighouse (standing centre) *and Jaques* (front) *at an RBSC fancy-dress ball.*

Such was the volume of business now handled by Tilleke & Gibbins that, in 1923, Brighouse and Atkinson decided there was a need for an additional lawyer and duly advertised in *The Times* of London. Atkinson went to England to interview applicants and short-listed two: Frank Babbage, who had recently qualified as a solicitor, and Victor Henry Jaques, a budding young barrister. After deliberation between the two partners the position was finally offered to Babbage, but this young man's career in Siam was to be a short one. Soon after his arrival in Bangkok he contracted a stomach complaint that proved persistent and, with continuing ill health, he was advised to return to England after scarcely a year in the East. Atkinson and Brighouse then contacted Jaques, who accepted their offer of a position as a junior.

A tall man at six foot four inches, Jaques was to have an outstanding career in Siam, both with Tilleke & Gibbins and in the British military as a secret operative during World War II. Known as a rather elusive character, a reputation perhaps enhanced by his wartime activities, Jaques was an adventurous man as well as a meticulous lawyer. He also had an exotic background, his father having worked in China for many years and died there while his son was at school in England.

Born in 1896, Jaques served in World War I, acquiring the rank of colonel and then, having distinguished himself in one profession, he turned to law and qualified as a barrister at Gray's Inn, London, in 1924. In 1927, three years after joining Tilleke & Gibbins, Jaques was made a partner in the firm.

His marriage to Millicent (Mollie) Watson, who was born in Bangkok in 1908, the daughter of a former British Consular Court judge in Siam, took place at around the same time as this promotion. The vagueness over the date of such a normally memorable occasion as a wedding stems from the fact that although Jaques officially announced his marriage in 1931 the ceremony, held in Colombo, Sri Lanka, had taken place some years previously. Jaques never explained the reason for the secrecy of his wedding, at least as far as the Bangkok community was concerned, and it has become a part of the mystique surrounding his near legendary life story.

Jaques and other expatriates newly arrived at Bangkok in the 1920s would have found an increasingly Westernized city. The Grand Palace, Wat Phra

Keo and other temples were still exotic sights, but new development was widely apparent, especially notable being the roads. Although the Chao Phraya River was still a main highway and thousands of sampans plied the

Victor Henry Jaques.

canals, paved roads were becoming more characteristic of the city. Ratchadamnoen Avenue, conceived by King Chulalongkorn as the capital's equivalent of the Champs Élysées, had set an urban pattern as remarked upon by impressionable 1920s visitor Ebbe Kornerup. Describing

a nocturnal drive through the city, Kornerup writes in *Friendly Siam*: 'Then the car swings through great avenues, as though we were in one of the great cities of Europe. . . . Again an avenue engulfs us, and under the big trees the going is marvellously smooth. . . . More avenues. Bangkok is a city of avenues, and its avenues are lovely; they close high up like Gothic arches.'

On the same evening tour, Kornerup spotted the foreign community at ease: 'In the European quarter, which spreads over the whole of Bangkok [actually centred on New Road but then beginning to expand] the bungalows are brightly lit; men in white sit on their verandas drinking whiskies and sodas with women in light frocks. . . . Another turn, and the car stops in front of the modern Sports Club. Here there is music and dancing; the veranda is full of people; men in white are drinking in the bar, the billiard rooms are full, the reading rooms too are full and a big athletic ground lies outside open to the seven winds of heaven.'

Kornerup clearly views Bangkok through rose-tinted

An expatriate social function during the interwar years.

glasses, but the city could easily have appeared as a colonial idyll in the first half of the twentieth century, as indeed Thailand is frequently seen by travellers today as a land of lotus-eaters. In many respects expatriate life, centred on the social and recreational clubs, was pleasurable and privileged, though there were drawbacks. Cholera was no longer the scourge it once was, thanks largely to the proper water supply provided by the opening of the Bangkok Waterworks in 1914, but as the unfortunate Babbage discovered, stomach ills were not uncommon, and it was essential that food be fresh and well cooked.

Lieutenant Colonel C.H. Forty, a British military officer who served with the Royal Siamese Army in the early 1920s, wrote in 1927: 'In England an incompetent cook may be the cause of indigestion, in the tropics his ignorance may land his master in the cemetery.'

Mosquitoes were another bugbear. Ladies usually wrapped a sarong around their legs to prevent bites as they sat out of an evening, while the men generally trusted to the prophylactic power of alcohol. The latter, however, was not always effective and English writer Alec Waugh, who visited Bangkok in 1925, made the mistake of sitting outside

one evening drinking a gin sling. 'Never anywhere', he wrote afterwards, 'have I been bitten so painfully. I was kept awake at night by my tormented ankles.'

Even in the days before air conditioning, the climate was considered tolerable, but did take its toll. 'Most of them [expatriate women]', Forty noted, 'stand the climate remarkably well, but rose-leaf complexions soon fade, and ankles are apt to lose their elegance.'

Above all, expatriate life was genteel. Mrs Atkinson remembered that if a newcomer 'blotted his or her copybook' they were asked to return home and, if they could not afford the passage, money would be raised for them. Helping an ordered society was, according to Forty, a lack of temptation. 'Visitors to Bangkok who expect to find the hectic scenes of vice and depravity sometimes described by novelists as the usual things of the East will be agreeably surprised by their absence, or chagrined as the case may be.'

The high profile of Tilleke & Gibbins and its partners during these heydays of expatriate life in Bangkok is well reflected in *The Siam Observer's* notice of Brighouse's fiftieth birthday on 11 July 1931. The paper devoted no

Exotic Sights

Royal Grand Palace, Bangkok.

'They [Bangkok's temples] are unlike anything in the world, so that you are taken aback, and you cannot fit them into your scheme of the things you know. It makes you laugh with delight to think that anything so fantastic could exist on this sombre earth. They are gorgeous; they glitter with gold and whitewash, yet are not garish; against that vivid sky, in that dazzling sunlight, they hold their own, defying the brilliance of Nature and supplementing it with the ingenuity and the playful boldness of man.'

Somerset Maugham,
The Gentleman in the
Parlour, *1930.*

less than 22 column inches to the occasion, using the opportunity to pen a candid portrait of the birthday celebrant.

'During his residence here', wrote *The Siam Observer,* 'Mr Brighouse has been a personality of force and influence. He has touched local life at many facets. . . . And throughout he has shown a spirit of downright independence for which one must express the fullest admiration. That sense of independence . . . has brought him controversy after controversy, but whatever the odds, he has been guided by what he has considered the right course, caring not what any man might think or say. And through all these contentious occasions he has disarmed his opponents by his unfailing good humour, his bonhomie and highly developed sense of the ridiculous. . . . We are certain that no one who has opposed his view has regarded him as but a clean, fair and chivalrous opponent.'

Scarcely could a lawyer have wished for higher praise or be accredited with better qualities.

In contrast to the seemingly sunny skies under which Bangkok's expatriates flourished, clouds were gathering over the Siamese world during the 1920s. King Vajiravudh died in 1925 and heavy spending during the latter years of his reign had left the

HM King Prajadhipok, Rama VII.

national coffers badly depleted. Economic problems dogged Vajiravudh's successor, King Prajadhipok, Rama VII, whose efforts at cost cutting had some initial impact but were ultimately doomed by the Great Depression. This financial crisis of the American and European markets shocked Siam in the early 1930s, most noticeably in the plummeting price of rice, the mainstay of the country's economy.

Paralleling the fluctuation of economic fortunes was growing political criticism. This was fomented mainly by young military officers and students,

nk.

our.

ations.

SERVICE]
July 11,
ent, Dr.
Paris are
erest and
the Press
Paris dis-
icate that
ke advant-
financial
nch parti-
ernational
nk, depen-
it being
overnment
onment of
with Aus-
the build-
ed pocket
nder con-

the Com-
Press, the
against the
e Catholic

Mr. S. Brighouse.

Celebrates His Fiftieth Year.

"A Bonnie Fechter."

Today Mr. S. Brighouse celebrates his fiftieth birthday, and has been the recipient of numerous messages of congratulation and other marks of appreciation and good will. With the many who have remembered the notable occasion we would like to associate ourselves. Of those fifty years, twenty-four have been spent in Siam, in hard work and in hard play, in business and social intercourse, and we are sure that many of our readers who were not aware of the occasion will wish Mr. Brighouse, perhaps not so intimately as his close personal friends but none the less sincerely, the best of luck.

During his residence here Mr. Brighouse has been a personality of force and influence. He has touched local life at many facets. He has given of his time and services generously in the interests of club life and sport. And throughout he has shown a spirit of downright independence for which one must express the fullest admiration. That sense of independence is a strong element in his character, and, frankly, it has brought him into controversy

Going on leave, Brighouse (above) aboard a steamship in May 1933 (courtesy of Joan Atkinson); and celebrated in the press (left) on the occasion of his fiftieth birthday.

predominantly law students pursuing their studies overseas. In the 1920s Bangkok's law school was the centre of advanced thinking, and it was from here that many students won scholarships to study abroad. Most went to England, but several opted for France. The latter group tended to be the more radical, fervently discussing amongst themselves ideas of socialism and popular democracy.

The most prominent of these students was a young lawyer named Pridi Phanomyong — who headed a secret association known as the Promoters of Political Change, later to become the People's Party — and a military cadet, Luang Phibul Songkhram. The political ardour of these two, dubbed by their friends as, respectively, 'The Professor' and 'The Captain', did not diminish on their return to Bangkok and by 1932 they were in a position to successfully stage a bloodless coup that changed Siam's political system from an absolute to a constitutional monarchy. 'No revolution in the turgid history of mankind', wrote Alec Waugh, 'has been carried through so swiftly, so efficiently and so pacifically.'

'Under the New Constitution', as the 1934 *Commercial Directory for Siam* described it, 'the Sovereign power emanates from the Siamese nation. The King, who is the head of the nation, exercises

HM King Ananda, Rama VIII.

the legislative power by and with the consent of the Assembly of the People's Representatives, the executive power through the State Council and judicial power through the Courts duly established by law.'

However, fundamental though the change was — laying the foundations of the modern state — the coup of 1932 had little impact on daily life. The executive powers that had previously been held by princes were transferred to military men and bureaucrats, but as far as the man in the street was concerned, the king remained the ultimate figure of respect and love, a deeply rooted veneration that continues to this day.

King Prajadhipok reigned as a constitutional monarch only until 2 March 1935 when, his relations with the new government having become increasingly strained, he abdicated and was succeeded by the young King Ananda, Rama VIII. Prajadhipok retired to England, taking a house at Virginia Water, just outside London, where Brighouse paid him a courtesy call when on home leave.

For Tilleke & Gibbins the only immediate effect of the changed political situation was the loss of its work with the Privy Purse, although Tilleke & Gibbins continued as adviser to the Treasury and Jaques was subsequently awarded The Most Exalted Order of the White

Keeping account: entries made in a Tilleke & Gibbins' Siam Commercial Bank ledger (courtesy of Siam Commercial Bank), displayed with 1930s' currency.

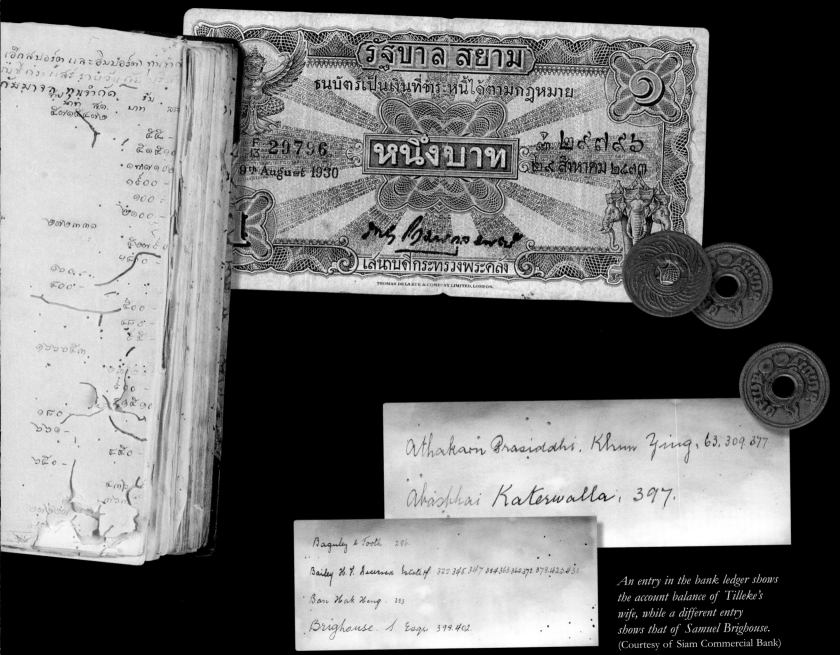

An entry in the bank ledger shows the account balance of Tilleke's wife, while a different entry shows that of Samuel Brighouse. (Courtesy of Siam Commercial Bank)

The Professor

Pridi Phanomyong, known as 'The Professor' among the revolutionaries who were behind the coup of 1932, was a child prodigy. Born the son of a rice merchant in a village near Ayutthaya, he finished at the prestigious Suan Kulap College and entered the Ministry of Justice's law school at the age of just seventeen. He was called to the Bar two years later. In 1919 he tried and won his first and only court case as a defence lawyer, that of an elderly Chinese merchant held liable by the Crown for damages to royal property during a boating incident on the Chao Phraya River. By the age of nineteen Pridi had already earned a reputation for legal and rhetorical skill. After further studies in Paris, he returned to Bangkok in 1927 and was assigned to the Ministry of Justice's secretariat, where he acquired extensive knowledge in the drafting of laws. He also wrote a compilation of Siamese laws from antiquity to modern times, which was published in several volumes.

The Captain

Like his revolutionary confrère Pridi, Luang Phibul Songkhram was a commoner, his parents owning fruit orchards just outside Bangkok. After his death, his widow emphasized this background to put into focus Phibul's early achievements. He had taken first-place honours at the Cadet School and won a King's Scholarship to study in France, and this was the more remarkable because, his widow wrote, 'in that period few commoners indeed could afford the expenses of sending their children to study abroad, and a very limited number of scholarships were available to their likes'. Although he was dubbed 'The Captain' by his revolutionary friends, Phibul was not just a simple soldier (he ultimately held the rank of field marshal); he had a scholarly disposition and became a noted teacher of and writer on military science. He is described in Thailand: A Short History by David K. Wyatt as, 'one of only a handful of people who definitely put their stamp on Thai history'.

Elephant (Class IV) for his legal services to the royal financial affairs. Also, several members of the royal family continued to use the firm for private matters such as the drawing up of wills. Other legal business remained strong and in 1937, the earliest date of related surviving records, the firm took part in 37 court cases, the figure rising to 61 in 1940. The litigation was wide ranging, from the formation of companies to debt, bankruptcy, motor accidents, murder, attempted murder, and one case involving the Asiatic Petroleum Company intriguingly referred to as 'dangerous or noxious trades'.

The expatriate social scene was also little affected, and Brighouse and Atkinson remained very active in club life. Two years before the 1932 coup, Atkinson cofounded the Rotary Club of Bangkok, becoming its first vice president, and later he established a local branch of the British Legion.

But by the latter half of the 1930s troubled times were plaguing Europe, and soon World War II would put paid to the quasi-idyllic days of the Bangkok expatriate. For the Atkinsons, family life was disrupted in 1936 when Mrs Atkinson moved permanently to

England to be close to their son and daughter who were at school there. Then in 1940, shortly after World War II had broken out in Europe, Reginald Atkinson, always the courageous patriot, returned home to join the Army. He was declined regular service due to age — he was then 58 — and instead he joined the Home Guard, in which he remained active throughout the war.

Not until 1941 did the war finally come to Thailand. On 7 December of that year, the Japanese requested of Thailand's government that its armies be allowed passage through Thai territory. It so happened that, at the time, Thai prime minister Phibul Songkhram was 'carefully unavailable', as one historian has put it, and so the Japanese received no response from the Thais. It made no difference; their request had been a mere formality and just before dawn on 8 December the Japanese landed in Thailand, meeting only light and brief resistance. The Thai government had little alternative but to accept the situation and, surmising that Japan would likely win the war, it was concluded that a military alliance with the invader was in the country's best interests.

Cover of an old Rotary Club magazine.

For Bangkok's foreign community the first intimation that they were soon to fall captive to the Japanese came on the evening of Saturday 6 December at a dance and fête held at The British Club. As Eric W. Deane recorded in a diary he was to keep throughout the war, the event was 'a combination of many of the seasonal activities: the annual Winter Dance, a postponed St Andrew's, a fête to raise money for the 'Spitfire Fund' and so on, and 'all Bangkok' was there. About midnight the British and American ministers were recalled to their respective legations

Not Convenient

E.W. Deane.

'*Monday, 8 December 1941. When we switched on the radio to Malaya, we heard the news of the attack on Pearl Harbour and the air raids on Hong Kong and Singapore. In the midst of this my telephone rang. It was Dr Viehofer, an American professor at the University asking if it would be convenient if he brought a Japanese friend to the Sports Club that evening to introduce him to me preparatory to putting him up for membership. Somewhat curtly I said it was not, decidedly not, convenient.*'

From the diary of E.W. Deane.

to receive signals from Whitehall and Washington.'

The following day, Deane, who spent the afternoon playing golf at The RBSC, recorded that there were all sorts of rumours but 'many of us were hardly in the right state of mind to give them serious thought after a long night of revelry'.

Matters became clear on Monday, 8 December, when it was learned that the Japanese forces had landed in Thailand — near Paknam at the mouth of the Chao Phraya River, and close to Songkhla in the South. That evening the British minister Sir Josiah Crosby addressed a meeting of the British community at The British Club. Brighouse would doubtless have attended, as did another English lawyer, Gerald Sparrow, who later described the minister's speech as 'the most lamentable exhibition of pompous complacency it has been my misfortune to witness'. Basically, Crosby said the Thai Foreign Ministry had assured him that all British subjects would be free to move about and continue their normal business activities. He added that for those who wished to leave, he had been promised a special evacuation train.

Crosby's complacency, however, did not fool many. 'The meeting was very sceptical', Deane noted in his diary, 'and started to ask awkward questions at which Crosby lost his temper and stalked off the stage to growls of strong disapproval.'

Of course, none of Crosby's optimism was justified. The Japanese took effective control of Bangkok and the Thai government remained the power in the land in little more than name. All nationals of the Allies were interned for the duration of the war.

Luckily, Atkinson had already returned to England, and Jaques had had the foresight to send his wife and his son Ralph to England in 1940 for safety. The following year he too left Thailand to join his Royal Sussex Regiment, in India at that time. Brighouse was less fortunate; he, his wife, and all but their youngest daughter Jane (who was at school in Malaya and managed to escape to Australia) were caught in Bangkok and interned. For the first time since its establishment, Tilleke & Gibbins ceased to practise.

CEREMONY AT SUAN KULAP

NON-AGGRESSION PACT SIGNED BETWEEN THAILAND, FRANCE AND BRITAIN

A SIMILAR PACT WITH JAPAN.

The Suan Kulap Palace which is the residence of H. E. the Premier was the scene of a historic ceremony this morning when Pacts of Non-Aggression were signed between Thailand and France and Thailand and Great Britain.

Treaty was signed with Fr... ceremony, too, was simila... conclusion Sir Josiah Crosb... speech and this was replied ... the Premier in the Thai lan... English translation being re...

His Excellency Monsieur P. P. Lép... sier, Envoy Extraordinary and Minist... Plenipotentiary of the French Repub... at Bangkok.

The Pact represents the desire ... ensure peace and develop the friend... relations between the two countries ...

Pictures taken on the occasion of the signing of the Non-Aggression Pacts between Thailand, France and Great Britain at the Suan Kulap Palace, Bangkok, on June 12th.
—*Photos by Courtesy of the Publicity Department.*

Press report (above) of the signing of the Non-Aggression Pacts, and (right) a Thai war propaganda poster.

พี่น้อง ชาวไทย

มีความสามัคคีกัน
เชื่อมั่นในรัฐบาล และ
กองทัพของเรา
มีความแน่ใจว่าเราต้องชะนะ
งระลึกเสมอว่าเข่าวที่มาจากสัตรูย่อม
เป็นการให้ร้ายต่อเรา และข่าวที่ไม่ดีสำ
หรับเรา ก็คือข่าวของสัตรู

กรมโฆษณาการ

*World War II poster exhorting Thais to be united and trust in their government and the army. They should be certain of victory
and know that news from the enemy is always bad news. (Courtesy of The Royal Bangkok Sports Club).*

Sine Die
1942–1945

HE Ambassador MR Seni Pramoj.

On 25 January 1942 the Thai government officially declared war on Britain and the United States. To the declaration Brighouse and others familiar with legal Latin might have forlornly added the phrase 'sine die' — literally 'without appointed day'. It would have echoed the uncertain future then facing Tilleke & Gibbins and other Allied-owned companies in Bangkok.

When would the war be over? Would it be possible to pick up the pieces in Bangkok once the hostilities finally came to an end? Imponderable questions at the time. And time must have weighed heavily on the mind of the 61-year-old Brighouse as he, along with all other nationals of the Allies, languished in a Bangkok civilian internment camp. Of the other partners Atkinson, also not far off retirement age, was guarding the home front in England, and Jaques, as will be seen later, was to face perilous times. The survival of Tilleke & Gibbins was by no means certain.

Thailand's position was ambivalent. The Thai ambassador to the United States MR Seni Pramoj had refused to submit his government's declaration of war and set about forming a Free Thai Movement, which supported the Allies and was initially centred in Washington, D.C. Yet for the moment this did not alter the situation in Bangkok, where the Japanese took control, closed down foreign businesses and rounded up nationals of the Allied nations.

Brighouse and his family, along with all other Allied nationals, were interned in Ta Prachan camp, which occupied the campus and buildings of the University of Moral and Political Sciences (now Thammasat University), and was then relocated during the later stages of the war to Vajiravudh College in the Dusit district, near the royal palace. Conditions were cramped and obviously not

Free Thai

'A communiqué has just come through today from Bangkok to the effect that the Japanese armed forces have entered Thailand by land and sea. . . . Under these circumstances it is no longer possible to be sure whether instructions reaching me from Bangkok are those of the Thai government or are dictated by the armed invaders. . . . I therefore deem it my duty as the representative of my King, and of the free and independent Thailand which sent me here as its representative, to carry on the struggle for the freedom of Thailand. . . . I have decided to work from now on for one thing and one thing only — the reestablishment of a free and independent Thailand.'

HE Ambassador MR Seni Pramoj, extract of statement to the US Department of State, 10 December 1941.

Ina Jorgensen. (Courtesy of Joan Atkinson)

was widely regarded as being sympathetic, even to the extent of unofficially allowing internees to have radios. Certainly, internment in Bangkok was a far cry from the horrors endured by the Allied military prisoners of war forced to work on the infamous 'Death Railway' and the River Kwai Bridge in Kanchanaburi province some 130 kilometres west of Bangkok.

Ta Prachan camp had separate quarters for singles and married couples, with rooms divided into small cubicles by ten-foot-high wooden partitions. The beds, as described by E.W. Deane, were 'not bad, but our mattresses, help!' Food was 'rough but not too bad', and was supplemented by fruit and eggs, along with other 'luxuries' and necessities supplied by friends of the internees, both foreigners of neutral countries and Thais. Among the expatriates not interned was Ina Jorgensen, secretary to Victor Jaques, who retained her freedom as a national of Denmark, a country occupied by the Axis powers. She was allowed regular visits to Ta Prachan camp, taking food and medical supplies to the Brighouse family, as well as carrying messages in and out.

Life for expatriates outside the camp was not easy. Deprived

luxurious, but since civilian internees came under the control of the Thai government and not the Japanese their treatment was by and large considerate and reasonable. The Thai commandant of the camp Mom Bongsephrom (usually shortened to 'Bhrom')

of regular employment Ina Jorgensen, who also had her mother to support, struggled to make ends meet by dealing in real estate, trading in gems and taking on any other moneymaking scheme that might present itself. Nonetheless, she was a resourceful and intrepid woman and was successful in not only keeping an eye on the Tilleke & Gibbins office, which had been occupied by the Japanese military, but also in preserving the documents of foreign companies and other clients held by the firm.

Details of exactly how Ina Jorgensen managed to keep things going and what activities she conducted on behalf of Tilleke & Gibbins are not known, although she clearly took extraordinary care.

Her nephew, Carl Zeytoon, who was in his early teens during the war, possesses to this day a 'partners' table' — one of those double-fronted desks that were once common in law offices of old and are now valuable antiques — which somehow Ina Jorgensen preserved from the Japanese occupation.

For the internees, life quickly settled into a routine once the shock of captivity had passed. Reveille was at 6 am; roll call at 7 am. Breakfast consisted of coffee and two slices of dry bread, usually supplemented by private supplies of fruit and eggs. Lunch, at noon, was typically a meat and vegetable dish, sometimes a curry. Dinner of soup and a meat course was at 5 pm, with lights out at 9 pm. The political and administrative life of the camp, for which the internees were allowed a fair amount of self-determination, was served by elected committees, and on a variety of these Brighouse, as a noted figure in the foreign community, featured prominently.

The only physical danger faced by the internees — and indeed by every other inhabitant of Bangkok — came from Allied bombing, first by the RAF flying out of Rangoon until its capture by the Japanese, and later by US B–24s ('Liberators') based in Calcutta. Targets were, however, generally limited to strategic installations such as the port and the railway yards, and the most significant hits were Memorial Bridge on the Chao Phraya River and the electrical power station (the latter blacking out the city for most of the war). But Ta Prachan's original site close to the river made it vulnerable and there were one or two near misses. It was for this reason that the camp was eventually moved to Vajiravudh College.

Bombing aside, the only other major upheaval Bangkok

Carl Zeytoon with friends at The RBSC.
(Courtesy of The Royal Bangkok Sports Club)

Death Railway

As part of its strategy to conquer Burma, the Japanese forced Allied prisoners, as well as Thai and other Asian labourers, to build a 415-kilometre railway between Thailand and Burma. A vital link in this supply line was a bridge to span the River Kwai in Thailand's Kanchanaburi province. Engineers estimated it would take five years to build the railway — the Japanese forced its completion in sixteen months. It cost the lives of 16,000 British, Dutch, Australian, American, Malay and Indian prisoners of war and an estimated 100,000 Thai and other Asian forced labourers, all of whom perished from inhumane treatment, malnutrition and disease. The line was in use for just twenty months before the Allies bombed the Kwai Bridge in 1945.

*Bomb-damaged shophouses
in Bangkok* (above) *and
scant defences* (right) *in the
city streets.*

The Allied bombing of Bangkok caused considerable destruction,
although it was localized and overall the city remained intact.
A B–24 'Liberator' bomber (right) was one of the aircraft
used by the Allies for bombing sorties over Thailand.

A Pretty Girl Called Ann

Ann Sorensen, née Brighouse, shortly after the war.
(Courtesy of Ann Sorensen)

It so happens that whilst I have been typing these extracts from my Diary I have been reading a book, lent to me by Johnny Marshall, entitled Prisoner on the Kwai *by Basil Peacock. This, with its stories of the many hardships and indignities (and the many deaths) suffered by those on the railway, has emphasized once again — if indeed emphasis were needed — of how most fortunate we were to have been in the hands of the Thai and not of the Japanese. This book describes an incident at the end of the war which had some connection with us, and I conclude these notes with this extract: 'Two hundred of us dressed in a queer assortment of garments dropped from relieving aircraft . . . filed noisily into a large hangar. . . . Then an astonishing thing happened. All fell silent as we caught sight of a table with tea urns and mugs on it in a corner. Standing there, smiling, was a pretty English girl with long fair hair sweeping in a wave over her neck, dressed in a crisp summery outfit. Two hundred toughs, clad like scarecrows, were hushed by the sight, and many were visibly affected. She signalled to us to file past to receive tea and sandwiches, and we did so quietly and even shyly. An elderly, unshaven private soldier immediately in front of me, when asked if he would like sugar, murmured with genuine feeling the old hackneyed reply, "Oh, miss if you just put your finger in it, it will be sweet enough". He stared at her in a doglike way, and stumbled past, blinded by the presence.' I was at Don Muang at the canteen when this happened. The girl, whose name has appeared more than once in my narrative, was Ann Sorensen, née Brighouse.*

Eric Deane,
Grayshott,
March 1975.

experienced in the war years was the famous flood of October 1942. At more than a metre high in the low-lying areas — The Royal Bangkok Sports Club, for example, became a large lake with the racecourse rails only just showing above the water — this was the biggest of regular inundations for some fifty years and it made the city and the internment camp extremely uncomfortable for several weeks. Fresh food supplies were seriously affected, while Carl Zeytoon remembered 'there were snakes everywhere.'

But mostly it was boredom the internees had to contend with, and to fill the yawning gaps in the long days they organized various activities and entertainments, among which amateur theatricals were particularly well supported. Eric Deane produced a number of plays and he devotes much space in his unpublished wartime diary to describing what was clearly a busy programme.

In one rather breathless entry covering a year's activities, Deane recorded: 'Last Christmas [1942] we had *Pygmalion*, which was a success. . . . Then we had a pantomime written by [Gerald] Sparrow, followed by monthly variety shows, some good, some indifferent. . . . Then some one-act plays and a fairly good effort by Sparrow and Braine-Hartnell on the theme of a murder trial.'

Following that, a number of 'more ambitious' comedies and farces were staged, the first being *Tons of Money*, which had been a famous farce at London's Aldwych Theatre. What Brighouse thought of these light-hearted entertainments is not recorded, although his daughters Ann and, to a lesser extent, Mary acted in several of the productions in which it seems their 'decorative qualities were more highly regarded than any true talent for the stage. Acting did, however, provide an opportunity for romance to blossom, and Mary Brighouse became attached to a fellow amateur thespian named Ffolkes whom she was to marry after the war.

On the subject of the Brighouse girls' romances, the war

Anton Sorensen. (Courtesy of Ann Sorensen)

had separated Ann from her beloved, Anton Sorensen, a Danish air force officer who was posted to North Africa at the outbreak of hostilities. Out of the blue, just three days after Ann was released from internment, he turned up in Bangkok and shortly afterwards the couple married,

initially staying in Bangkok until Sorensen's work took them to Phuket and then Borneo.

In many ways, apart from the privations and loss of freedom, the internees tended to live in a microcosm of the society they had inhabited before the war. An extract from Deane's diary makes the point: 'By and large . . . the Camp settled down to a general amicable existence. Perhaps inevitably circles seemed to form and although these in our limited space impinged on one another at times, one saw more from day to day of the members of one's own particular "set". During 1944 mine seemed to hinge round the "golfers", the bridge and the poker circles and those who had been concerned with the plays I had produced.'

The less savoury elements of community life did, of course, raise their ugly heads from time to time. In the early days of internment, for

Soldiers Not Spies

Instructed by Winston Churchill to 'set Europe alight', the Special Operations Executive (SOE) was established in 1940 with the principal task of fostering and supporting resistance movements in enemy-occupied territory with the aim that they would take effective action against the enemy and eventually join invading British armies. Intelligence gathering, although inevitably a by-product, was not SOE's primary role and its personnel were soldiers not spies.

example, there was a particularly acrimonious and protracted case of a matrimonial breakup, which for a time caused some unpleasantness for the friends and acquaintances of the feuding couple. Brighouse, displaying his characteristic high moral standards, had initially given some professional advice to the husband over the legal aspects of the dispute, but was later disgusted and would have nothing more to do with him when he found the husband had written scurrilous notes to his estranged wife.

Of course, it was not a normal life in the camp, and the psychological pressures of internment inevitably had their effect, even if the sufferers weren't necessarily aware of it at the time. This is wonderfully spotlighted by an incident in 1943 recorded by Deane. By then, a number of military prisoners of war, mostly airmen whose planes had been shot down, were detained at a separate camp on the perimeter of Ta Prachan. These were not supposed to have general contact with the civilians, but one afternoon one joined the internees' queue at the canteen.

'Hi!' called one of the expats. 'You're in the wrong queue.' To which the military prisoner replied, 'It doesn't matter. I'll just act silly and they won't know the difference.'

Samuel Brighouse at The R.B.S.C.

Deane could scarcely believe the inference of the comment, but after the war an old friend told him, 'Well, you all seemed a little bit off centre, you know'.

In spite of it all, Brighouse and his family remained popular figures in camp life and a great

source of strength under difficult circumstances. But in early 1944 Brighouse developed a cancerous growth in his throat and he expected the worst as the disease had already proved fatal to a close family member. When his condition worsened he asked to be sent to Saigon, Vietnam, where his brother was a doctor, and he was placed in an internment-camp hospital where radium treatment was available. The authorities granted permission for Brighouse's wife to be with him in Saigon, and Ina Jorgensen also visited him there, having the misfortune to be detained briefly by the Japanese on suspicion of being a spy.

The radium treatment failed to contain the cancer and Brighouse died in Saigon on 18 May 1944. Both Tilleke & Gibbins and Bangkok's foreign community thus lost a man who had been a pillar of strength for close on forty years.

Mrs Brighouse remained interned in Bangkok until the end of the war which, in Asia, came with the Japanese surrender on 15 August 1945. During that last year she was 'admired by everyone, not only for herself but for the very gallant show she has put up since Samuel Brighouse's death'.

A very different war from that of the internees was experienced by Victor Jaques. A highly decorated veteran of World War I, Jaques was 43 at the outbreak of World War II and could reasonably have been expected to serve out the new hostilities in some nonmilitary capacity. But that would have been out of character for this adventurous man, though it was not primarily his past military achievements that eventually brought him back into active service, rather the local knowledge and language skills he had acquired during his years in Bangkok with Tilleke & Gibbins.

As already noted, Thailand's political position in World War II was ambivalent. Much of this revolved around the characters of Phibul Songkhram and Pridi Phanomyong, the two leaders of the revolution of 1932. As the prime minister in 1941, Phibul first conveniently absented himself when the Japanese requested permission to enter Thai territory and made no reply. Then, when the Japanese actually invaded, he ordered a cease-fire and eventually signed a pact with

them. Pridi, on the other hand, who had been foreign minister and then finance minister, was known to be strongly anti-Japanese.

Since their revolutionary days, Phibul and Pridi had grown apart,

Victor Jaques in British Army uniform.

the former, with the support of the army, looking more and more like a dictator as time went on. After allying himself with the Japanese, Phibul was shrewd enough to realize that Pridi could be a problem, but he also knew that his colleague was too popular

with the public to be simply dismissed. As so often happens in such situations, Phibul sought to neutralize Pridi by promoting him — in this case to head of the Regency Council (for the young King Ananda). Pridi, a man who in the revolution of 1932 had proved himself capable of organizing and mobilizing a large secret underground movement, was not to be so easily sidelined.

This is not the place to give an account of modern Thai history other than as it impinges on the principal figures in the story of Tilleke & Gibbins. Suffice it to say that with Pridi a potential resistance leader in Thailand, and with the Free Thai Movement — which, as the war continued, drew support from thousands of students and other overseas Thais in the US and Britain — already in existence, the Allies saw that bringing the two together was one way to undermine Japanese control. The link for this as far as the British were concerned (the Americans had their own, not always parallel, agenda), was Force 136 of the Special Operations Executive (SOE).

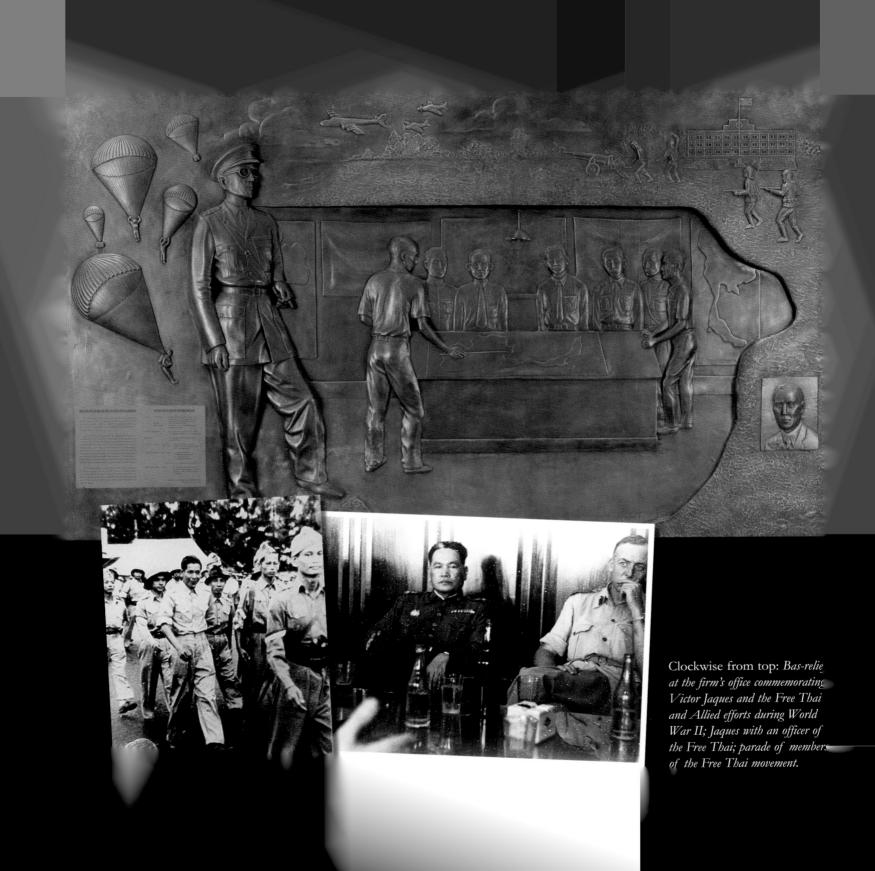

Clockwise from top: *Bas-relief at the firm's office commemorating Victor Jaques and the Free Thai and Allied efforts during World War II; Jaques with an officer of the Free Thai; parade of members of the Free Thai movement.*

Based in India and Sri Lanka, Force 136 was the arm of the SOE assigned to operate against Japan. Its activities in Thailand have been detailed by Andrew Gilchrist in his book *Bangkok Top Secret*, from which the following details have been largely drawn.

As far as it touches on the history of Tilleke & Gibbins, Force 136 came into the picture in late 1944 when the authorities were looking for a suitable candidate to infiltrate Thailand. His mission would be to make contact with Pridi, the overall leader of the Free Thai Movement since 1943, and to act as a liaison between the Free Thai and Allied Command. The required qualifications for the job were: British nationality; fit, active, and capable of parachuting; full knowledge of Thailand and the language; some political background; and, finally, the successful candidate should be a genuine soldier capable of discussing military plans on a high level.

Andrew Gilchrist, who was in charge of the operation, describes in *Bangkok Top Secret* how he was despairing of finding a single candidate with all the right qualifications. Then, Major A.C. (Peter) Pointon MC, head of Force 136's Siam Country Section solved the quandary: "'Andrew,' he said, "I've got an idea. What about Jaques?" "Jaques?" I asked. "Yes, Victor Jaques — you know, the legal eagle." I drifted out to think things

Victor Jaques, right, at Don Muang Airport.

over. I had known Victor Jaques for years — a brilliant lawyer, one of the leaders of Bangkok society, a light-hearted gambler, a man of the highest intelligence. . . . I realized at once that Jaques was the one man who in his own person covered all of my conditions.'

Jaques was at the time a staff officer with the rank of acting brigadier. Some doubted that, given his rank, he would be willing to accept the assignment. To which Gilchrist replied, 'Nuts. I know Jaques, he's mad enough for anything'. And indeed, in January 1945, Jaques accepted the job.

In an operation code named 'Panicle' and with a personal code name of 'Hector', Jaques was flown by Catalina seaplane to a rendezvous off the coast near

Victor Jaques (centre of seated row) *pictured with fellow British officers and members of the Free Thai movement.*

POWs leave Don Muang Airport after the end of World War II.

Hua Hin. There he was met by Free Thai agents who took him to Bangkok, where he made direct contact with Pridi. 'The operation was carried out with entire success,' wrote Gilchrist. 'Jaques came back five days later, after an astonishing expedition, and made his report to Mountbatten [the Allied Commander in Southeast Asia].'

Subsequently, Jaques was 'reinserted' and remained as Mountbatten's representative with Pridi and the Free Thai Movement until the end of the war. As Gilchrist describes it, 'It was a fantastic episode. For the most part Jaques was kept in strict seclusion, but sometimes he had to shift quarters hurriedly, and sometimes he had to move elsewhere for important interviews. The only car available was an ancient Ford Anglia, and how to get the six-foot-four brigadier inside was a serious problem.'

Most audaciously of all, in the last days of the war Jaques made his headquarters in the administrative building of the civilian internment camp, commandant Bhrom by then being involved with the Free Thai. As a refinement to the conditions, Bhrom's secretary Maureen James acquired curtains for the upper windows, not for décor but so that Jaques need not crawl on hands and knees when moving along the corridors to avoid being spotted by the internees or the Japanese.

Although working clandestinely and always kept hidden until close to the end of hostilities, Jaques was a professional soldier through and through, and he made it a matter of principle that he always wore his uniform lest he might be accused of being a spy if caught by the Japanese. In spite of having to live rough at times and surviving on meagre rations, Jaques later referred to his experiences with Force 136 as the best time of his life.

The end of the war came swiftly with the Japanese surrender, and there was no last-ditch stand by Japanese troops in Thailand, which some had feared might happen. Jaques was promoted from acting to full brigadier and was briefly the temporary British military governor of Thailand until the appointment of General Evans. The internees regained their liberty and there was now peace, but it was not until 1946, when Jaques was demobilized, that the sine die closure of Tilleke & Gibbins finally came to end.

A lunch given in honour of Admiral Lord Louis Mountbatten at the Prime Minister's Office. Right: Acting Brigadier Victor Jaques (far left) and a fellow British officer visiting Direk Jayanama's house at Soi Santisuk, Sukhumvit Road, on 30 August 1945.

Left to right: Herman Seiler, Alexander MacDonald, Jim Thompson and Jorges Orgibet in the garden of Orgibet's home on North Sathon Road in 1948

America Ascendant
1946–1967

Anyone wandering around Bangkok after World War II would have seen a city scarred in places but less damaged by Allied bombing than might have been expected. One notable casualty, however, seems symbolic, almost prophetic. This was the grand old building of the Borneo Company. Having its offices reduced to rubble did not spell the end of one of Thailand's most illustrious foreign trading companies (indeed, it survives today as part of the Inchcape Group), but it did signal the passing of an era. After the upheaval of the war, times were to change; the old quasi-colonial and characteristically British-dominated pattern of expatriate life and work in Bangkok had seen its day.

For Tilleke & Gibbins, as for the Borneo Company and other foreign businesses, life carried on, although after a period of picking up the pieces the picture of the jigsaw was never quite the same.

Bangkok scarred from World War II.

The biggest change after the war was the ascendancy of American influence over that of the British, both in the political sphere and in the nationality of the individuals who were to have an increasingly greater impact on postwar foreign business in Thailand.

Curiously, several of the Americans who settled in Thailand in the late 1940s and made names for themselves — most famously silk tycoon Jim Thompson, at one time a client of Tilleke & Gibbins, and Alexander MacDonald, founder of the *Bangkok Post* in 1946 — were former members of the Office of Strategic Services (OSS), the forerunner of the Central Intelligence Agency (CIA), though their common OSS connection was doubtless coincidental.

British and American political moves towards normalization in the immediate postwar period were vastly different in that the US had never officially been at war with Thailand, whereas Britain, although recognizing the Free Thai Movement, had considered itself at war with the Phibul government. As a consequence, the British tried to pressure the new government under prime minister Seni Pramoj to accede to onerous war reparations, including the right to station British and Commonwealth troops in the country indefinitely. Weeks of tense negotiations were only resolved when the US intervened and managed to persuade Britain to reduce its demands. Finally, in January 1946, an 'Anglo–Siamese Agreement for the Termination of the State of War Between Siam and Great Britain and India' was signed, Victor Jaques being one of those involved in the drafting of the document.

The ending of the war was also the beginning of a new regional outlook. 'In the 1945–6 negotiations', historians Chris Baker and Pasuk Phongpaichit write, 'the US became Siam's protector, warding off any extension of British colonial influence. Initially, the US was interested in Thailand as part of a regional plan for rebuilding Japan's economy. With the explosion of leftist anticolonialism in neighbouring countries in 1947–8, the "loss" of China to communist revolution in 1949, and the commitment of US and UN troops in Korea in 1950, the US grew steadily more interested in Thailand as an ally and base for prosecution of the Cold War to stem the spread of communism in Asia.'

A year after peace was secured, Victor Jaques, now demobilized from the British Army and awarded a CBE (Commander of the Order of the British Empire), MC (Military Cross) and DSO (Distinguished Service Order), set about reviving the business of Tilleke & Gibbins. Except for the assistance of Ina Jorgensen, he

The Legendary American

Of all the Americans who fell under Thailand's spell and who made their careers in the country after World War II, Jim Thompson achieved truly legendary status. Fascinated by the beauty of handwoven Thai silk — a traditional craft in steep decline — Thompson saw the potential of the material and set about revitalizing the weaving industry in partnership with M.C. Sanith Rangsit. By the 1950s he had succeeded in not only restoring local production but also

(Courtesy of The James H.W. Thompson Foundation)

in establishing international markets for the fabric. Today, the Jim Thompson label is a hallmark of fine Thai silk. The man himself, however, disappeared in 1967 while vacationing with friends in Malaysia's Cameron Highlands. One afternoon he went out for a walk and was simply never seen or heard from again. Despite exhaustive searches, no trace was ever found and Thompson's disappearance remains one of Asia's greatest unsolved mysteries.

Null and Void

'Whereas by a proclamation made in Bangkok on August 16, 1945 the Regent of Siam did, in the name of His Majesty the King of Siam, proclaim the declaration of war made by Siam on January 25, 1942 against the United Kingdom to be null and void in that it was made contrary to the will of the Siamese people and in violation of the constitution and laws of Siam.'

First clause, Anglo–Siamese Peace Agreement, January 1946.

had to start up alone since Atkinson had decided — in spite of Jaques' attempt to persuade him otherwise — to remain in England due to failing health. Atkinson died in 1953 at the age of 72.

There was no shortage of work, however, and Tilleke & Gibbins' usual caseload was augmented by war claims against the Thai government on behalf of individuals and European companies. In 1946, Jaques brought into the firm a young trial lawyer, Roland (later Rojvit) Periera, the son of a Singhalese father and Singaporean mother, who was to have a long and illustrious career with Tilleke & Gibbins.

The pressure of work at this time was nonetheless great. By 1951, with his health deteriorating and at his wife's insistence that he take life more easily, Jaques decided to sell Tilleke & Gibbins (minus the trademark side of the business which he had assigned to Ina Jorgensen in 1947 as a reward for her loyalty in safeguarding the firm's interests during World War II). He subsequently entered into partnership with Ina Jorgensen under a new company, Jorgensen & Co., but it was to be a short-lived association as Jaques' health rapidly

Roland (later Rojvit) Periera.

A Royal Tragedy

HM King Ananda, Rama VIII.

Just as Thailand was beginning to recover from the upheaval of World War II, the nation was devastated by a royal tragedy. On 9 June 1946 the young King Ananda Mahidol was found dead from a gunshot wound in his palace bedroom. The true circumstances of his death have never been publicly established. The all-important role of the monarchy was, however, secured when King Bhumibol Adulyadej, Ananda's younger brother, acceded to the throne. His reign has subsequently become the longest and one of the greatest and most revered in Thai history.

declined. At first it was thought he was suffering from tuberculosis, and in 1953 he went to Switzerland for treatment. But there he was diagnosed with lung cancer. He died two years later in England.

Jaques' sale of Tilleke & Gibbins marked what could be described as the end of the firm's British era. All of its previous partners had been British —even Tilleke himself though by nationality not birth — but now, like many other foreign businesses in Bangkok, Tilleke & Gibbins was to assume an American persona.

Purchasing the practice from Jaques was Mr Albert Moses Lyman. Like Tilleke, but unlike all other previous partners (who had joined the firm as newly qualified lawyers), Albert Lyman brought a wide range of experience to the business.

Born in Boise, Idaho in 1905, Lyman grew up from the age of twelve in Washington, D.C. There he attended Central High School where, among other distinctions, he was the only boy in a class for shorthand and typing, skills that were later to prove invaluable and pivotal in his professional life. He went on to study law at the George Washington University Law School in Washington, D.C., although he never took a degree, having sat and passed the Bar exam before finishing his university course. As a student he worked for two years with the Lincoln National Bank (now Riggs National Bank) before setting up as a sole practitioner in his own law firm in Washington, where he remained in successful general practice until 1943.

The year of 1927 was momentous for Albert Lyman, and not only for him as it was the year in which he married Freda Ring. Herself a lawyer, Freda had graduated from the George Washington University Law School

In Loving Memory

In proud memory of my husband Colonel V. H. JAQUES, C.B.E., D.S.O., M.C. & Bar The most exalted order of The White Elephant of Thailand 4th class Bangkok 1925-1940; Barrister-at-Law Royal Sussex Regiment 1914-1919 & 1940-1946 1896 ~ 1955

The memory of Victor Jaques is honoured in a plaque placed by his wife at Bangkok's Christ Church. It is a most fitting location as Christ Church, built in 1905 on Convent Road, was in Jaques' day, and so remains today, the religious focal point for the British and other Protestant residents of Bangkok. The building has changed little over the decades and, although now dwarfed by modern high-rises, its small square tower is still a city landmark.

Above: *Freda Lyman, née Ring, aged four* (right) *with her sister Gretchen, aged six, circa 1904.* Right: *Albert Lyman in 1908, aged three.*

albert Lyman

about 1908

Left: *Freda Lyman in 1946, aged 46.*
Below: *Freda, aged 17, at her high
school graduation.* Right: *The couple
shortly after their arrival in Bangkok.*
Far right: *The young lawyer Albert
Lyman on his wedding day, aged 22.*

with Honours — in 1921 at the tender age of twenty. She was too young for admission to the District of Columbia Bar, and had to wait a year before she was accepted. Albert was admitted to the same Bar in 1929.

Although Albert and Freda had studied at the same law school and were members of the D.C. Bar, it was not law but swimming that first brought them together. Albert Lyman had been a gold-medal springboard diver at high school and continued in the sport afterwards as a swimming instructor. Freda signed up for lessons and so the two met. But as she was to say in later life: 'Albert makes a better husband than he did swimming instructor as I still don't know how to swim.'

The marriage of Albert and Freda Lyman was an unqualified success and, most remarkably, their personal relationship was matched by an equally successful professional partnership. To the marriage lines of 'in sickness and in health' could have been added in their case 'in home and in

office'. As their son David, today the Chairman and Chief Values Officer of Tilleke & Gibbins, describes his parents: 'My father was the problem solver, my mother the organizer, and they both had enormous respect for each other.'

It was this ideal combination of personal qualities that, to

The birth certificate of David Lyman.

a great extent, accounted for the vast success and expansion of Tilleke & Gibbins in the latter half of the twentieth century. Albert Lyman would affectionately refer to Freda as the 'straw boss', while his own approach to the law business was, in words he might well have spoken himself, 'to keep the clients out of goddamn trouble'. Indeed, there were those who would affectionately refer to Albert

as 'Mr Goddamn', for he was a crusty and quick-tempered character, but always with a good heart and a love for his work that manifested itself in a genuine desire to help.

Before this partnership reached full fruition with Tilleke & Gibbins in Bangkok, Albert and Freda Lyman made their early life together in Washington, D.C. In addition to running his one-man business, Albert also taught at Tarrell Law School (now Howard University) and held Bar review courses for predominantly black students. From these early years he developed an appreciation of people of all races and ethnic origins, as well as a hallmark character that has been described as 'colourful yet unpretentious, profane, witty, articulate, cantankerous and old-shoe style'.

Freda also established her characteristic pattern of efficiency that she later described as 'work, children and home'. Daughter Lucy was born in 1932 and David in 1936, while her work at this time was with the Children's

In at the Deep End

Above: *Swimming and diving coach Albert Lyman (standing seventh from right).* Left: *Albert performs a half gainer from the 3-metre springboard at The Royal Bangkok Sports Club.*

Since his youth, *Albert Lyman was a keen swimmer and champion diver, as were two of his younger brothers, and he retained a passion for the sport throughout his life. In Thailand, at the Naris Club pool, he founded and coached a national girls' swimming team, but even as he grew older he was not content just to give instruction from the poolside. As a friend recalled: 'To watch Albert Lyman jump off the high divingboard at The Royal Bangkok Sports Club at the age of nearly seventy was an alarming sight for anyone who didn't know him. Wasn't he too old for that sort of thing? Then he would do a fancy dive and come up smiling like he always did.'*

*Proud parents: Freda Lyman with baby Lucy (left)
in 1932, and Albert (above) with David and Lucy
in a swimming pool in Chevy Chase, Maryland, USA.*

Bureau of the US Department of Labour, where she advised on the writing of child legislation.

The practice of law came to a temporary halt for Albert Lyman during World War II when, in 1943, he joined the US Navy for three years, being promoted to Yeoman 1st Class, and was initially stationed at the Amphibious Base in Norfolk, Virginia. Given his professional qualifications, it was not surprising that he was assigned duty as legal assistance officer handling mostly courts martial. What did surprise the Navy was Lyman's strong preference to associate himself with the defence, in which he proved, to the chagrin of his superior officers, remarkably skilful. Military thinking was generally that any sailor brought before a court martial was guilty, should be declared so, and punished in the interests of discipline. Once Lyman became involved, however, the conviction rate at Norfolk dropped markedly.

Acquittals increased until the base commander warned Lyman 'to remember what you're here for and who pays your salary'. The champion of the underdog was not deterred. In a brilliant famous last case he advised defence counsel of a Native American who was charged with persistent drunk and disorderly conduct every time he left the base with a navy wartime ration card to buy beer.

Lyman dug deep into the statutes of the State of Virginia and found that from the seventeenth century it had been against the law to sell alcohol to a Native American; 'firewater and the Red Man don't mix,' as they would have said in the old days. Thus, Lyman argued, the navy was at fault for providing the defendant with a ration card to buy off-base, in Virginia territory, the beer he could not resist. Presented with such a case, the court martial, taking judicial notice of the local statute, had no alternative but to bring in a verdict of Not Guilty. This was the last straw for the commanding officer; shortly after the court martial, Lyman and his client quickly found themselves on a train headed west, having been transferred to the amphibious forces in the Pacific theatre — about as far from Norfolk as the base commander could send them.

Thus in early 1945 the lawyer came to be disgorged from the doors of a landing ship tank (LST) during the invasion of Okinawa. But he was saved from the horrors of life in a foxhole by his legal and

Albert Lyman as Yeoman 2nd Class, US Navy.

clerical skills (that shorthand and typing he had so wisely taken at high school), and was snapped up by the US Naval Military Government (USNMG) in whose service Lyman saw out the rest of the conflict and the immediate postwar period with distinction.

Among those distinctions was work on the drafting of the first Constitution for the Southern Ryukyu Islands of the Islands of the Nansei Shoto and Adjacent Waters, of which Okinawa is the largest. Indicative of Lyman's characteristic humanity, his draft included universal suffrage and equal rights for all men and women;

freedom of the press and public criticism of government, including the USNMG; the right to strike and unionize; complete religious freedom for all; and vesting the power of government in the people.

Lyman's unexpected transfer to Okinawa was to prove a turning point in his life. Quite simply, he fell in love with Asia. Following his repatriation to the US in March 1946 for demobilization, he found himself inexorably drawn back to the Orient and almost immediately sought and accepted a job as a civilian lawyer with the Department of Justice assigned to the US Military Government in Korea (USMGIK). There he remained from September 1946 to late 1948, being joined early in his sojourn by his wife, daughter and son.

During this Korean period of Albert Lyman's career almost single-handedly he established the juvenile courts and reformatory system, and also compiled and edited all legal opinions of the USMGIK, which were subsequently published. For his work he received a commendation from his commander, and was made a life member of the Korean Bar

Association. But the honour he probably cherished most was the number of commemorative plaques in his name made and installed by boys at several of the reformatory schools that he had founded.

Post-World War II Bangkok street scene.

In October 1948, with South Korea under threat of invasion by its northern neighbour, Albert Lyman was appointed to the Judge Advocate Section of the US Eighth Army in Yokohama, Japan, while Freda and the children

returned to Maryland, USA, for a few months until accommodation could be found for them in Japan. In Yokohama Albert worked on the Class B War Crimes Trials Review Board and although kept busy he was nonetheless able to spend periods of leave exploring other parts of the region, including Shanghai, Hong Kong, Manila and Bangkok, nowhere having a greater impact on him than the latter, which he visited several times. After the subzero winters of Korea and Japan, Bangkok's attraction was its tropical climate, but Lyman was also captivated by the city's inescapable charm and the smiling hospitality of its people.

'I'm crazy about Bangkok,' he wrote to Freda. 'There are no American lawyers here at all, but there are three British lawyers, all old-timers and about ready to quit. . . . Two of the British lawyers were very friendly and cordial . . . both said American business is greatly increasing in Siam, whereas the British [business] is barely holding its own. . . . My heart is set on going to Siam and practising law there as it offers the most promise.'

Freda Lyman also toured extensively through Asia and

similarly became enamoured of Thailand. So, having explored the options, the choice of where next was a foregone conclusion for the Lymans — the lure of Bangkok proving as irresistible to them as it had to all of Tilleke & Gibbins' previous partners. When Albert Lyman's contract with the US government expired in early 1949 he travelled ahead of his family to prepare the way, flying from Japan to Bangkok on a British Overseas Airways Corporation (BOAC) — forerunner of British Airways (BA) — flying boat in April 1949, landing on the Chao Phraya River. It was a bold move for a man with no assured employment and only 750 US dollars in his pocket.

Prospects of financial gain were not immediately forthcoming. Lyman pinned his hopes on a tentative offer of a partnership in the law firm of Baguley & Tooth, but a month after his arrival, at around the time his family joined him, he learnt the offer had been withdrawn, the sons of Baguley & Tooth's managing partner apparently persuading their father there was no need for a new partner.

It was a blow. Still, the family managed to get settled and set up a temporary home at the Oriental Hotel, as did, coincidentally, the prior partners of Tilleke & Gibbins.

That was not as grand as it might sound; the Oriental being in that immediate postwar period a mere shadow of its former self and a far cry from the oasis of

The BOAC flying boat that brought Albert Lyman from Japan to Bangkok in 1949.

luxury it has now become. Such were the hotel's shortcomings that David Lyman, then not thirteen years old, recalls, 'We rapidly became members of The Royal Bangkok Sports Club so as to have a place where we could take a hot shower'.

As it happened, the Lymans' stay at the Oriental became part of its history, with Freda Lyman contributing in no small way to the hotel's steady reemergence as a premier hostelry. The American presence in Bangkok was growing at this time and the Oriental needed to provide culinary fare with a Western flavour if it was to satisfy its burgeoning new clientele. Running the hotel after World War II was Germaine Krull, a Frenchwoman who had been a photojournalist and who was resourceful in many ways but was at a loss when it came to coping with American tastes. In her reminiscences, *Bangkok: Siam's City of Angels*, she admitted, 'I did not know how American sandwiches, hamburgers and cheeseburgers should taste, so I could not teach the cook'.

Fortunately, Freda Lyman was at hand. 'An American couple who were both lawyers, Mr and Mrs Lyman, were staying at the hotel,' Krull wrote. 'Freda Lyman, who later became one of my closest friends, agreed readily to instruct the cook how to prepare American sandwiches and show the boys how

Snapshots and mementos of life in Korea and Japan,
clockwise from top left: *Freda Lyman's Armed
Forces Pacific ID card; Albert pictured in late 1945
in Okinawa; 1946 certificate admitting Albert to practise
before the Supreme Court of Korea; and a snapshot of
Freda and friends on a visit to Korea in 1962.*

Nearly a Shattered Dream

Gov't Forces Strike Back; Premier Still Captive

The Postmen Say:

THAT, the political climate today being what it is, we decided to give Kittridge, the office changeboy, a day off and let it, instead, if how it took us three hours to reach the office this morning, ... we have had such transportation trouble.

It began at 6:15 when we sallied out Soi Lek K i Bangkapi and headed eastward on the Sukumus Road.

The sun, among other things, we witnessed.

We negotiated three lanes eastward by car. There, on the outer of our army officers, we parked the Chevrolet and continued on foot. Seniors were not allowed.

A Sol Samben a flustered soldier turned the corner, followed by what seemed a horde out of bullets. We followed him promptly into the lanes.

The shooting was getting thicker and thicker along the railway line a couple of hundred meters ahead and artillery pieces were sounding from the Wireless Road area. Occasionally a shell whistled overhead.

Taking the back road parallel to the highway we reached as far as Soi Chuea Chitra where the shooting again thickened. We pushed further inland until we arrived at Klong Bangkapi.

Maybe, we thought, we could get through the "no man's land" shoes by water.

A passing boat had a man abreast with the same idea in mind. Tony Thorogood of Cooper-Johnston Co. was desperate, I've some reason, to get to his office today.

We joined him in the little dinghy

Post Vol. 5, No. 273. Saturday, June 30, 1951. Price 1.50 Baht

Ridgway Getting Truce Directive

LATE NEWS: General Ridgway has broadcast an invitation to the Red commander to meet him for armistice talks aboard a Danish hospital ship in Wonsan harbor.

WASHINGTON, — UP —Instructions on a possible field negotiation of a cease-fire in Korea have been approved by President Truman and are being sent to General Matthew B. Ridgway, Far East Commander.

Deputy Defense Secretary Robert A. Lovett disclosed this at a Pentagon news conference Friday.

Lovett refused to give any details of the instructions but he said any settlement reached by Ridgway and the commanders of the North Korean and Chinese Communist forces would be subject to approval.

IRAN BACKDOWN ON ANTI-BRITISH BILL INDICATED

TEHERAN,—(UP)—Premier Mohammed Mossadegh promised

COUP GROUP BACKED BY NAVY UNITS

Fighting Intensifies After All-Night Radio War

Armed forces supporting the Phibun Government and Royal Navy forces supporting the "Save the Nation" coup group were still battling for control of the kingdom this afternoon.

The coup group opened their attack on the government with the kidnapping of Premier Phibul Songkram at 3:30 p.m. yesterday. The Premier was attending a ceremony during which the dredger Manhattan was turned over to the Thai Government.

Premier Still Held

This afternoon the coup group, with a variety of forces embattled at their bases in Thonburi, at the radio base and at the Royal Landing, still held Pibul Marsal Pabin in their hands.

The Phibun Government is temporarily under the leadership of Mal Venkuron Banoh, Minister of Foreign Affairs, and is being supported by the Army, the Royal Air Force, and the

COUP SCENE: In upper picture, the Premier, with U.S. Charge d'Affaires William Turner, left, and ML D j Saniwong right, walks aboard the dredge Manhattan at the Royal Landing. Lower picture shows Navy men in control as the crowd disperses immediately after the Premier was taken prisoner.

MOVEMENT IN BANGKOK PARALYZED

Thousands Stranded Overnight By Barricades

Following declaration of a state of martial law last night, civilian movement in Bangkok today was virtually at a standstill.

Many business houses stayed closed from yesterday evening when barricades were set up at bridges and other strategic points in the city. A number of office jobs also have not been able to go home through areas taken over by the military last night.

Cars were stalled and persons caught between barricades had to pass the night in front of houses, in stationary tram rail in offices. Many men and women thus caught stood all night in front of houses where radio receiver sets were blaring on amusement.

Trams and bus lines still were not running this morning and most city streets were devoid of motors or books of books set up at various intersections.

O ir a f e e d off shops opted for business today. Even

The purchase of Tilleke & Gibbins by Albert Lyman was almost scuppered by what became known as 'The "Manhattan" Coup'. On 29 June 1951 a group of Thai naval officers attempted to overthrow the government of Field Marshal Phibul whilst he was attending a ceremony on the Chao Phraya River aboard the dredger Manhattan, *gifted to Thailand by America. Negotiations with the coup plotters failed and fierce fighting broke out in Bangkok the following day between the government, supported by the army, police and air force, and the navy and marines. The attempted coup was eventually suppressed but with over 3,000 casualties, including 1,200 dead. When the fighting began, Victor Jaques and Albert Lyman were on the balcony of the firm's offices in Hongkong Bank Lane and about to sign the T&G sale agreement. A sudden nearby explosion caused them both to duck under the table, the trained reaction of these two World War II veterans. Only after the danger had passed did they realize they had sought cover under a glass-top table which, if shattered, could have put paid to the sale in a very permanent way.*

Divorce Thai Style

'One department of law developed more than any of the others. And that was divorce. There seemed to be a great deal of European as opposed to Siamese divorce in Bangkok. The hot sun, the good pay, and the everpresent bar, made the men less faithful than they would otherwise have been. And the fact that all the women, wives as well as unmarried girls, had very little to do, always a car and a chauffeur at hand, gin squashes at call, and a large number of bachelors just around the corner, made them more amorous than they would ever have been at home.'

Gerald Sparrow,
Lawyer at Large.

suited both parties. The young trial lawyer, Roland Periera, remained with Tilleke & Gibbins after the purchase and was soon made a partner by Albert Lyman, while Freda later joined her husband as the other senior partner. The firm remained an unregistered partnership, and staff at the time, including the Lymans and Roland Periera, totalled just six.

Once the purchase was complete, Lyman moved the firm into new offices at 1169 New Road, the old Whiteaway Laidlaw store building, diagonally opposite the General Post Office and still

within the then heart of Bangkok's foreign business district. The same prestige in location was maintained when, in 1960, expanding business led to another move, this time to the Wang Lee Building on Suriwongse Road.

With Bangkok growing in size — between 1936 and 1960 the metropolitan area increased from 43 to 120 square kilometres — and in prosperity, with established commercial companies expanding and new firms setting up business, Tilleke & Gibbins found no shortage of work in the 1950s. To the old established British trading

borrowed from Freda, purchased Tilleke & Gibbins from Victor Jaques, the firm's sole remaining partner after the war. The two would have known each other well — it was a small foreign community and Lyman had been introduced to Bangkok's few foreign lawyers on his earlier visits — and with Jaques seeking retirement due to poor health, the sale of the firm

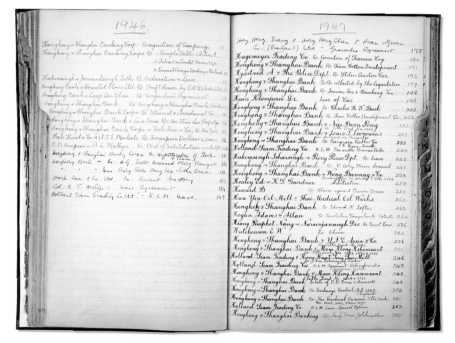

Company records in the days before office computers.

BAGULEY & TOOTH,
ADVOCATES & SOLICITORS.

Telegraphic Address.
"BAGULEY, BANGKOK."

A. B. C. Code 5th. Edn.

TELEPHONE:

Registered Airmail

Bangkok, 13th January 1949

Dear Mr. Lyman,

Thank you for your letter of the 17th October last. My sincere apologise for the delay in answering it due to my feeling that, if I may say so, you would be handicapped at your age by having to acquire the language as is necessary to practise in the courts. Your fellow-countrymen are, however, acquiring substantial interests in Siam and the fact may be beneficial to you. Our firm also does valuable trade mark work for ~~the~~ United States firms as well as those in other foreign countries.

A Siamese lady-barrister, who is capable and energetic, daughter of Prince Wattyakorn who kindly allows me to use rooms
... h me prior
... another
... ess known
... owledge
... e invaluable
... a male
... ou are
... the lady
... emaining

WESTERN UNION

JOSEPH L. EGAN
PRESIDENT

CLASS OF SERVICE
This is a full-rate Telegram or Cablegram unless its deferred character is indicated by a suitable symbol above or preceding the address.

1201

SYMBOLS
DL=Day Letter
NL=Night Letter
LC=Deferred Cable
NLT=Cable Night Letter
Ship Radiogram

The filing time shown in the date line on telegrams and day letters is STANDARD TIME at point of origin. Time of receipt is STANDARD TIME at point of destination

PA104

P.SFA023 INTL=SF YOKOHAMA VIA RCA 33 26 1205S= 1949 JAN 26 AM 4 44

NLT FREDA LYMAN=

MAIL 4824 EDGEMOOR LANE BETHEDA(MD)= DUPLICATE OF TELEPHONED TELEGRAM

RECEIVED OFFER OF LAW PARTNERSHIP IN BANGKOK WITH BRITISH LAWYER AND SIAMESE PRINCESS BARRISTER AM FASCINATED PREPARE FOR LIFE OF ROYAL ROMANCE AND HIGH ADVENTURE=

ALBERT=

Wi 4594

ADD

FK 737A-26 MAILED

4824=.. THE COMPANY WILL APPRECIATE SUGGESTIONS FROM ITS PATRONS CONCERNING ITS SERVICE

Albert Lyman worked hard at seeking a position in Bangkok, although high hopes were not quickly fulfilled.

Left: *1169 New Road (Bank of America Building), where Albert Lyman relocated the offices of Tilleke & Gibbins following his purchase of the firm in 1951.*

New premises in the Wang Lee Building, on Suriwongse Road, were acquired in 1960 as expanding business demanded more space. Looking insignificant today, the building was Bangkok's first custom-designed multistorey office block.

Bangkok traffic in the 1950s.

concerns such as the Borneo Company, and foreign banks like the Hongkong & Shanghai and the Mercantile Bank, the firm added more recently arrived and mainly (though not exclusively) American companies, including Caltex, Getz Bros & Co. and Pan American World.

The case files for the 1950s show that Tilleke & Gibbins was not only extremely active but also diversified in the type of business handled. From the mundane — such as divorce, last wills and testaments, trademarks, company formation and licensing, taxation, maritime and airline business, even the loss of a Neilson Hays library book — to more complicated cases like embezzlement, perjury, libel and child adoption, the firm's undertakings covered a wide range of legal proceedings.

The largest number of cases, however, related to debt settlement, it being against Thailand's taxation laws to write off debts without a court suit, while one of the biggest single cases was an action between Curtis-Wright Corp. and KLM regarding the burning of a KLM plane at Don Muang Airport in 1955.

Not surprisingly, given Bangkok's notorious traffic congestion (though it was far less in the 1950s than now), automobile accident cases were common, but what does stand out from the list is an action against careless driving. This is remarkable in that, today, mere observation leads one to believe there cannot possibly be a law that allows for a careless driving charge to be actionable.

Success in the courts did not always mean financial success, and like many other law firms Tilleke & Gibbins has had over the years its share of difficulties in receiving payment. These resulted not necessarily from clients without means (although Albert Lyman would take on criminal cases simply to help those in need). For example, Air India, which Tilleke & Gibbins had successfully represented in a case involving the Customs Department, took nineteen years to settle the fees. Another notable incident was with the Bank of America. Successfully represented in a case of deferred taxes, it proved difficult to persuade the bank of the monetary value (and hence fees) of taxes deferred for nineteen years.

Criminal law was always Albert Lyman's main area of interest, but much of his attention in the 1950s and '60s was taken up with legislation and activities concerning trademarks and their infringement. This was a business he had to build up from scratch,

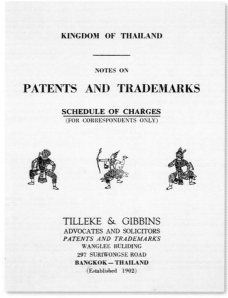

Albert Lyman rebuilt the patents and trademarks business after purchasing T&G.

Neilson Hays Library

(Courtesy of Neilson Hays Library)

A client of Tilleke & Gibbins once involved in a case of a lost book, the Neilson Hays Library was and remains a venerable Bangkok institution. Its roots date back to 1869, when the Bangkok Ladies Library Association was founded to serve the needs of the city's English-speaking community. Initially, the library was housed in a private residence and subsequently in various other locations until the present building was erected in 1922. This charming, domed colonial-style library was constructed by Dr T. Heyward as a memorial to his wife, Jennie Neilson Hays, who had been a mainstay of the Bangkok Ladies Library Association.

Roland Periera (right) *with Albert Lyman* (centre) *and Washington, D.C. lawyer Evan Berlack, pictured in the mid-60s.*

In the history of Tilleke & Gibbins, Roland Periera — a quiet, kind and generous man of the old school — is rather overshadowed by the flamboyant Albert Lyman, and later by the equally strong and extrovert personality of his son David Lyman. Nonetheless, Roland Periera was a cornerstone of Tilleke & Gibbins for more than half a century until his death in 2002. As David Lyman noted in a funeral address: 'In my law school I learnt well the admonition of one of my professors that "finding a good business partner is ten times more difficult than finding a good spouse". Mr Periera and the Lymans have met and exceeded that test.'

Even before it came to the practice of law, Roland Periera was a boon to Albert Lyman right from the start. Coming to Thailand directly from the Pacific war zone in the years immediately following World War II, Mr Lyman had had no opportunity to learn the language and thus found the bilingual (English- and Thai-speaking) Periera an indispensable partner. Mutual respect and absolute trust were the basis of the partnership, so much so that the forty per cent interest Periera held in the firm remained only a verbal agreement until as

as all such Intellectual Property work that Tilleke & Gibbins had previously handled had been sold off to Jorgensen & Co. after World War II by Victor Jaques. Borrowing the idea from a similar procedure used by the Western colonial powers in China, Albert Lyman also developed consular registration for patents, which went some way to providing protection for patent holders. The groundwork laid by Lyman in these areas bore abundant fruit in later years when Tilleke & Gibbins became one of the foremost legal experts on

intellectual property (trademarks, patents and copyright).

Assisting Albert and Freda Lyman in the practice was Roland Periera, who acted as the firm's principal trial lawyer, foreigners being allowed to act only as solicitors and not barristers in the Thai courts. Born in Bangkok in 1920, Roland Periera took his LLB degree at Bangkok's University of Moral and Political Sciences (now Thammasat) in 1942, although he did not begin to practise until the end of World War II when he joined Victor Jaques at Tilleke & Gibbins.

Rojvit (formerly Roland) Periera (right) and (below from the right) Nati Choonahakasikarn, Somchit Boonyapravet, Prince Wattayakornkasemsri (Mom Chao), Sutham Pathamadilok and Savee Saisuwan, lawyers working for Tilleke & Gibbins in the 1950s.

Legal Repercussions

When Albert Lyman represented Jim Thompson in a case against a Lao national who had tried to appropriate Thompson's company during the silk tycoon's absence, he could not have foreseen its repercussions. Some time after the case, Lyman had business with the Lao minister of justice in Vientiane. On his introduction to the minister the latter responded, 'Ah, you're the man who jailed my brother in Bangkok'. So ended Tilleke & Gibbins' foray into Laos.

late as 1973 when Tilleke & Gibbins became a registered ordinary partnership following the introduction of a new Aliens Business Act.

In his long career with the firm, Periera appeared in more than 1,000 cases, many of them ranking among Bangkok's most notable post-World War II trials. One of these cases was, at the time, the largest in Thai history, involving a 400-million-baht suit between Siam Kraft Paper and Parsons & Whitmore, a construction company, concerning the Siam Kraft factory in Kanchanaburi. Periera succeeded in securing a satisfactory outcome to the litigation for Parsons & Whitmore.

In the words of David Lyman, Periera was a 'litigator par excellence. He did not like to lose in court and rarely did'. Lyman adds that thorough preparation and an intimate knowledge of the law and procedure were the keys to Periera's success, assisted by the hallmark characteristics of a keen intellect, vivid imagination and quick mind.

Outside the office and the courts, Periera took an interest in business and civic affairs. He played an instrumental role in the formation of the Franco–Thai Chamber of Commerce, and was also an active Rotarian, achieving the distinction in 1982 of becoming Rotary International's first district governor for Thailand.

On the social front 'Bangkok was always a lively city with all-night parties and lots of visiting back and forth', recalled Freda Lyman in later life, and the physical and social setting in which Tilleke & Gibbins expanded in the 1950s and early 60s was not altogether different from that in which the firm flourished under Brighouse and Atkinson.

Bangkok was a sprawling city with no definable centre and its architecture was all low-rise, most characteristic being rows of three- or four-storey shophouses (*hong taew*), which alternated with temple compounds, houses and patches of open land. Bangkok was nonetheless evolving and, as D. Insor wrote in his 1963 book *Thailand: A Political, Social and Economic Analysis*, 'The Thais have created in their public buildings a genuine synthesis of the art of East and West. Long, sloping roofs, often of green tiles, slightly overlapping at the ends, derive from the characteristic three- or four-tiered temple roofs.'

At this time, the city could still lay claim to its old 'Venice of the East' tag, with many of its canals still intact. Close to the Tilleke & Gibbins office were canals along Si Phaya, Suriwongse and Silom roads, all of which connected with the Chao Phraya River. As Albert

Rama IV Road in 1945.

Lyman was to recall, 'a lot of folk went swimming in them'.

As a teenager growing up in Bangkok, David Lyman remembers the city as being 'hot, smaller than now and very Oriental, much more so than Japan or Korea [his previous homes in the East] because it was tropical'. The traffic was 'heavy' as opposed to congested, which it became from the 1960s onwards. He also recalls, with a pained look, that there were no real dentists in Bangkok, 'only an old German who did not understand anaesthesia'.

Lucy Hill, David's sister, has a vivid recollection of the city in the 1950s as 'peaceful and with trees everywhere'. She also has fond memories of formal dances at Amporn Gardens, 'so pretty with coloured lights illuminating the fountains'.

Generally, social life and expatriate entertainment revolved around The Royal Bangkok Sports Club (where Lucy made the most of her attraction as the eldest of the very few American teenage girls). Entertaining at home was typical and dinner parties were frequent,

guests comprised largely of foreigners — mainly families of embassy and UN staff and business people, plus a smattering of Protestant and Catholic clergymen. Not surprisingly, the Thais who were part of the expat social scene were

David and sister Lucy (above), *and David's first Thailand resident's card* (left).

usually those who had been educated overseas.

Beyond Bangkok, Thailand was something of an adventure. The beach resort of Pattaya was then a fishing village, reached via a four-hour drive from Bangkok. To the north, it took about a week to reach Chiang Mai by car.

On the international front, Thailand was perceived by strategists as one of the last bulwarks in Southeast Asia against the spread of communism out of China. It was this more than anything else that served as a catalyst for change. Norman Bartlett sums up the balance between old and new in the decade after the end of World War II. 'By 1955', he wrote in *Land of the Lotus-Eaters*, 'Bangkok had a two-way appeal: it was a lingering, seductive, glamorous relic of the passing mysterious East and, at the same time, promised the intriguing interest associated with the dangerous chess of twentieth-century atomic international politics.' Accepting this duality, the latter aspect of Bangkok was to grow, especially with the escalation of the Vietnam War in the 1960s. But the exotic façade was, regrettably, to decline, although it was not to vanish entirely until the economic boom of the late 1980s (and even then it partially survived in out-of-the-way pockets of the city).

In domestic politics, the prevailing climate was largely one of

Ethnic Chinese in an illegal opium den in early twentieth-century Siam. (Courtesy of Hall of Opium, Mae Fah Luang Foundation)

military coups followed by dictatorships, in spite of the nation having had a succession of constitutions since 1932. Only with significant economic progress in the 1980s did the pattern begin to change as business interests, along with an emerging middle class, came to eclipse the power of the military.

For the time being, however, domestic politics was played out by a power elite and had little impact on daily life, certainly not that of the expatriate community. Bangkok remained a never-never land, 'an intriguing clutter of old and new, East and West . . . a wily yet guileless city . . . deeply devoted to the arts of pleasure', as Alexander MacDonald once remarked.

One blot on the Thai landscape was drugs. 'Opium, at that time,' wrote Norman Bartlett in 1959, 'was a basic element in understanding Siam although few Thais smoked it.' He added that the 'foul tendrils of corruption and easy money spread far and high and not only in Bangkok'. Until relatively recently, the so-called Golden Triangle, comprising parts of northern

Patpong

The first address of the American Chamber of Commerce, which Albert Lyman cofounded, was Patpong Road. That would be inconceivable today, with Patpong and its attendant streets being famous (or infamous) for go-go bars, sex shows and the night bazaar. But it was not always that way. Originally, the land had belonged to an American firm run by a certain William Hunt, who was engaged in shipping. When the Japanese took over Bangkok during World War II, the land was confiscated as enemy property and sold to a Thai, Mr Udom Patpong. Initially, just one

street was built up as a private road, which after the war emerged as the city's most prominent foreign business centre. Here were the offices of leading companies, among them Caltex and KLM, as well as the American Chamber, and several restaurants such as Mizu's Kitchen and the Red Door. Only with the escalation of the Vietnam War in the latter half of the 1960s did Patpong start to develop and expand as an entertainment district catering to American servicemen. Patpong roads I and II are still today the property of the Patpong family.

T&G's American Chamber of Commerce membership certificate.

Thailand, Burma and Laos, was the world's largest producer of opium and its derivative, heroin. Drug cases, especially those involving foreigners charged with heroin smuggling, frequently made the headlines and, as will be seen later, it was the defence of a drugs charge that became one of Tilleke & Gibbins' most high-profile cases, grabbing international headlines.

Without diminishing the drug problem, it should be noted that foreigners in the 1950s tended to view opium smoking as a titillating example of Oriental 'wickedness'. Many visitors tried it and Lucy Hill well remembers that the opium dens of Bangkok's Chinatown (legal until 1959) were 'a standard stop on the visitor's tour'.

For Albert and Freda Lyman, life in Bangkok was not all days of legal practice and evenings of partying, and both contributed enormously to the business and social life of the city, drawing on their energy and talents to help achieve positive and lasting gains. In 1950 Albert Lyman was a founding member of the American Association of Thailand which, in 1957, evolved into the American Chamber of Commerce, with Lyman one of its cofounders and its legal adviser for many years.

Fellow cofounder Walter Meyer remarked in a 2001 interview that the Americans thought the already established British Chamber of Commerce was 'old style and didn't do enough'. The Americans would show the way, and they did. One of the American Chamber's first self-appointed tasks was, with USAID cooperation, to help formulate a new Revenue Code, although sadly this document was to vanish in one of the drawers of the Revenue Department. More successful was a push to get the then Business Tax levied on imports to be collected at the port before the goods were released. This was aimed at preventing widespread cheating on the tax. For a while the Chamber met with a blank wall as the Revenue Department claimed that the port was the Customs Department's turf and it could not interfere. However, the Americans eventually got their argument accepted and the Revenue Department did open an office at Bangkok's port, which had the effect, according to Meyer, of practically ruling out cheating on business tax.

Again in the business world, Albert Lyman was the inspiration

American Style

'We are all a bit discouraged just on general principles. However, we continue aiming at improvement of the American community in the face of difficulties, such as the prevalent refusal of the American group to wear neckties and long sleeve shirts; an encouraging sign is that few Americans go around in public wearing shorts. Just between us, we have noticed quite a few of our British cousins hastening through the streets to their 'fish and chips' with their bronzed and coarse-haired limbs amply shown by their usually immaculate business or sports shorts, an evil custom which fortunately we more civilized folks have not yet deigned to copy.'

Albert Lyman,
Bulletin 20, The American Association of Thailand.

for the founding of the Bangkok Stock Exchange (now the Securities Exchange of Thailand) in 1961, and served as its chairman for ten years. Other distinctions include being a founding member of the Bangkok Cigar Club (Lyman's own favourite puff was a Philippine Tabacalera Manila Blunt), the select membership of which included some of the country's most eminent personages. He also helped establish the Mariner's Club at Klong Toey port in 1952–3 — to provide merchant seamen of all nations with a place to relax and play sports while in Bangkok. He also remained active in the legal aspects of maritime matters.

On the social scene, Lyman was not only a prominent member of The Royal Bangkok Sports Club, where he taught youngsters swimming and diving, but also he joined the Bangkok Riding and Polo Club, not because he was any sort of horseman (though he did buy a horse, Mary, for his children), but because his enthusiasm and

personal magnetism was needed to spark the club along.

Between his busy professional and social commitments, Albert Lyman managed to find time to engage in journalism. He initiated, and for several years authored, the Polo Club's

Albert Lyman, confirmed cigar smoker and founding member of the Bangkok Cigar Club.

tongue-in-cheek newsletter *Boots and Saddles*, while in more serious vein he contributed articles in the 1950s to the *Far Eastern Economic Review*. Among the latter were pieces on Thailand's judicial system and on the country's income

tax regulations. Both articles are highly informative and flavoured by Lyman's candid light-heartedness, as in such asides as, 'The general story is that such [irresponsible] firms keep three sets of books — one for the tax authorities, one for their partners and one for themselves'.

As energetic as her husband, Freda Lyman was equally active in Bangkok life outside the office. Indeed, she helped to expand the social sphere, especially where women were concerned. 'While women were active in business and they did accompany their husbands, there wasn't too much in the way of activities for them,' she commented in a 1984 newspaper interview. To redress the situation, Freda was instrumental in starting the American Women's Club, the Soroptimist Club, and the Toastmistress Club, 'just to get women out of the house and involved in projects to improve themselves or their community'.

Through her work with the American Women's Club, Freda

Price $1.60 per copy

FAR EASTERN

ECONOMIC REVIEW

Vol. XVIII   Hongkong, June 30, 1955.   No. 26

THE HONGKONG AND SHANGHAI
BANKING CORPORATION
(Incorporated in the Colony of Hong Kong)
The Liability of Members is limited to the extent and in manner
prescribed in Chapter 70 of the Laws of Hong Kong

Capital Authorised .. Hong Kong $25,000,000
Capital Issued and Fully Paid Up Hong Kong $25,000,000
Reserve Fund .. .. .. Sterling £7,687,500
Reserve Liability of Members .. Hong Kong $25,000,000

Board of Directors
C. BLAKER, M.C., E.D., Chairman,
H. D. BENHAM, Deputy Chairman,
H. D. M. BARTON   J. H. HAMM
The Hon. J. A. BLACKWOOD R. J. SHEPPARD
B. T. FLANAGAN   The Hon. MICHAEL W. TURNER
HEAD OFFICE:— HONG KONG
The Hon. MICHAEL W. TURNER, Chief Manager

BRANCHES:
BURMA   INDIA
Rangoon   Bombay
CAMBODIA   Calcutta
Phnom Penh   JAPAN
CEYLON   Kobe
Colombo   Osaka
CHINA   Tokyo
Shanghai   Yokohama
DJAWA (JAVA)   MALAYA
Djakarta   Cameron
Surabaja   Ipoh
EUROPE   Johore Bar
Hamburg   Kuala Lum
Paris   Malacca
HONG KONG   Muar
Hong Kong   Penang
Kowloon   Singapore
Mongkok   Singapore
               (Orchard
               Sungei Pat
               Teluk Anse
LONDON OFFICE:— 9, Gr

Banking business of ev

A comprehensive service na
is undertaken by the Ban
in
HONG KONG   LOND

Peninsular & Oriental S. N. Co.
British India S. N. Co., Ltd.
Eastern & Australian S. S. Co., Ltd.
will be glad to assist with
Passage and Freight space
To
STRAITS and CEYLON
INDIA and PAKISTAN
EAST AFRICA and PERSIAN GULF
RED SEA and MEDITERRANEAN PORTS
UNITED KINGDOM and CONTINENTAL PORTS
AUSTRALIA, NEW GUINEA
AND

18 DAY SERVICE

VESSEL

KOREAN BEAR (MARINER)
CALIFORNIA BEAR
INDIAN BEAR

REFRIGERATION ❖ D

For full particulars call (

*Occasional journalism was one of
Albert Lyman's many interests beyond
his professional commitments.*

FAR EASTERN

ECONOMIC REVIEW

Vol. XVIII   Hongkong, June 30, 1955   No. 26

THE JUDICIAL SYSTEM OF THAILAND

By Albert Lyman

The Kingdom of Thailand possesses a modern judicial system. Its general structure includes a Supreme Court, called the "Dika Court," and an Intermediate Court of Appeals, plus numerous city and provincial courts of original jurisdiction, the latter being called District Courts. In Bangkok, the capital city, there are located both the Supreme Court and the Intermediate Court of Appeals. All the courts sit in continuous session through the year, taking only one month for vacation, and that is during April, it being the hottest month of the year in Bangkok. During vacation periods the court is always open for emergency matters, routine motions and attachments. The Supreme Court has a bench of twenty-two judges. The Intermediate Court of Appeals has a bench of forty-six judges. The appellate courts sit in panels and divisions accord

when the two lower courts agree in their decisions as to matters of fact, then the Supreme Court confined itself to appeals on matters of law alone. Also appeals come as a matter of right, and not by petition for a writ of certiorari.

Sentences in criminal cases, as well as judgment in civil matters, can be altered by the appellate courts, including increasing or decreasing penalties and changing awards made by civil judgments.

The judicial system of Thailand is independent of the legislative and executive branches of the government. There have been little, if any, attempts by the executive authorities to interfere with the functioning of the courts. Governmental Ministries and the various Departments are subject to suits in the courts the same as ordinary private defendant

PUBLIC NOTICE

Announcing the Formation of the

BANGKOK STOCK EXCHANGE

(Operated by the Bangkok Stock Exchange, Limited Partnership)

Wanglee Building, Room 304, No. 297 Suriwongse Road, Bangkok, Thailand.   Telephone 34991

Acting as a Clearing House and offering facilities to Share Broker members thereof for trading in the shares and securities of Thailand Registered Limited Companies.

Firms desiring listing on the Exchange for their shares and securities, and parties wishing to become members thereof, should apply for particulars to the secretary of the Stock Exchange.

Chairman and Managing Partner : **Mr. Albert Lyman**

Secretary : M ---

It Is Hereby Certified That

Mr. Albert Lyman

Is A Member Of The

BANGKOK STOCK EXCHANGE

and a Shareholder in

Bangkok Stock Exchange, Ltd.

Bangkok, Thailand.

Richard A. Moore

Director

Director

Date 17th April 1964.

In business as in law, Albert Lyman was a pivotal figure, most notably being the inspiration behind the formation of the Bangkok Stock Exchange, for which he served as chairman for ten years.

COMMERCIAL NEWS

Stock exchange moves to Silom building

The Bangkok Stock Exchange has moved its office from Wang Lee building, Suriwongse Road, to Room 607 Silom Building, Silom Road. Members met at the new premises yesterday, following the official opening on Tuesday.

POSTPIX above shows some of the members at the new office yesterday, including near left Mr Mrs Vera Cykman and Mr P.J. Alexander.

The Bangkok Stock Exchange Ltd., established in June 1962 with six members, now has forty members, including 10 non-residents. Market value of shares listed on the exchange is 1.2 billion baht. Turnover of 25 million baht last year is expected to nearly double this year.

there are few speculators and mostly investors.

According to Exchange findings the Thais are the heaviest investors, followed by Indians, Chinese and foreign communities.

Directors of the Exchange are Chairman, Mr Albert Lyman; President, Mr Willis H. Bird; Dr Rak Panyarachun, Mr Pancha Sayalakshana, Mr Isaac Djemal, Mr Surin Osathan-

Left: *Gretchen Ring, Freda's elder sister* (to the left of the picture) *with Albert and Freda and friends, during a Bangkok social function in the mid-1950s.* Below: *Organizing committee of the Foundation for the Handicapped, at Wang Sapathum Palace, Pakkred, Nonthaburi. The picture was taken during the 1960s. Freda Lyman is seated in the back row, fifth from the right, next to HM the Princess Mother, sixth from the right.*

Order of the Crown of Thailand 5th Class in 1961, making her the first foreign woman to be decorated by His Majesty King Bhumibol Adulyadej.

With Albert and Freda Lyman contributing so much to the welfare of the local community, it might be thought that Tilleke & Gibbins suffered some neglect. But that was not at all the case. Both partners put in more than a full day's (and many a late night's) legal work and the firm flourished. Such was the growth that by 1967 there was room for their son David to join the practice as a fully qualified lawyer, so consolidating Tilleke & Gibbins as a true family affair.

Freda Lyman (immediate left of centre) *played a key role in the running of various charity programmes.*

became actively involved with charitable activities aimed at aiding crippled children. She played a large part in the creation of the Foundation for Crippled Children, which in turn led to other welfare projects such as the Cheshire Homes. In recognition of this work, Freda was awarded the Most Noble

American Women's Club

In May 1955 the wife of the then US ambassador to Thailand, Mrs John E. Puerifoy, called a meeting of all American women interested in answering a need for some form of organization of American women in Bangkok. A year later, on 18 May 1956, the American Women's Club of Thailand was officially handed its charter by Thanpuying Phibul Songkhram, wife of the then prime minister Field-Marshal Phibul Songkhram. Freda Lyman was not only the club's first secretary and second president but also she allowed her house on Soi Polo, off Wireless Road, to be the organization's initial home. Club activities were numerous and varied, ranging from painting and sketching to monthly lectures on Thai art and culture. Members also undertook charitable work, raising funds and supplying equipment for such institutions as the Phra Padaeng leper colony and the Foundation for the Welfare of the Crippled. As the outgoing president in 1957, Freda Lyman wrote, 'I'm sure the American Women's Club will expand and extend its usefulness and influence'. It was a forecast that has been admirably fulfilled.

เสรา...สยามินทราธิราช บรมคล
คสบ ผู้เป็นประธานของเครื่อง
...ไทย
ผู้จึงจะได้พบประกาศป้ายักรมนี้ให้ทราบท่า
น
...ทรงพระกรุณาโปรดเกล้าโปรดการหม่อม
ชั้นที่ ๕ ชื่อ เบญจมาภรณ์
...ล้วสวัสดิ์ทุกประการเทอญ
...ลิกายน พุทธศักราช ๒๕๐๔

Above: *The Most Noble Order of the Crown of Thailand 5th Class, with certificate, was awarded by HM King Bhumibol Adulyadej to Freda Lyman in recognition of her outstanding charitable work.*

A Family Affair
1967–1986

True to Mr Tilleke's original stipulation when he sold his practice, the firm's name has never been changed, regardless of shifts in ownership and partnerships. It has always been simply Tilleke & Gibbins, and such continuity highlights what has been effectively, if not literally, a family business. The various partners from the late nineteenth century and through the first half of the twentieth century had not been blood relations, but they did conduct their business according to a strong paternalistic pattern, as was the case with many foreign companies of the period in Bangkok.

In 1967, however, a true family line was established when Albert and Freda Lyman's son, David, joined the firm as an associate.

Father and sons: Rojvit (formerly Roland) Periera (second right) with sons (from left) Santhapat, Thanes and Rachasith.

In 1984 he became a partner. The pattern would be reinforced when two of Rojvit Periera's three sons, Thanes and Santhapat, entered

the practice in 1981 and 1990 respectively. Thanes was a law graduate of the University of Wales, while Santhapat had taken his first degree at Thammasat University and then obtained two master's degrees — one in international trade and commercial law and the other in international banking law — from the universities of Miami and Boston.

Yet, in a way, David Lyman's career with Tilleke & Gibbins has been paradoxical. He is a third-generation lawyer and, in due time, he succeeded his parents to what he describes as a 'benevolent dictatorship', a father figure. While accepting this role he did, at the same time, work steadily to steer the firm away from being a family-owned business and established it as a limited liability company that was more orientated to expansion through the addition of new partners. This would not be fully achieved until 2000, when Tilleke & Gibbins was finally restructured in that fashion.

Describing his 'benevolent dictatorship' style, David comments, 'Within the firm, we bring as many people into the decision-making process as possible, but you can't have a true democracy, it just doesn't work in a business organization. Though you must delegate decision-making authority, ultimately somebody has to take full responsibility. That's me. I brook no violations of

The young David Lyman.

fundamental principles. I'm understanding, tolerant, and sympathetic to human shortcomings, but when it comes to the basics of honesty,

trustworthiness, loyalty and respect I have zero tolerance for any deviation.'

As one CEO guru has remarked, 'A person doesn't build a business. A person builds an organization. The organization builds the business.' Certainly, David Lyman is the first to insist that many have contributed to the extraordinary growth of Tilleke & Gibbins in the latter half of the twentieth century, and teamwork has been very much a key to continuing success. 'This is a team,' Lyman said in a 1997 newspaper interview. 'We are not just multifaceted but multitalented and interdisciplinary. So that when a client comes in with a problem, he doesn't categorize it as just being in one small niche. You have to analyze

Very Interesting, Counsellor

Judges, you would think, have heard it all. Not so. In representing the Thai branch of a UK pharmaceutical retail chain in a suit of wrongful dismissal brought by its local manager, David Lyman prepared a long and detailed account of the plaintiff's misdeeds for which he had been fired. After listening intently to Lyman's defence over a series of hearings, the court dismissed the case on the grounds that the plaintiff was suing the wrong company, his contract being with the parent company and not with the local firm he was suing. Later, in private conversation, Lyman asked the judges why they had let him present his arguments when they must have known all along they would dismiss the case. 'Well,' the chief judge said, 'the man's misdeeds were so intriguing that we just had to hear it all.'

it, and we find it usually takes a team of different disciplines to satisfy a client's problem, whatever it happens to be.'

That said, and not detracting from the contributions of his numerous colleagues, David Lyman is a confirmed workaholic — regularly working fifteen or sixteen hours a day — and it has been his exceptional drive and direction that has guided the firm to its preeminent standing into the third millennium. The figures speak for themselves: from a staff of 33 when David joined the firm in 1967, Tilleke & Gibbins today employs close to 360 in all four offices, full- and part-time staff serving more than 5,000 clients.

The achievements of Tilleke & Gibbins during David Lyman's 42 plus (and still counting) years with the firm have been many and far-reaching. But, to keep within the chronology of Tilleke & Gibbins' history, David did not initially embark on a legal career, the profession having no attraction for him at all.

'Law was the last thing I wanted to do,' he says of his youthful ambitions. He explains that he had seen how hard his parents worked and how 'the law totally absorbed them'. So far was his father immersed in the practice that when David was a teenager at school in southern

At Duke University, David Lyman with tape recorder.

India, his father's letters were always very formal and signed 'Sincerely yours, Albert Lyman'. Even after David had complained of this to his mother, there was little improvement: later missives were signed 'Sincerely yours, Your old man, Albert Lyman'. It was not a question of lack of love in the family, only that law and its necessary formality of tone was all-embracing. This was Albert

Lyman's style; he was strictly by the book, addressing everyone as sir or madam, or only by their surname as Mr X or Mrs Y. Even when addressing old school friends he would generally use both their first and last names.

So a lawyer's life was not as yet an appealing option for Lyman fils. After one year (eighth grade) at the Seventh Day Adventist School in Bangkok, David attended Highclere, the missionary school in Kodaikanal, southern India, for his first two years of high school before more happily completing secondary education at the École International de Genève between 1952 and 1954. While at high school in Switzerland, he came to two decisions regarding his future: he wanted to study electrical engineering and he would join the US Navy. The navy was already established as something of a family tradition second to law, and Albert Lyman was full of encouragement for his son to join the service that he himself, along with two of his brothers, had entered during World War II.

David applied for a scholarship from the Naval Reserve Officers' Training Corps (NROTC). He did not win the scholarship but was accepted as a Contract Student, which meant much the same thing although without financial support except for a stipend in the last two years of the four-year programme.

With the rank of midshipman (thus outranking his father's wartime status), David entered Duke University in Durham, North Carolina where, from 1954 to 1958, he completed a four-year degree course in electrical engineering, at the same time fulfilling the drill and orientation courses required by the NROTC. It was not all plain sailing as David gave full expression to a characteristic sociability, being very active in various university societies, with the result that his studies suffered. To make up his grades he had to attend summer school at the University of Southern California between his third and fourth years, which boosted his final year's academic performance for graduation with a 'B' average.

Embarking on active naval service as a junior officer, David was first assigned to a minesweeper, the USS *Illusive* MSO448, based at Long Beach, California, on which he served for sixteen months before volunteering and being selected to become a submariner. He admits that the decision was based largely on a romantic view of submarines,

U.S.S Illusive MSO448. (Courtesy of NavSource)

along with the fact that the submarine service then accounted for only two per cent of the US naval forces, and its personnel, all volunteers, were considered 'la crème de la crème' of the corps. There was also an added bonus in that submariners, like aviators, received extra 'hazardous duty pay'.

Lyman proved worthy of the submarine service's high reputation and completed his six months' officers' basic training course in

the upper ten per cent of his class (thus redeeming himself for his lacklustre university academic performance). This success gave him his choice of ship and home port. With his youthful experience of living in the tropics of Asia, he opted to be stationed on a Pacific Fleet diesel-powered submarine, the USS *Pickerel* SS524. Her home port was the US Naval Submarine Base, Pearl Harbour, Hawaii.

Although the young Lyman loved the Navy, he had a nagging feeling that it was perhaps not quite the right career for him. He came to believe that a naval officer required a certain military personality, one that would unquestioningly follow orders and was not argumentative. David, by his own admission, is exceedingly outspoken, and this he realized would sooner or later land him in trouble with his superiors. So when, in 1962, his contracted years of service were up, he decided not to extend or to convert his status from the Naval Reserve to the Regular Navy, but rather take up the option of three years' tertiary education, any time during which he could, if he wished, return to the Navy with no loss of seniority.

Clockwise from above: *David's submarine the USS* Pickerel *SS524 at sea and during practice of emergency surfacing manoeuvres. In the navy: David Lyman as the smart young officer* (right) *in June 1962; a bearded and more casual-looking submariner at sea* (below right — front row, second from the right) *in October 1961.*

During his time in the US Navy, David Lyman had more than once served as defence counsel in military courts martial. This suited his personality in a way normal service did not. 'In a court martial', he says, 'you are expected to be assertive and argumentative, to challenge the system from within the system. I found I enjoyed it very much; the law wasn't so bad after all.' It was, therefore, no surprise that when David took up his tertiary education option he chose to study law, in his own words 'to give it a shot'.

Accepted by the Hastings College of the Law in San Francisco (part of the University of California system), it took only one semester for David to realize that he had found his niche. It was a challenge nonetheless — only 256 students out of a 750 intake successfully completed the exams three years later, with Lyman finishing in the upper twenty per cent of those graduating. The challenge was something he relished, especially after his underachievement at Duke University, and it was part of the attraction of law itself. 'It's a career in which you are expected to challenge, and I love an intellectual challenge,' he

The graduate: David Lyman with classmate Vorawee Wang Lee in June 1958.

remarks. He also learnt that the law 'is a living thing, it's never complete, always evolving and changing as social norms change. It combines imagination and practicality in applying knowledge to a specific set of circumstances.'

Once David had passed the California Bar exams in 1965, he thought less about returning to the Navy as a full-time career. He would, however, continue to fulfil his Naval Reserve affiliations and duties. While in the Navy he became an avid scuba diver, having earlier learnt the basic skills in a swimming pool in Las Vegas in

1958, and subsequently achieved high proficiency in the sport he pursues to this day. But if he never totally severed all connection with the sea, he did finally become part of what was the paramount family tradition, followed not only by both his parents, but also by his paternal grandfather and two of his paternal uncles, one of whom married a lawyer.

There was, however, no easy entry into a comfortable partnership with Tilleke & Gibbins in Bangkok. Albert Lyman wanted David to stay in the US for some years and work with small law firms in order to 'get his ears pinned back', meaning to make mistakes and learn from experience. From 1965 to 1967 the younger Lyman did precisely that, working first for the firm of Fitzsimmons & Petris, and then with Lempres & Seyranian, both in Oakland, California.

When he did move to Bangkok in 1967 (with an American wife now and taking a two-thirds cut in salary), David found no difficulty in settling back into the city he had known since his early teens. In appearance it remained mostly low-rise; in character it was still quintessentially Thai; and in ambience its oddly alluring sense of impending chaos had altered not at all. Nevertheless, fundamental change was in the making. Its full impact would not become manifest until the late 1970s, but the indicators of change were already highly visible on the streets of Bangkok — American GIs.

In 1965 the US sent its first ground troops into Vietnam, thus escalating the war that would rage for the next decade. As the region's staunchest American ally, Thailand became both the recipient of US military aid (the amount quadrupling during the 1960s and peaking at 123 million dollars in 1972) and the host to some 45,000 American servicemen

Undergraduate David Lyman with girlfriend Pat Dunnigan, late 1957.

and civilians stationed in the country. Their numbers doubled by the constantly rotating presence of US combat troops visiting on rest-and-recreation (R and R) leave. All this was in addition to the substantial American assistance provided to help Thailand cope with and overcome its own communist insurgencies.

Some commentators argue that the biggest outcome of the American presence during the Vietnam War was the creation of Thailand's well-known sex industry. That is not true. Prostitution had been widespread long before — for centuries, in fact, in one guise or another — and Bangkok's Chinatown, for example, was known for its many licensed brothels. Nor were American GIs responsible for originating what

All at Sea

Although declining in recent years, maritime cases had always accounted for a considerable share of Tilleke & Gibbins' business. For David Lyman there was a certain irony in this when, out of the navy and practising as a lawyer, he frequently found himself handling legal matters relating to ships in trouble. To mention but three, there was the Alinda, *which hit a floating crane in the Chao Phraya River, spilling its highly inflammable cargo, and narrowly avoiding setting the city alight; the* Lord Byron, *which is immortalized in the firm's history as the '6 S Job' — a falsely claimed cargo of Siamese sugar financed by a Soviet bank in Singapore and exported from Bangkok, Siam, to Somalia; and the* Australia Tide, *a salvage ship arrested at sea by the Royal Thai Navy for allegedly wrongfully raising sunken treasure from the ocean floor. Tilleke & Gibbins successfully defended the shipowners in the first two cases, while the owners of the* Australia Tide, *although advised they had a case, declined to pursue the matter due to financial reasons. Among other notable maritime cases were two separate incidents of ships deliberately scuttled in the deepest water off the Burmese coast with nonexistent, fraudulently claimed cargoes — one of Thai Buddha images and the other of 'one-third of the world's annual supply of cloves'.*

US servicemen stationed in Northeast Thailand during the Vietnam War.

has become an almost obligatory fiction genre for aspiring foreign writers in Bangkok — the cautionary tale of a Westerner who falls for the charms of a Thai girl. That trend also predates World War II and was established back in 1956 when Jack Reynolds wrote *A Sort of Beauty* (later reissued in paperback as *A Woman of Bangkok*).

Certainly the sex industry grew and became more visible in the 1960s and 70s, but it was not the fundamental legacy of American influence on Bangkok. Rather, it was increasing wealth and shifting social attitudes that would ultimately bring about the greatest change.

Without denying Thailand's own fiscal performance, American money that poured into the country during the Vietnam War years greatly boosted the economy, largely through infrastructure development, both military (such as the huge airbase constructed at U-Tapao on the Eastern Seaboard and others upcountry) and civil works (that included roads and accommodation facilities). All this created a new moneyed class, along with managerial and administrative personnel and trained blue-collar workers. The major economic impact of it all was the development of a tourism industry. Between 1959 and 1970, visitor arrivals to Thailand grew from 40,000 to more than 600,000, making tourism the country's fifth largest foreign exchange earner. Sustained growth would see that ranking jump to first place by the 1980s.

Less visible, though equally a catalyst for change, was the exposure of the Thais to Western culture. Until the arrival of the American forces in the 1960s, only a small social elite (mostly educated overseas) was familiar with Western ideas, values, and fashions; now these became known to a much wider section of the population. From rock 'n' roll and youth culture to hamburgers and blue jeans, new lifestyles came

Popular Bangkok nightclub in the 1960s and '70s.'

to challenge traditional Thai ways. 'The city [Bangkok] changed in shape, style and tastes,' write Chris Baker and Pasuk Phongpaichit in *A History of Thailand*. 'New suburbs clustered around the schools, shops, cinemas and clubs catering to Westerners. Elite Thai families were attracted to the same areas because of their perceived status and their rising property values. Foreign goods — and especially American brand names — acquired new status value. The American era

At Ease in Bangkok

In the latter half of the 1960s and early 1970s, thousands of battle-weary American troops stationed in Vietnam opted to spend their periods of rest and recreation (R and R) in Bangkok. It is not difficult to understand why. With their finely tuned sense of hospitality, the Thais made the GIs welcome, offering a package deal that included a hotel room, a rented 'wife', and a car with driver for the duration of their stay. Much of this industry was focused on New Petchaburi Road, which saw a 1960s building spree of hotels and massage parlours, while Patpong Road developed the go-go bars for which it still remains famous.

redefined what was modern and aspirational, especially for the urban middle class.'

Economic and social change was, however, a matter of evolution not revolution. For the moment the old ways persisted, and for Tilleke & Gibbins the side effect of the Vietnam War was only noticeably manifest in the increased work that came with representing civilian contractors employed by the US military and with several courts martial defence cases

Although David Lyman was well acquainted with life in Bangkok, a period of adjustment was inevitable. He needed to make himself familiar with Thai law and the legal system, and to learn the systems (in some cases the lack of systems) of the Tilleke & Gibbins office. Always a realist, David set himself five years to find his feet, and initially worked in all areas of office work, from filing upwards, while he made use of his electrical engineering degree and skills learnt in the navy in fixing the office machines and keeping them in running order.

David's main worry was that he would not be able to talk over issues and the application of the law with anyone. Such a fear, he quickly discovered, was unfounded and the Thai lawyers

Khun Udom Benrosmon.

in the firm were welcoming and helpful. The sense of a family business may have been reinforced by David's arrival, but it was the very nature of the firm. Khun Udom Benrosmon, who joined Tilleke & Gibbins in 1959, remembers, 'it was like working with a family; Albert and Freda were always very kind to the staff'.

That a friendly, family office atmosphere should prevail was due in large part to Albert Lyman's ability to adapt to Thai social mores. Practising as a lawyer is one thing, practising successfully as a lawyer (or as any other professional) in Thailand can be something else. Whereas Westerners are culturally attuned to encourage equality,

Bride and groom Nancy and David in 1965.

David Lyman, well adapted to Thai ways.

heart")'. The article added that, 'In Thailand, successful employee relations are based upon *bunkhun*, a "meritorious debt" concept rooted in Buddhism. This obliges the boss to care well for his workers and the workers to repay the boss with loyalty and tangible effort.'

Both Albert and Freda Lyman, and subsequently David, adapted perfectly to Thai ways, taking a genuine interest in the local community, as well as treating employees at all levels with care and respect. It is something that goes beyond general business practice, such as staff bonuses. Albert Lyman, for example, made a habit of taking a staff member or two with him on business trips more as a vacation than out of any real professional need. Freda, also, was kindness itself, always bringing token gifts for employees when she returned from overseas. Kind consideration further extended to her style of working, and Khun Suwalee Kuruchittham, who joined the firm as Freda's secretary in 1971, remembers her saying, 'It's not a secretary's job to make coffee. You're not a maid. I make my own coffee.'

Adapting to a different culture is not always easy, as David's

constructive criticism and argumentation, Thai society tends to reward people for obedience, diffidence, politeness and allegiance. Many a foreigner has found his business failing simply because he or she has neglected to appreciate cultural differences.

On the face of it Albert Lyman, with his crusty forthright manner, would appear ill-suited to the Thai world, where a smile achieves far more than a gruff word. Lyman succeeded, however — as pointed out in an article on foreign business people in Bangkok in the January/February 1982 issue of *Asia* magazine — because he was 'widely known to have the prized characteristic of *jai dee* ("good

American-born first wife Nancy Wilson, whom he married in 1965, quickly discovered. For the first two years she hated Bangkok, and only after returning from extended leave back in the US with a more positive attitude did she learn the need to participate. She became involved in animal conservation, cofounded the Bangkok Community Theatre (she held a

A Question of Identity

A man accused of murder was recommended by David Lyman to plead guilty. 'After all,' David said, 'you were identified by witnesses in a police line-up.' The man replied, 'Of course I was picked out, I was the only one wearing handcuffs.'

Nancy Lyman, or 'The Virginian Nightingale' as she was dubbed in this British Club playbill, was an active, popular star and theatrical director in Bangkok's amateur dramatics circle.

BRITISH CLUB

21st December : 8 p.m. tickets B/30

unique dramatic presentation

NEVER BEFORE SEEN IN THE ORIENT

MR. MICHAEL O'SHEA'S
CELEBRATED DRAMA

VIRTUE IN PERIL
OR
a drunkard's deliverance

Featuring for positively   the last time

Mrs. Jean Sommerfield's   RENOWNED

DEATHBED   SCENE !

Replete with the evil genius OF

Mr. John Davies

in his world acclaimed role as
DR. CALLIGARI

Direct from our sister colonies
in the Americas the adorable

Nancy Lyman

The Virginian Nightingale

**Famed throughout
the Continent of EUROPE
The Heroic Posturings of**

D.V. LANDER ESQ.

With the facial contortions and vocal distortions of

DAVID FISHER ESQ.
the darling of the English stage

Come one, come all and see the prize Drama

Yubol 'Buk' Pumsathit, David Lyman's second wife.
Married in 1979, the couple divorced in 2001.

master's degree in theatre arts), worked as a radio DJ and busied herself with other local activities (including raising otters, much to the disruption of the Lyman fils household). Subsequently, in 1974, David and Nancy were divorced. Five years later David married his second wife Yubol 'Buk' Pumsathit.

To come to terms successfully with living and working in Thailand emphatically underscores the old saying that life is what you put into it, and all the partners of Tilleke & Gibbins throughout the firm's history have made considerable contributions to society.

Cultural clashes have of course occurred, and David notes that it has at times been difficult to teach Thai barristers greater sophistication of argument and the finer points of logic — intellectual attributes that are not stressed in Thailand's nonconfrontational culture. 'Traditionally,' he says, 'Thai law students have not been trained to solve problems. They are trained to tell you what the law is. But most often our clients come to us with problems. You have to teach both the professional and support staff how to practise law to suit our foreign clients, and what these clients need and want.'

An amusing nonlegal example of cultural differences occurred in 1967, when Albert Lyman and Rojvit Periera entered a joint venture to build T&G Apartments. These were designed for foreign residents, but Periera insisted the refrigerator should go in the dining room. For him this was quite logical since, at that time, possession of an electric fridge was a status symbol in Thai society and thus should ideally be placed where people could see it. It took much persuasion by David and Nancy Lyman to convince their Thai partner that, for Westerners, fridges belonged in the kitchen. Periera eventually compromised by having the fridge in the kitchen — but placed opposite the door so it was easily visible from the dining room when the door was open.

The incident reminded David Lyman of a summer programme in Comparative Law that he attended in 1974 at Columbia University in New York, where one of the professors told his students that everything anybody does is logical. It's just that we all have different starting points for our logic.

Cross-cultural clashes were not, however, David Lyman's principal challenge when he began work in Bangkok. Rather he was faced with the classic confrontation of the younger generation versus the old. Albert Lyman was proud of his son

Thanes Periera.

professionally and there were no differences over legal cases, but arguments did arise over processes and procedures. David has his own notions as to how the firm should develop and, as Thanes Periera notes, 'his style was very different from that of his father'.

The situation was certainly not easy. Since 1960 the firm had occupied just the fourth floor at the Wang Lee Building on Suriwongse Road, and when shortly after David's arrival more space was secured on the fifth floor, conditions remained cramped. But David was the proverbial 'new broom' and he had the determination to sweep clean.

'It was a big change when David arrived,' Khun Udom says. 'Before, the office was not really organized, and he introduced a lot of improvements that made a great difference.' These included some office procedures never previously used. For example, David initiated time sheets, a system for files open, and even colour-coded file folders to replace the outdated lawyers' custom of tying up rolls of documents with red tape. As for getting a modern photocopier installed, the tussle between father and son can be left to the imagination.

Notwithstanding David Lyman's efforts to establish order and procedures, a freewheeling atmosphere characterized the early 1970s. Opportunities were there for those able and willing to turn their hand to anything. This was as true for Tilleke & Gibbins

David Hallmark.

as much as for Bangkok at large, and is well illustrated by the example of English lawyer David Hallmark.

At the age of 23 and with the ink still wet on his law certificate, Hallmark set out from England with a group of friends intent on driving their Land Rover as far as

Love's Labours Lost

The foreign male who comes to Thailand and falls disastrously in love with a young Thai bargirl has become a travel cliché. It still happens, but naïvety seems to have been greater back in the 1970s and '90s, when Tilleke & Gibbins received numerous clients, mainly European, seeking assistance in finding a lost love. Typically, a letter would arrive from Germany or England with a request that the firm find a girl called Lek or Noi or Daeng, or some other very common Thai nickname, and, of course, she would be described as having light-brown skin, dark eyes and long black hair. Sometimes a photograph would be enclosed to help identification — and some of the photographs identified all of the girl's anatomy. These sorry fellows had visited Thailand and fallen in love with a bargirl in Bangkok or Pattaya. The girls had expressed their undying love and willingness to marry, but later. The men returned home, wrote love letters back, and usually sent money, while the girls promptly forgot them. All Tilleke & Gibbins could do was proffer advice on the facts of life. It was not always appreciated, or believed.

Mysterious Death

UK seaman innocent of murder

LREM Andrew Robert Tombs, an English naval seaman (charged with killing a girl while sleeping with her in 1970) who has fought his case through the courts, was finally pronounced innocent by the Supreme Court yesterday.

TOMBS

The English naval seamen was first charged with killing Miss Kularb Thongburi in a hotel in Yannawa District by the Criminal Court which found him guilty and sentenced him to two years' imprisonment.

The Public Prosecutor appealed to the Appeals Court that the penalties should be increased and claimed that LREM Tombs had intentionally committed the murder. However, the naval seaman told the Court of Appeal that Miss Kularb, presumably a prostitute, died accidentally while having intercourse with him.

The Appeals Court, after a detailed consideration of the case, ruled that Sgt Tombs did not have any intention of killing the girl and decided to drop the case.

However, the prosecutor brought the case to the Supreme Court, asking it to impose penalties on the naval officer. After thorough consideration of the case, the Supreme Court yesterday upheld the Appeal Court verdict and released the naval seaman.

The death of a prostitute in 1970 was as much a mystery to Radioman 2/C Andrew Robert Tombs of the British Royal Navy as to the police, yet he confessed to her murder. The simple facts of the case were that Tombs had taken the prostitute to a hotel and after making love he fell asleep. When he awoke he found the girl lying dead next to him. The cause of death proved to be lack of oxygen. Tombs was found guilty of culpably, though not intentionally, causing the girl's death. The case then went to the Court of Appeal at which time, by a remarkable coincidence, David Hallmark of the Tilleke & Gibbins defence team found quite by accident a newspaper story of a similar case in Spain where an American airman had been found not guilty of strangling a prostitute. The solution to both cases was that the girls had died from accidental pressure on the vagus nerve during passionate lovemaking. Any temporary blockage of this vital junction of nerves in the neck can cause loss of consciousness or death if the person is in weak health. A relieved, though probably still confused Radioman Tombs was acquitted.

News story of the Tombs case, and photograph of the victim.

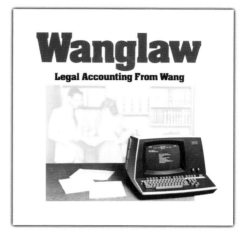

Cover of Wang Word Processor brochure.

their money would take them. He arrived in Bangkok in April 1970 with no money, nowhere to stay and no friends. But in those days there was a serendipitous quality to the city. Chance encounters led Hallmark to a meeting with Albert Lyman, who offered him a job, and to a garden party at the British Embassy, where an introduction to the naval attaché later resulted in Hallmark's first case, the defence of a British naval rating charged with murder (see box story, 'Mysterious Death').

'All of a sudden my life plan, such as it had been, was changed,' Hallmark says. 'I had no experience as a qualified lawyer and awaited my first client. My legal career could not have started in more dramatic circumstances.'

Not only was the start of Hallmark's career dramatic, the eighteen months he spent with Tilleke & Gibbins offered a more varied experience than any young lawyer could reasonably expect. In addition to the murder case he, by chance, brought to the firm, he was engaged in company and commercial law, as well as odder cases such as the theft of an elephant and a dispute over the ownership and operation of a DC-3 aircraft.

In the division of labour at Tilleke & Gibbins, Albert Lyman parcelled out the work, himself handling specifically the intellectual property and trademark side of the business as well as taking a keen interest in corporate and criminal law. Freda Lyman supervised client relations and all office administrative matters, and Rojvit Periera was the chief trial lawyer. David Lyman's new input, in addition to organizational matters and rationalizing staffing, was primarily twofold: to develop international business and to secure the firm's financial footing.

The system worked and essentially the firm was sound. However, a general upward trend, with gradual staff increases and office upgrades (the firm's first

computerized Wang Word Processor was on order by 1980), was subject to fluctuations during the 1970s. As evidenced by management memos announcing annual bonuses, there was a pattern of 'one of the most successful years for the firm' being followed by a lean year. For example, the firm went into overdraft 'for a short period' in 1973; in 1976 it 'suffered an operating loss for the first time in many years'.

Fundamentally, the success of Tilleke & Gibbins' legal practice was not reflected in the firm's profits. Albert Lyman loved the practice of law but not the business of law, and he took a cavalier approach to billing. 'He never cared about clients paying or not,' says Leonie Vejjajiva, who started

Leonie Vejjajiva.

An Engraved Issue

TILLEKE & GIBBINS
REGISTERED ORDINARY PARTNERSHIP
ADVOCATES & SOLICITORS

(FOUNDED A.D. 1902)

One custom that Albert Lyman refused to give up in a modernizing business world was having Tilleke & Gibbins' stationery specially engraved on bonded paper by Waddies, a printing firm in Scotland. He clung to this simply because he thought it brought good luck, as Waddies had supplied Tilleke & Gibbins since the early twentieth century. What it certainly did was to increase costs as fresh stationery had to be ordered every time a new lawyer's name was added to the letterhead. Eventually, in the 1980s, it all became too much, and engraved stationery became a thing of the past. Yet if not engraved, the firm's redesigned letterhead remains highly distinctive with a subtle design that, if one looks closely, contains a wealth of information about contacts, services and affiliations, as well as a map of Southeast Asia.

with the firm in 1972 as David Lyman's secretary. 'He'd send out a bill and hope for the best, holding that a lawyer should never go after a bill.'

Far more businesslike than his father, David Lyman realized that money problems were not just a question of billing, but also related to the types of business the firm was handling. The policy, he argued with Albert, was the need to concentrate on the more profitable work and abandon the lossmakers. Specifically, he pinpointed commercial collections and criminal cases — most especially those concerning narcotics charges — as areas that involved much work for little, if any, return in fees. To convince his father and Periera of this, he initiated in the late 1970s and early '80s, meticulously detailed studies to prove his point.

Commercial collection cases, it was shown, lasted an average of 36.17 months and each on average produced a counsel fee of just 779 baht. For narcotics cases, a statistical analysis of the 179 cases undertaken between the end of 1975 and the first quarter of 1980 revealed an overall expenditure of 8,183,699.62 baht and an overall remittance of 9,392,884.64 baht.

These figures give an arithmetical mean of 45,718.99 baht and 52,474.22 baht respectively, producing a net average earning of merely 6,755.23 baht per case, which covered out-of-pocket expenses only. The firm essentially worked for free. As David Lyman wrote in a memo to his colleagues, there was an obvious need to see how the firm could revise its systems, otherwise 'if we don't look after ourselves then we won't be around to look after our clients'.

In addition to revising the firm's systems David Lyman actively sought new clients and by the mid-1970s business was expanding noticeably, especially in the fields of intellectual property and commercial and corporate business. Increasingly, large international contracts were secured and, for example, Tilleke & Gibbins handled the formation of Diners Club and American Express in Thailand, marking the first major entry of credit card companies into the country.

With a mix of persuasion and argument, David Lyman's way of thinking gradually came to prevail and small commercial collections and narcotics cases, along with minor criminal cases, began to be phased out from the practice.

Before that policy took effect, however, the firm was engaged in some headline-making drug cases.

If narcotics cases produced little by way of financial return they certainly brought publicity. Grabbing wide public attention in both Thailand and the UK was the case of Rita Nightingale, a 22-year-old British woman arrested on 19 March 1977 at Bangkok Airport, when 3.4 kilograms of heroin were found hidden in her suitcase and a transistor radio. She was charged with illegal possession of the drug and endeavouring to smuggle it out of the country with the intent to sell.

Nightingale pleaded not guilty, claiming she had no knowledge that the heroin was hidden in her suitcase. Tilleke & Gibbins took up the defence, and during the trial Albert Lyman was quoted in characteristic tone by a British newspaper as 'doing my damnedest for Rita'. Nonetheless, the prosecution had a strong prima facie case and Nightingale was found guilty and sentenced to twenty years imprisonment. That was not, however, the end of the matter, and Albert and David Lyman, backed up by their team, continued to work hard with a steady belief in Rita's innocence.

David went to England, where there was a much publicized campaign for Rita's release, to brief her champion, Member of Parliament Barbara Castle.

On 21 July 1978 the verdict on Nightingale was upheld by the Court of Appeal, and yet still Albert and David Lyman did not give up hope. With the appellate process completed, the only avenue left open to the defence was a clemency petition for a royal pardon. To support the petition the Lymans worried away at the facts of the case to try to find new evidence. In this they were markedly successful.

The difficulty with Nightingale's original defence was the lack of supporting evidence for her claim that the heroin had been placed in her luggage by a Chinese drug syndicate without her knowledge. She had travelled from Hong Kong, where she had been working, in the company of two Chinese men, one a friend of her Chinese sweetheart and the other an alleged drug-syndicate security man. But although the two men were arrested along with Nightingale, they were quickly released, reportedly for lack of evidence, and were not at the trial to confirm or deny Rita's professed innocence.

Gun for Hire

In spite of its prosaic title, intellectual property can be an exciting, even dangerous field for lawyers, as the young Thanes Periera quickly discovered. One of his earliest cases after joining Tilleke & Gibbins in 1981 involved counterfeit products. It happened that one morning the counterfeiter's agent came to the office to negotiate. His opening gambit was, without saying anything, to place a gun on Thanes' desk. What seemed set to become a heated discussion was suddenly defused when the two men discovered a common interest in the teaching of a particular Indian guru they both admired. Business was forgotten and, after a philosophical chat, they parted amicably. 'A little while later', Thanes recalls, 'I heard the man had been shot dead.'

The new evidence the Lymans eventually brought to light focused primarily on two areas. One was a telex message from the Hong Kong Preventive Service (Customs) to Bangkok advising the Thai officials to intercept Nightingale as a suspected drug courier. The reasonable assumption

I'm going home!

NURSE RITA'S JOY AS SHE IS FREED FROM JAIL

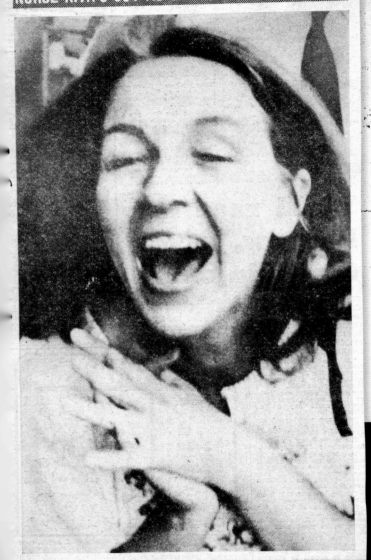

THE prison gates swing open and out steps Rita Nightingale, clapping her hands and shedding a tear in her excitement at being free.

"This is the happiest moment of my life. Fairy stories really do come true," said the 26-year-old British nurse as she was released in Thailand yesterday from a 20-year sentence for heroin smuggling.

"Now I'm going home to my mother in England."

HOUSE OF COMMONS
LONDON SW1A 0AA

16 September 1977

Personal

Dear Mr Lyman

The enclosed letter from me is to put before the Court, if you think it is desirable. I am today giving a press conference in London about the petition in which I have been careful not to criticise the Thai authorities but rather to show confidence in the fact that Rita will receive justice.

I understand from Dave Allin, the reporter from my local constituency paper who recently visited Bangkok, that when he was over there he saw a film which the Thai Customs Officers took of her arrest at the Airport and that this film, when seen in its entirety, completely convinced him of her innocence.

I am wondering whether it would be possible for you to look at the film yourself and get it shown to the Court? I am very grateful for all you are doing to help Rita.

Yours sincerely

Barbara Castle

Rt Hon Mrs Barbara Castle M.P.

Mr Albert Lyman
Tilleke and Gibbins
Wang Lee Building
5th Floor
297 Suriwongse Road
BANGKOK Thailand

The Rita Nightingale case made headlines in both England and Thailand. Efforts for her release also included the direct involvement of the Rt Hon. Mrs Barbara Castle, the Member of Parliament for Rita's constituency in England.

THE FIRST INTERVIEW SINCE SHE WAS SENTENCED TO 20 YEARS FOR HEROIN S

My nightmare li in a Bangkok ja

Rita Nightingale sobs after her sentence.

RITA NIGHTINGALE talking to ALWYN TAYLOR

RITA NIGHTINGALE, a 26-year-old nurse from Blackburn, was jailed for 20 years eight months ago in Thailand convicted on a charge of trying to smuggle 7 lb. of heroin, worth £650,000, out of Bangkok in a transistor radio and false-bottomed suitcases.

Two Chinese men arrested with her were released for lack of evidence. Rita Nightingale claims she was the unwitting tool of these men and her Chinese boyfriend in Hongkong . . .

THE steel-barred main gates of Lardyso Women's Jail were opened by a beautiful Thai wardress in a neat khaki uniform. She smiled as she slipped back a bolt and allowed me into a covered forecourt.

Across the courtyard we came to a room with one wall covered with a fine steel grille. Through it I could see Rita Nightingale.

She was standing in an oatmeal-coloured short-length linen dress with an open crochet top. A silver cross hung around her neck on a gold chain, on her left wrist were two bracelets made of a golden-coloured fabric finely plaited.

On her feet she wore sandals. She looked fit, plump; her hair was clean and brushed; the whites of her eyes were bright and white.

Rita answered questions readily and with the pace of a machine-gun. She hardly paused for breath during the 35 minutes I was with her. This is her story.

"I haven't heard what's been happening in the outside world since July 17 second to

pouring water over ourselves with a dipper.

"My dormitory is one of several in a long, wooden building on stilts located in the centre of the prison compound. I sleep on the floor with no mattress or bunk. But I've got four blankets given to me by the British Embassy people and

make special dainty sandwiches for them.

"I suppose this sounds all very cheery and they certainly call this a model prison—it probably is by Thai standards—but it is still very unpleasant being here.

"People come and tour around the prison and go away to talk about the beautiful

at the trial was that Hong Kong Customs had prior knowledge that Nightingale was involved in narcotics. What was not explained at the time, and which the Lymans subsequently discovered, was that the Hong Kong advisory was simply a lucky guess without any solid basis for its claim. The other key point concerned a security camera videotape of Rita's arrest. As discovered in Tilleke & Gibbins' post-trial examination of the case, when the tape had been presented to the court, a key section showing Nightingale's apparently genuine surprise at the discovery of the heroin — thus giving support to her claim that the drug had been hidden without her knowledge — had been deleted.

Although all judicial procedures had been exhausted by now, the fresh light Tilleke & Gibbins' research shed on Nightingale's case did assist her in her pursuit of a royal pardon. This proved successful and finally, in January 1980, after spending nearly three years in jail, Nightingale was freed by an act of royal clemency. The first thing she did on her release was to throw her arms around the man who had doggedly believed in her innence, Albert Lyman.

A royal pardon is exactly what it says and does not overrule a court verdict, but as David Lyman commented to the press at the time: 'We feel that on the basis of the information we received after the fact, even after the first appeal, that had this evidence been presented, the court might just have gone the other way.'

The Nightingale affair was the most famous of the numerous narcotics cases handled by the firm in the 1970s and early 80s, but one other deserves mention for the unexpected result it had for Albert Lyman. This concerned 45-year-old Mrs Luisa Gonzales, a Spanish charwoman, who was arrested at a Bangkok hotel on 10 August 1977 and charged with the possession of 15.9 kilograms of heroin found hidden in six woodcarvings. Her Portuguese male companion was arrested at the same time, but died of blood poisoning before he could be brought to trial.

In pleading not guilty, Gonzales claimed she had been approached by the Portuguese man, her neighbour, who invited her to visit Thailand at his expense. When in Bangkok, she was told to receive 'gifts', which duly arrived in two suitcases

Snatch

Fraud cases have commonly featured among Tilleke & Gibbins' litigation work, but of them all none has been quite so amusing as what may be titled 'The Diamond Snatch'. In simple terms, the firm represented a Hong Kong company that was the victim of an attempted fraud over a shipment of diamonds sent to Bangkok. The details of the crime, however, are worthy of a comic Hollywood caper. It went like this: the company's Bangkok representative switched the pack of real diamonds for a bag of fake stones, which he placed in his briefcase. As arranged, his accomplices rode by on a motorcycle and snatched the briefcase. According to plan, the representative would then claim the diamonds had been stolen. But unfortunately for him, an off-duty motorcycle cop saw the snatch, gave chase, and apprehended the 'thieves'. So the scam was exposed before it even got off the ground.

brought by two Chinese men. Gonzales said she had no knowledge of what was in the cases.

Here, there was less of a prima facie case than in the Nightingale

You Can't Win Them All

Lawyers can give their clients the best legal advice and still lose. In that way it came about that Tilleke & Gibbins lost the business of long-standing client the Hongkong & Shanghai Bank (now HSBC). A minor had somehow managed to obtain a loan from the bank, and the bank wanted Tilleke & Gibbins to handle the collection of the debt. Because the bank had failed to follow proper legal procedures in lending to minors, the firm advised against proceeding, but the client insisted. The case was duly lost and Tilleke & Gibbins duly fired.

trial, but nonetheless Gonzales was found guilty and sentenced to a jail term of forty years. The Criminal Court's verdict was upheld by the Court of Appeal, but in his customary dogged way Albert Lyman continued to pursue the case. Finally, in February 1980, he succeeded in getting the verdict overruled by the *Dika* (Supreme) Court.

In acquitting Mrs Gonzales, the *Dika* Court ruled that the prosecution's evidence was insufficient to prove guilt. In particular, it was pointed out that the suitcases had been locked when handed over to Mrs Gonzales, and the Chinese men had given the keys not to her but to her Portuguese companion. This indicated that a deal had been made between the three men without Gonzales' knowledge, and that she was merely a poor — if naïve — woman who wanted to come to Thailand without having to pay any expenses.

For Tilleke & Gibbins, however, the case did not end with Gonzales' release. All along, Albert Lyman had understood that the Spanish government would pay his firm's legal fees, as Mrs Gonzales had no money of her own. Later, an embarrassed Spanish ambassador in Bangkok had to inform Lyman that, while his government was extremely grateful for all he had done in defending one of its nationals, it was not policy to pay the legal fees and expenses of Spanish citizens who found themselves in trouble abroad, except in the case of a capital charge. But this is where a misunderstanding had arisen, since Mrs Gonzales had been charged with a potentially capital offence.

David Lyman conceived and proposed a face-saving solution for all concerned whereby, in lieu of payment of the legal fees and expenses, Spain would award Albert Lyman a royal honour in recognition of his services. This was agreed and the award was duly given and gratefully received.

Nonetheless, the Gonzales affair was further proof, as if needed, of David Lyman's argument that narcotics cases were a financial liability for Tilleke & Gibbins. It was in Albert Lyman's blood to fight for the underdog, to ensure anyone in need had legal

Spain awards lawyer

AMERICAN Albert Moses Lyman, Thailand's most prominent foreign lawyer, was yesterday awarded a royal Spanish medal for his work on behalf of the Spanish Government and its citizens.

Albert Lyman honoured.

ACCOMPLICE DIED BEFORE TRIAL

Spanish woman gets 40 years for heroin

BEFORE THE VERDICT

Surprise freedom for Spanish lady

was a farce. He indicated in his letter that Thai companies should gain access to the manufacturing contract. His full letter is on Page 9.

Late News

ROME — The UN World Food Programme (WFP) has lifted its suspension of food aid shipments to Kampuchea because food previously sent there is now being distributed, executive director Garson Vogel said yesterday. — Reuter

40-year term lifted

A SPANISH woman who was sentenced to 40 years' jail on a charge of possessing heroin for sale is to be set free.

The Dika (Supreme) Court yesterday acquitted the woman, Mrs Luisa Gonzales, 45, of the charge, overruling two lower courts' verdicts which sentenced her to the 40 years' imprisonment.

Announcing its verdict, the Dika ruled that the prosecution evidence was insufficient to prove she was guilty.

Mrs Gonzales and an alleged accomplice, Portuguese national Jose Crescencio, were apprehended by narcotics policemen attached to the Crime Suppression Division at the Victory Hotel in Bangkok on

LUISA Gonzales behind bars at Taopoon police station after her release from Lard Yao Women Prison.

The Gonzales narcotics trial was another high-profile case for Tilleke & Gibbins, and again its fortunate outcome for the accused was due to the dogged efforts of Albert Lyman and his legal team.

Mrs Luisa Gonzales leaves a detention cell at the Criminal Court to hear the Dika (Supreme) Court's decision yesterday.

Equal Merit

JUAN CARLOS I, REY DE ESPAÑA

Sr. Albert Lyman

la Cruz de Caballero

Albert Lyman finally saw himself his wife's equal when he received the Spanish royal honour of Knight Cross of the Civil Merit, bestowed in recognition of services in the Gonzales narcotics case. In his acceptance letter to King Juan Carlos I he explained: 'Several years ago my wife . . . was awarded a decoration by His Majesty the King of Thailand. . . . Now that you have kindly granted me a Royal decoration, I am now even with my wife in being granted Royal awards. You realize that in the later years of married life it is of great benefit that the husband and wife should be on an equal status in all their endeavours and rewards, they leading to a harmonious marital life especially important in their declining years.'

representation, and this, to his credit, he did supremely well; but it simply was not good business.

Unrecorded in the case files is Albert Lyman's personal as well as professional triumph. Almost against the odds he fought some of his toughest cases, such as those of Nightingale and Gonzales, when his health was fast failing him. The diabetes from which he had long suffered began to take its toll when, in February 1976, it led to the amputation of his right foot. In late 1980, further complications of the disease resulted in the loss of sight in both eyes. In spite of these severe handicaps, he continued to draw on his boundless energy and inner strength to practise the law that was both his vocation and his only hobby, aside from swimming and his fancy diving.

Still in harness, conducting work from his hospital bed, Albert Lyman finally succumbed at the age of 78, on 10 April 1984. He had guided Tilleke & Gibbins for 33 years and had taken due pride in the firm's sustained reputation as Thailand's leading and largest foreign law practice.

Anecdotes abound attesting to the high regard in which Albert

Lyman was held by all who knew him; but let one suffice here. As part of the after-dinner entertainment at a party hosted by the British ambassador, eight British and two American guests were posed the hypothetical question of whom they would contact if they suddenly found themselves in a dangerous or

New Year office party, 1977. From top left, clockwise: *David Lyman, Rojvit Periera, Albert and Freda Lyman.*

threatening situation (in Thailand) and could make only one telephone call. Not one of the guests gave the obvious answer (of getting in touch with their embassy), but six of them did agree — they would call Albert Lyman.

Freda Lyman survived Albert by two years. For some time she

had been troubled by a heart problem, although like her husband, she refused to allow ill health to curtail her professional life. Literally attending the office to her dying day, she suffered a fatal heart attack in the early hours of 18 July 1986, a couple of weeks before her 86th birthday.

In a royal audience granted to David Lyman shortly after his mother's death, His Majesty King Bhumibol kindly recalled Freda Lyman as 'a dynamic and gracious lady'. Indeed, she was a remarkable woman of wide-ranging accomplishments — as good a cook, for example, as she was a lawyer — and is fondly remembered by all who knew her. More telling than affectionate memories, however, are the many and varied personal qualities that have stayed in peoples' minds. Khun Jeeravan, one of Freda's filing clerks, recalls, 'She didn't like people to say "I'll try my best". She would say to them, "You do it, don't say you'll try, but you do it". She somehow always got the best out of people. That is why Tilleke & Gibbins is what it is now.'

PASSED AWAY PEACEFULLY
AT 05:10 A.M. ON 18 JULY 1986

FUNERAL RITES WILL BE HELD AT WAT MAKUT KRUNGKASEM ROAD (NEAR UN BUILDING) SALA 9 ON FRIDAY 18th, SATURDAY 19th AND WEDNESDAY 23rd, JULY 1986 AT 19:30 P.M. ROYAL CREMATION WILL BE HELD AT THE SAME WAT ON THURSDAY 24th, JULY 1986 AT 18:00 P.M. JEWISH SERVICES AND BURIAL WILL BE HELD ON FRIDAY 25th, JULY 1986 AT THE PROTESTANT CEMETERY ON NEW ROAD, YANNAWA DISTRICT AT 09:00 A.M. NO INVITATIONS WILL BE ISSUED.

FLOWERS NOT NECESSARY. THE FAMILY HAS RENAMED THE "ALBERT LYMAN MEMORIAL FUND" TO BE THE "ALBERT AND FREDA RING LYMAN MEMORIAL FUND" TO AID DIABETIC RESEARCH AND FOR OTHER SIMILAR PURPOSES. DONATIONS MAY BE SENT C/O TILLEKE & GIBBINS, R.O.P., WANG LEE BUILDING, 4TH FLOOR, 297 SURIWONGSE ROAD, BANGKOK 10500.

Lady lawyer 'extra special'

FREDA is 83, and she is still putting in a full day at the office, with the help of a nurse.

"The nurse? That's to help me from falling down, my balance isn't as good as it used to be." But that's the only concession Freda is making to encroaching age. At the office or at home, she is still in command; Thanksgiving dinner for 25, husband Al's birthday, gifts for everyone in the office and lunches or cocktails for guests who are always dropping in unexpectedly.

You can always count on a good dinner at Freda's; turkey with all the trimmings, a fine big roast ham, cauliflower in cheese sauce, rum or pumpkin pie. There's Freda's pride in what she serves, in running a good household. That will never change.

But here's Freda's own story:

"The most significant thing that ever happened to me was a public piano recital I gave at the age of 12. I still have the programme. It was in Washington DC, and everyone, family, friends and relatives came. Actually we're Baltimore people but we moved to L Street in Washington DC, opposite the Dewey Hotel, where all the baseball players stayed, when I was six.

"At 14, I taught piano to Ruth McKee who lived upstairs for 15 cents a week. Her sister Felipa played the violin, but so badly, I began to teach her too. I never learned how to play the violin myself but 'music is music' and it was all the same to me.

"In fifth grade, I wrote a play. The teacher said there wouldn't be a Christmas play that year because we didn't have one ready. So, I sat down and wrote one. It was all about a lost child who returned on Christmas Eve. Then I made a story out of it and this was published in a local magazine.

"I went to George Washington Law School but on graduation, couldn't take the Bar exams because I was too young and had to wait a year. Why law? Professor Maurer was my favourite teacher in high school and I had taken an undergraduate law course with him and liked it. Then I went to work in the federal government's Children's Bureau, advising the states on what kind of child legislation to write.

"I met Albert Lyman at a local swimming pool. He was thinking

"I'm not special at all. I've really accomplished very little. I'm not interesting." Freda Lyman, the first *farang* woman lawyer to set up a practice in Thailand, tries hard to evade the glare of publicity. But Freda's story is a good one and you can't hide it for long behind all "those men's doings." Here she talks to JOYCE RAINAT.

Above: Freda (left) and Al, along with a friend, on a klong boat trip. "Bangkok was really the 'Venice of the East' in those days; there were klongs along Sathorn, Silom, in front of the Erawan Hotel (before it was built) and in Soi Polo where we live today." Left: Freda at 83, still puts in a full day at the office.

town and he didn't think we would have any trouble getting started. He said it would cost a family of four about US$4,000 a year to live here comfortably well, and when I heard that I said 'sold.'

lawyer, Mr Victor Jakes, who was running Telleke & Gibbons wanted to retire and he was looking around for someone to take over the law office. He liked Al and struck up a deal for something like 5,000 baht

PASSED AWAY PEACEFULLY ON 10 APRIL 1984.

RITES WILL BE HELD AT WAT MONGKUT (NEAR UNITED NATIONS BUILDING), SALA 9, ON 11, 12 AND 13 APRIL 1984 WEDNESDAY, THURSDAY AND FRIDAY RESPECTIVELY AT 7:00 P.M. CREMATION AT THE SAME WAT ON SUNDAY, 15 APRIL 1984 AT 6:30 P.M. JEWISH SERVICES AND BURIAL ON MONDAY, 16 APRIL 1984 AT THE PROTESTANT CEMETERY ON NEW ROAD, YANNAWA DISTRICT AT 10:00 A.M. NO INVITATIONS WILL BE ISSUED.

FLOWERS NOT PREFERRED. THE FAMILY HAS ESTABLISHED "THE ALBERT LYMAN MEMORIAL FUND" TO AID DIABETIC RESEARCH AND OTHER SIMILAR PURPOSES. DONATIONS CAN BE SENT C/O TILLEKE & GIBBINS, R.O.P.; 297 SURIWONGSE ROAD, BANGKOK.

Freda and Albert Lyman were both very special, as lawyers and as highly respected members of Bangkok's expatriate community. The contribution they made in their own distinct ways to the development and ongoing success of Tilleke & Gibbins is inestimable.

Commemorative bronze busts of Albert and Freda Lyman sculpted by Venetia Walkey and displayed in the firm's offices.

Bridging the Millennia 1987–2009

Tilleke & Gibbins had been reenergized by Albert and Freda Lyman after they took over the firm in 1951, and their passing inevitably marked the end of an era. Their memory is honoured in two bronze busts displayed in the firm's offices, as well as in portraits and conference rooms bearing their names, and their paternal style of business has in essence been continued. Yet change was inevitable in the face of what was becoming, and continues to be, a fast-changing world.

By the 1980s Thailand was beginning to put behind it the difficulties of the previous decade, characterized by the Vietnam War, communist pacification, dictatorships, repeated military coups and the bloody suppression of student demonstrations. Now increasing political stability and advances towards greater democracy provided a better climate for economic growth which, fuelled by a concerted export drive, the wooing of foreign investors and determined tourism promotion, resulted in a new and unprecedented period of prosperity.

From the late 1980s to the mid-'90s the Thai economy heated up like never before, hitting double-digit growth and doubling in size in just seven years. Giving concrete expression to such an extraordinary economic performance was the rapidly and radically changing face of Bangkok. In the 1950s, the city had numbered fewer than 25 buildings over six storeys (perhaps the most famous being the seven-storey Hoi Tien Lao Chinese restaurant in Chinatown); by the end of the century there were close to 1,000 high-rises over ten storeys — office towers, condominiums and luxury hotels — the tallest, Baiyoke Tower II, soaring to eighty-five storeys.

Around this vertical city snaked new multilane expressways, while an

Boom Times

'Between 1985 and 1990, the flow of foreign investment into Thailand multiplied ten times. . . . In 1980 three-fifths of exports originated from agriculture. By 1995, over four-fifths came from manufacturing. Over a decade the urban population doubled and the average per capita income doubled.'

Pasuk Phongpaichit
and Chris Baker,
Thailand's Boom and Bust.

Higher and Higher

When the 23-storey Dusit Thani Hotel opened in 1970, it was, along with the Chokchai Building on Sukhumvit Road, Bangkok's tallest edifice, a status that went unchallenged for more than a decade. From the hotel's top-floor Tiara restaurant you could look down onto a traffic-clogged Rama IV Road and out beyond to an uninterrupted bird's-eye view of a relentless flatness stretching to a hazy horizon. By the end of the 1990s, the hotel was dwarfed by new neighbours, lost in a forest of thrusting high-rises. Nor was it just buildings that had altered the location: the midsection of Rama IV had risen in a flyover, been crossed by the Skytrain and undergone deep excavation for the construction of an underground station.

elevated train mass transit system was completed in December 1999, to be followed in 2004 by an underground railway. What had once been the 'Venice of the East', Bangkok, City of Angels, was now rapidly reshaping itself in the image of its US namesake Los Angeles.

Powering the building boom and the massive infrastructure projects was the creation of giant cement and agro-industry companies along with a host of related industries and businesses, accompanied by vastly increased investor activity by both Thais and foreigners. Also, Thailand was witnessing for the first time the emergence of a true and effective urban middle class.

Economic expansion and social change proved a boon to Tilleke & Gibbins, particularly for its corporate and commercial department. Now added to the firm's traditional market of clients in established fields such as banking, shipping and airlines were others engaged in a huge diversity of businesses from construction to farm equipment, from pharmaceuticals to jewellery, from engineering to fashion.

Before the boom times fully arrived, however, Tilleke &

Gibbins was already sensing the need to respond to business growth and the shifting focus of Bangkok that was to accommodate it. When, in 1960, the firm moved its offices on New Road into the Wang Lee Building on Suriwongse Road, the area was at the heart of Bangkok's business district and the building itself was state-of-the-art as the city's first purpose-built, multistorey office block. But what was prime in the 1960s had become hopelessly outdated by the '80s.

In two decades Tilleke & Gibbins had progressively taken up more and more space and finally had to face the fact that it was outgrowing itself. So crowded were the offices that there was little room to walk around comfortably, while storage of files, books and papers was going beyond the problematic and reaching the intolerable.

Clearly, physical constraints were now seriously hampering business development and profitability, and if the firm were to progress new offices would have to be found. In 1983 the Lymans and Rojvit Periera agreed on the need to relocate; a less easy decision involved the where and how. At that time rents were escalating by ten to twelve per cent annually and after some deliberation it was decided the firm's needs would be best met not by moving into an existing office block, but by designing and constructing an office building of its own.

Rojvit Periera was charged with finding a suitable site and he duly selected a plot of land on Soi Tonson, off Ploenchit Road. This in itself was a somewhat radical move for although Tilleke & Gibbins had occupied various premises over the past ninety years, they had all been within the close confines of the New Road / Suriwongse / Si Phaya matrix that formed the hub of Bangkok's original foreign business quarter. However, by now the city had expanded so far — and was

Soi Tonson preserves an element of Bangkok's traditional ambience.

continuing to expand — that many companies, including a number of Tilleke & Gibbins' clients, had shifted to new, diverse locations in a metropolis that could no longer claim any one definable central business district.

The matter was literally one of moving with the times. The partners envisaged further expansion of the city, and rightly saw that leapfrogging to an office on Soi Tonson would offer ready access to Bangkok's southern hub centred on Silom and Suriwongse roads as well as to the northward and eastward development that has Sukhumvit Road as its principal axis. Parallels with the past persisted, however, as Soi Tonson preserves an element of the city's traditional ambience, flanked by a tree-lined canal and with close neighbours including the American, Dutch, Spanish and other embassies.

The rights to lease the Soi Tonson site were secured with the approval of the Crown Property Bureau, owner of the land, but various factors delayed the final design and the start of construction until the beginning of 1987. Work then progressed rapidly on the four-storey building, and the new offices were officially opened by the then deputy prime minister

Victoria's Precedent

(Courtesy of the British Embassy)

A precedent for Tilleke & Gibbins' move to the Ploenchit area of Bangkok had been set as early as 1927, when the then British Legation (now the British Embassy) relocated from its original site by the Chao Phraya River to its present location at the junction of Ploenchit and Wireless roads. Moved along with the diplomats was the legation's pride, a statue of Queen Victoria that had been erected in 1903. The dumpy but indomitable monarch's likeness continues to cast a stony eye over the embassy compound.

Legal Links

MEMBER

LEX ⬤ MUNDI

THE WORLD'S LEADING ASSOCIATION OF INDEPENDENT LAW FIRMS

Tilleke & Gibbins is the Thailand member of Lex Mundi, the world's leading association of more than 161 independent law firms; of Multilaw, a multinational association of over 65 independent law firms; State Capital Law Firm Group, an international organization of nearly 120 independent law firms; TAGLaw, a worldwide network of 117 independent law firms; Pacific Rim Advisory Council (PRAC), a strategic alliance of 31 independent law firms; World Services Group, a multidisciplinary network of more than 130 leading professional service firms; Counterforce Network of the International Chamber of Commerce's counterfeiting intelligence bureau; and TRACE International Inc., a nonprofit membership association of multinational companies committed to the highest standards of transparency.

HE Bhichai Rattakul on 23 November 1987.

'Soi Tonson at that time was very quiet and had only one noodle cart,' Khun Ubolratana Sitakalin recalls, reflecting that most typical of all concerns voiced by Bangkok office workers: where to eat. But that was the only perceived drawback and otherwise the staff was as much pleased with the smartness of the custom-built offices as clients were appreciative of the convenience. 'We were all excited about the move,' says Khun Ubolratana, who remembers being most impressed by the previously unknown luxury of wall-to-wall carpets. Space, too, was a luxury and unlike before, when even Albert and Freda Lyman had had to share a room, each lawyer now had his or her own office.

Excitement and expectations at the time of the relocation have been more than justified by history. 'Since we moved in November 1987', David Lyman remarked in 2005, 'our firm's gross income has grown 2,700 per cent thanks in part to Rojvit Periera's foresight in finding the right location for us.'

Following on the heels of the move into new offices were efforts to extend the scope of Tilleke & Gibbins' professional reach. Two significant elements in Thailand's burgeoning economy were foreign investment and regional markets, both of which generated greater demand and scope for legal services with an international capability. In the past, Tilleke & Gibbins had resisted attempts by overseas interests to buy into the firm, preferring to maintain its independence. Nonetheless, it had been Rojvit Periera's long-held view that Tilleke & Gibbins, while remaining independent, would benefit from an association with a respected American, British or Australian law firm that had a worldwide network of offices.

Periera's most persistent endeavours were directed at forging links with Freehill, Hollingdale & Page of Australia, and Jones, Day, Reavis & Pogue of the US, but ultimately the hoped-for relationships failed for reasons beyond the control of all parties concerned. Then, in 1989, Lex Mundi unexpectedly contacted David Lyman, which resulted in Tilleke & Gibbins joining what is the world's premier international grouping of independent law firms. This membership grew to give the firm access to the expertise

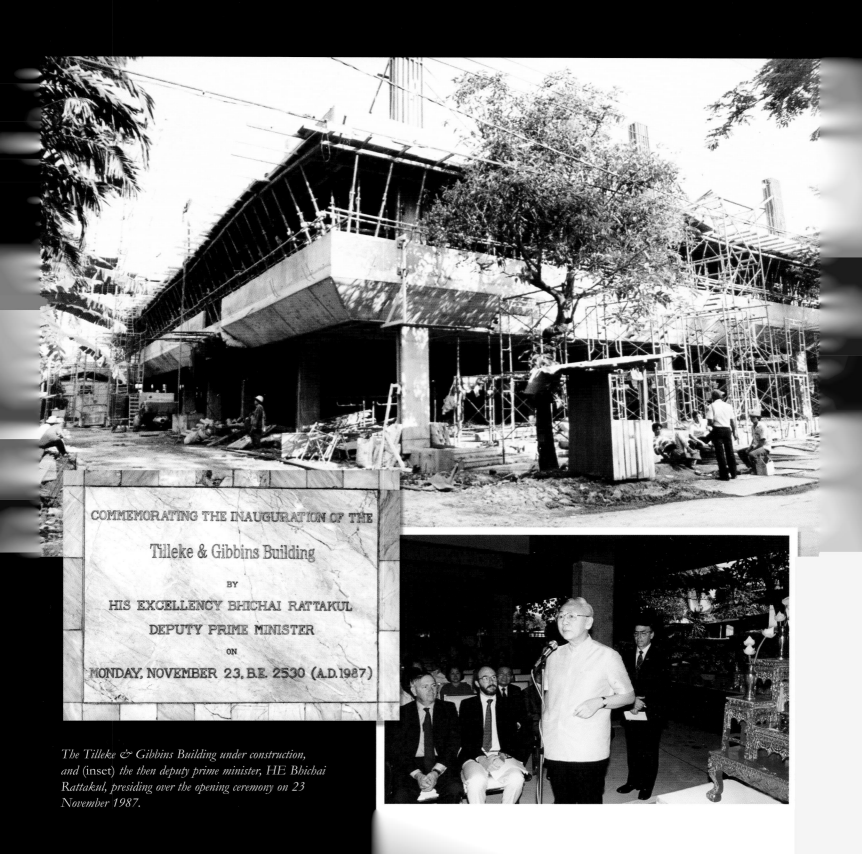

COMMEMORATING THE INAUGURATION OF THE

Tilleke & Gibbins Building

BY

HIS EXCELLENCY BHICHAI RATTAKUL

DEPUTY PRIME MINISTER

ON

MONDAY, NOVEMBER 23, B.E. 2530 (A.D.1987)

The Tilleke & Gibbins Building under construction, and (inset) the then deputy prime minister, HE Bhichai Rattakul, presiding over the opening ceremony on 23 November 1987.

Torajiro Ohashi.

and experience of more than 22,000 attorneys in over 160 countries and states, thus vastly enhancing its services in handling cases involving transnational jurisdictions.

In becoming a member of Lex Mundi (and subsequently several other international lawyers associations) Tilleke & Gibbins anticipated the trend towards globalization that continued through the last decade of the twentieth century and into the new millennium.

'In the global business of today you need to be able to provide global services for your global clients,' David Lyman said in a 2003 interview, 'and joining global networks enables you to "hang on" to a client. Since most independent law firms cannot directly service a client who wants to go abroad, because of the high expense of running overseas law offices, networks allow them to serve local clients by being able to provide them with the name of a known reliable law firm in the country they want to go to or do business in.'

Aside from legal affiliations, also indicative of an international service ethic are distinguished individual personnel employed by the firm, a notable current example being Japanese national Mr Torajiro Ohashi. After retiring as president of one of Thailand's largest truck manufacturers, with career achievements that include being decorated by the Japanese minister of communications, he now serves as a senior counsellor at Tilleke & Gibbins.

Indeed, the distinction of counsellors employed by Tilleke & Gibbins has always been extraordinarily high. Torajiro Ohashi's predecessor Junjiro Nishino, a classmate of Rojvit Periera at Thai law school, was the most senior Japanese in Thailand for many years until his death in 2001. He had been president of the Japanese Association of Thailand and director of the Japanese Chamber of Commerce, and in 1987 he received the decoration of Commander — Sacred Treasure of Japan from the Emperor of Japan.

Similarly, Dr Charoen Kanthawongs, who has long served

Death Threat

In the course of his long legal career David Lyman has encountered the gamut of the odd and at times unpleasant experiences that go with the profession, including death threats. Most memorable was an anonymous note fashioned in classical poison-pen style out of letters cut from newspaper headlines. It read, 'Death to Jewish' and was signed 'PLO'. Although the note was accompanied by revolver bullets, David was unworried, merely commenting that, 'if there is one word the PLO knows how to spell in English it's "Jews"'.

the firm, first as a young lawyer and then as a government liaison consultant, has been elected a member of parliament for eight terms and positions held during his distinguished career include minister of science, technology and the environment, and deputy minister of education. He is also the founder of Bangkok University — one of the largest of Thailand's private universitites — and was its President for 26 years.

The broadening of Tilleke & Gibbins' reach through personnel of exceptional individual distinction and through worldwide representation was paralleled by the firm's efforts to expand into neighbouring Indochina, specifically Vietnam and Cambodia. Focus on a region that had until 1975 been ravaged by war was in keeping with the political and economic climate prevailing in the late 1980s, when the Thai government of Prime Minister Chatichai Choonhaven famously urged Thai businesses to 'turn battlefields into marketplaces'.

At Tilleke & Gibbins, Rojvit Periera saw wisdom in the Chatichai dictum and investigated the possible setting up of an office in Vietnam. After many exploratory trips starting in 1982, the first concrete move, in 1989, was to establish Tilleke & Gibbins Consultants Limited (TGCL) to provide investment and legal consulting services for businesses engaged in commercial activities in Vietnam.

With perseverance, the firm succeeded in surmounting many obstacles in a country that was only just beginning to open up to international business. After three years trying, efforts were rewarded in July 1992 when Tilleke & Gibbins became the first foreign law firm to be granted a licence to establish a representative office in Vietnam. The new office, located in Ho Chi Minh City, the commercial heart of the reunified Vietnam, was followed by the establishment in January 1994 of a branch office in Hanoi, the nation's capital. Both offices were awarded full branch office licences in 1996.

Further expansion into what had now become generally known as the Mekong Subregion — comprising Vietnam, Cambodia, Laos, Myanmar and southern China's Yunnan province, and seen as an area of nascent political and economic importance — came in January 1995, when Tilleke & Gibbins entered into a law firm partnership in Phnom Penh, Cambodia.

Dr Charoen Kanthawongs.

Called Tilleke & Gibbins and Associates Ltd (TGAL), the Cambodian partnership employed American and local staff and drew on the resources of both the Bangkok office and a legal practice that had been set up in Cambodia in 1993.

As with Vietnam, Tilleke & Gibbins believed that there was strong business and investment potential in a rapidly developing nation like Cambodia, though realizing that potential could be problematic in a country only tentatively rediscovering normalcy after the tragedy and trauma of its recent past. Hence a law firm with experience in dealing with the public and private sectors and possessing a knowledge of the local legal structure could offer valuable client services to would-be investors.

Both Vietnam and Cambodia were pioneering moves, but as they used to say in the old American West, it is the pioneers who catch all the arrows, and towards the end of the 1990s Tilleke & Gibbins was finding that while its aims were justified, the productivity of its regional offices was not meeting expectations. Results reaped were disappointing, if not to say catastrophic. Partly it was a matter of timing; it was just too soon and neither the Vietnamese nor Cambodian governments were prepared for, or capable of accommodating foreign investment as initially believed. Also, Tilleke & Gibbins

David Lyman and Rojvit Periera visiting the newly opened office in Ho Chi Minh City, 1992.

had been extremely unfortunate in its choice of local personnel; loyalty as well as efficiency were lacking and in Vietnam the firm lost some 2.5 million US dollars through mismanagement and related causes. In Cambodia, losses amounted to 500,000 US dollars.

The end result was that ties with the Cambodian partner were completely severed, and in Vietnam the entire staff was fired. 'Neither pioneering Vietnam nor Cambodia was a mistake,' David Lyman says with hindsight. 'The decision to go in was right; the decision on how to operate once we were in was wrong. We had chosen the wrong people and didn't have the necessary controls or experience to monitor and manage properly.'

Plans to expand into Indochina were not totally abandoned, and although the idea of a Cambodia office was shelved indefinitely efforts in Vietnam continued with new minimal staffing taken on in order to keep the firm's licences active. A patient waiting game was

Burmese Money

Tilleke & Gibbins' regional work is generally successful and productive, though dealing with some of Thailand's neighbours can be unusually stressful, like the time when the formidable head of Rangoon's secret police demanded Tilleke & Gibbins tell its Thai client to return the 25,000 dollars she had been asked by a Burmese friend to keep for him. Described by David Lyman as 'not the kind of man you'd want to cross', the secret police boss was forceful in his demand. Undeterred, David met with him and said his client would certainly return the money once the Burmese authorities proved the entitlement to it was theirs and not that of the man who had deposited it, as his client obviously did not wish to pay back the money twice. They were unable to comply with this basic principle of law, nor were the Burmese authorities prepared to let David talk personally with the man in Rangoon. Eventually, the Burmese dropped the claim, although not until after much nerve-racking posturing.

played until September 2007 when, with Vietnam's economy once more on the rise, TGCL reopened in Hanoi with offices in the city's new and imposing HAREC Building.

John E. King was appointed TGCL's managing partner, and new lawyers and office staff were recruited. With a staff in early 2008 of 25 and rising, business was expanding with a focus primarily on intellectual property rights and commercial advice. Also in 2008, TGCL in Ho Chi Minh City moved to new facilities in the Citilight Tower.

Tilleke & Gibbins further strove to spread its wings locally but, as with Indochina, suffered setbacks before enjoying success. In 2001 a small field office opened at the Laem Chabang industrial estate on the Eastern Seaboard. What seemed a good idea on paper proved impractical; the office closed three years later due to insufficient business. Although many companies operated at Laem Chabang, legal work tended to be handled by offices in Bangkok.

Undeterred, the firm continued to view domestic expansion

optimistically and in June 2005 it established an office on Thailand's southern island of Phuket. Owned 51 per cent by Tilleke & Gibbins International and 49 per cent by its managing director John R. Howard, Tilleke & Gibbins International Phuket Ltd has thrived, and

The Phuket offices, headed by John R. Howard (inset).

continues to do so, on the commercial significance of Phuket for local and overseas investors,

especially the island's buoyant property sector.

With much of his career spent in the South Pacific, principally in Fiji, where he headed his own law practice, John R. Howard, an Australian, brought not only legal expertise and fresh ideas to the new Phuket office but also his considerable experience of island economies. He was initially supported by long-time Tilleke & Gibbins partner Tim Wales, who was director of legal services until his retirement in 2006.

Ventures into overseas and domestic expansion are indicative of the firm's strength and aspirations, but of more significance is the enormous growth Tilleke & Gibbins has sustained in Bangkok during the last two decades. In that time the firm's staff more than tripled from 114 to approaching 360 today, while the number of lawyers and consultants rose from 42 in 1987 to 97 in 2009. During the same period gross revenue increased from 33 million baht to in excess of 800 million baht. To cope with this rapid growth, the

New post

Dr. John R. Hanlon, a veteran of 17 years in the international rubber industry, has been appointed Chairman of the Board and Managing Director of Goodyear (Thailand) Limited, it was announced by Richard V. Thomas, President of Goodyear International Corporation. Mr. Hanlon will be the Chief Executive Officer of the newly formed Thailand company which plans to build a 350,000,000 Baht ($16,735,000) tire factory in Bangkok.

This 1967 press clipping shows John Hanlon, who 20 years later joined Tilleke & Gibbins.

firm took over and refurbished three floors in the Tonson Building ('TG North') located a short walk along Soi Tonson from its main offices ('TG Main').

Under David Lyman's leadership Tilleke & Gibbins was expanded, consolidated and modernized during the last years of the twentieth century to a greater extent than at any other period in its history. New, more efficient work systems were set up, and rationalization of core services, which had started back in the early 1980s with the shedding of largely unproductive criminal, narcotics and commercial collection cases, was extended. 'It all compared favourably with the New York law firm I'd been working with previously,' was the impression of Santhapat Periera on his joining Tilleke & Gibbins in 1990.

Greatly assisting Lyman in the reorganization of the firm was John R. (Jack) Hanlon, whose arrival in September 1987 was most timely. A senior director of the Support Services Department until his retirement in 2004, Hanlon joined the firm at Lyman's invitation just after its finance director had resigned, and he more than adequately stepped into the breach. Indeed, there could scarcely have been anyone better.

An American, Hanlon was a qualified lawyer, admitted to the Ohio Bar, and had a solid business background, including a degree in finance. He had held various executive positions with Goodyear Tyre & Rubber Co. Inc. from 1951 to 1987, during which time he was twice posted to Thailand, both times as managing director of the Thai subsidiary. Moreover, he was well acquainted with Tilleke & Gibbins, a working relationship that stretched back to December 1967, when Goodyear engaged the firm to secure a licence and Board of Investment privileges for the tyre factory it was then building in Thailand.

'With excellent advice and substantial help from Mr Albert Lyman, Goodyear was granted both the licence and the promotional privileges,' Hanlon says. 'During the next two formative years of the company I conferred at least weekly with Albert Lyman and increasingly with David Lyman, who had recently joined the firm, for the formation of the company selling shares to the public, purchasing land, construction contracts, employment policies, dealership agreements, and other myriad details of

IN MEMORY OF

V. H. Jaques.

Victor Henny Jaques
Partner · 1927 – 1946

Interior of TG North Building on Soi Tonson in 2007. Meeting rooms are named after past and present partners, with a personalized plaque complete with replicated signature on the wall outside each room, while within each room is featured a painting of the relevant partner. Commissioned by Tilleke & Gibbins, the paintings are all by British artist Paul Barton.

Freda R. Lyman

getting an industrial and marketing operation underway.'

The success of the working relationship was reciprocal. 'When the Goodyear operation was progressing well', Hanlon notes, 'I was able to devote some spare time with David assisting Tilleke & Gibbins' clients, particularly in cases related to the US military presence in Thailand.'

Hanlon retired after 36 years with Goodyear, just at the time when Tilleke & Gibbins was preparing to move to its new offices on Soi Tonson.

'I don't recall exactly how the discussion started, but I believe that while we were talking about my retirement from Goodyear David Lyman said something to the effect that he would love to have me with the firm but couldn't afford me, meaning he could not match what I had been receiving as an expat with Goodyear. But with my retirement package I did not need a matching arrangement.

'We went from there. We had a natural and experienced fit and so were off and running from the start. David gave me all the authority and backing that I needed to get the jobs done, to make changes to meet the growth that

was underway and to develop the technology needed for efficiently meeting client requirements.'

Hanlon was instrumental in many ways in the success of Tilleke & Gibbins following its move to new offices. Most dramatic of the changes he

David Lyman in 1986 when he was president of the American Chamber of Commerce.

initiated was to expand and upgrade computerization, a development that 'came just in time to save our billing system that was then limping along with hardware for which we could no longer get spare parts and software that was dependent on a programmer who was no longer available'.

The modernization of the firm was not, however, achieved without conscious, perhaps for some painful, effort. Relocation to new offices in 1987 served as a wake-up call. Six months after the move David Lyman issued a six-page memo to all solicitors, trial lawyers, department heads, paralegals and senior staff. It was headed 'The Revitalization of Tilleke & Gibbins'.

Effectively, this was a reading of the riot act. Lyman complained of slackness in the work ethic and sluggishness in the business. The blame for this, he admitted, lay in his own lack of proper leadership, but having accepted that blame he minced no words in saying the buck stops here.

'We have a long way to go to climb back and I intend to get us there,' Lyman wrote to the staff. 'That is my promise to you. It's also my responsibility to do so. . . . You have a choice. You can come with me sharing the burdens, the problems, the time, the sacrifices and the rewards, or you can leave Tilleke & Gibbins. . . . This is the beginning of a new era for Tilleke & Gibbins. You are either with me or you are no longer here.'

The memo included a form that gave those who wished to do so the chance to resign. 'For those of you who decide to stay', Lyman concluded, 'you understand that you have committed yourself, along with me, to do whatever is necessary to make us winners, to make us the best law firm in this country and to make us all considerably richer than we are today'. There were few resignations, and the rest, as they say, is history.

To further enhance lawyers' performance and productivity, on 4 January 1994, Lyman introduced an incentive system by which a lawyer's remuneration was 30 per cent of whatever he or she billed and collected against a guaranteed minimum wage package. That is still the standard on which some lawyers have done very well and others try to achieve.

Even when Thailand's economic bubble burst in 1997, law practice continued to flourish. 'Some clients went bankrupt', David Lyman remarks, 'but what we lost in the investment area was made up by gains in the restructuring field.'

With the streamlining that was carried out in the late 1980s, Tilleke & Gibbins' business was consolidated into three clearly defined departments: Corporate & Commercial; Dispute Resolution; and Intellectual Property, each headed by one of the firm's partners, supported by group heads of law practice subdivisions. This was not a new departure — department heads had been first established in the mid-1970s, prompted initially by the need to have someone in overall charge of the trial lawyers — but departments were now better, more solidly organized than before and assumed the structure they have today.

The Corporate & Commercial Department provides advice and assistance covering the myriad and complex laws and regulations governing trade in Thailand, as well as the promotion and development of new and expanding commercial interests and business investment. In addition to general commercial agreements, banking and finance, tax, and insolvency and restructuring are areas of expertise for which the firm is noted.

In the commercial sector, Tilleke & Gibbins has a traditional strength in maritime law and has been servicing shipping activities in Thai waters for more than half a century. In recent years, however, real estate and construction, initially

The Bubble Bursts

No one thought Thailand's economic 'miracle' would continue forever, though the severity of the bust that came in mid-1997 was greater than anyone expected. Over two million people lost their jobs; the baht fell some 40 per cent against the US dollar, and by 1998 the economy had shrunk 11 per cent, ending a forty-year period during which growth had never fallen below four per cent. The causes of the crash were multiple, summed up by commentators Pasuk Phongpaichit and Chris Baker as resulting from 'the explosive chemistry' of mixing careless lending by international finance and 'the pirate instincts of Thai businessmen and politicians'.

in Bangkok but also of late in Pattaya, Phuket, Hua Hin and Koh Samui have far exceeded maritime business in terms of number of cases and fees generated. Another growth area is telecommunications and information technology, with recent cases including acting as counsel to a major Japanese telephone company in its investment in a Thai counterpart, acting as counsel to a leading

Ms Piyanuj 'Lui' Ratprasatporn (top) *and Mrs Cynthia Pornavalai* (above).

international computer company in the sale of some of the assets in its Thai subsidiary, and providing legal assistance for a variety of Internet-related activities.

While possible to pinpoint areas of expertise, the principal feature of Tilleke and Gibbins' corporate and commercial activity as it stands today is its diversity, with the firm's list of active corporate and business clients numbering over 5,500 from 109 countries.

Now with 25 fee-earners, the Corporate & Commercial Department is headed by five partners, each with their own fields of expertise as well as impressive backgrounds.

Best known among the department's leading personalities are Ms Piyanuj 'Lui' Ratprasatporn (Corporate/M&A and Corporate Immigration), who was nominated as one of the leading lawyers in the corporate area in the *International Who's Who Legal* Series 2001–7, and who is listed in the *Asia Pacific Legal 500* 2002–9; and Mrs Cynthia Pornavalai (Banking & Finance, Japanese Unit) a partner fluent in Japanese, who was invited to be a founding member of the International Insolvency Institute in 2003. In 2009 she is scheduled in *Who's Who of Professionals*. Ms Sriwan

Puapondh (Taxation & Customs) is a partner who was formerly with the Revenue Department and has many credits, including listing in the *Asia Pacific Legal 500* and ranking as a 'recommended individual' in the tax area by *Which Lawyer Yearbook,* annually since 2006, and in 2009 by *PLC Cross-Border Tax or Corporate Transactions Handbook*, as well as being a member of the Working Group for Studying and Advising on the Amendment of the Revenue Code of the Federation of Accounting Professions under the Royal Patronage of HM the King. Also, Ms Pimvimol 'June' Vipamaneerut, a partner and head of the Transportation and Labour groups, is a notable alumna, as it were, of Tilleke & Gibbins, having been part-sponsored by the firm during her studies in the UK, which culminated in her taking her master's in Maritime Law. On the male side, Santhapat Periera (International Trade), a partner who is an Honorary Fellow of the Association of Fellows and Legal Scholars of the Centre for International Legal Studies, is also an adviser to two Thai Parliament subcommittees.

Other equally distinguished personalities are to be found in the firm's Dispute Resolution Department, which at present has fourteen fee-earners. Heading the department is Ms Tiziana Sucharitkul; she succeeded partner John E. King, one of Thailand's top dispute resolution lawyers, when he took sabbatical leave in 2005. He has been recognized by *PLC* in 2009/10. Tiziana's promotion gives a good example of the career advancement opportunities that Tilleke & Gibbins provides. During her training with the firm, she won a company-sponsored scholarship to study law at Hastings College of Law in San Francisco. After qualifying in California and spending a year back at the firm, she then furthered her work experience in the California and Singapore offices of a major New York law firm before settling back with Tilleke & Gibbins. Among her recognitions was being named as one of Thailand's leading dispute resolution lawyers in the 2005–9 editions of the *Asia Pacific Legal 500*.

A similar listing in the 2003–9 editions of the *Asia Pacific Legal 500* was awarded to the department's other partner, Mr Thawat Damsa-ard, the firm's chief litigator whose career combines six years' experience as a finance/account manager for CP Group, one of Thailand's leading businesses, and more than ten

years as a highly successful trial and arbitration attorney. He is also the recipient of an award from the Court of Appeal for his contribution to the law journal, *Extradition: Theory and Procedure.*

Tilleke & Gibbins has long had a solid arbitration practice, but the greatest gains, both in new arbitration claims and in enforcing foreign arbitral awards, have come in the first years of the new millennium. The biggest of the firm's Dispute Resolution Department's cases was in 2003, when Tilleke & Gibbins was retained to represent one of the world's largest multinational brewery corporations in a 500-million-dollar joint venture termination dispute. Through the firm's strategy and tactics, the case was settled in mid-2006 in the client's favour. Following this, the department was named as one of the four 'top-tier' dispute resolutions departments in the 2004–5 edition of the *Asia Pacific Legal 500*.

Of Tilleke & Gibbins' three main legal departments, Intellectual Property (IP) accounts for the lion's share of the practice, in terms of both revenue and employees. It is a field in which the firm has been a pioneer, filing some of the first trademark and patent applications

Ms Pimvimol 'June' Vipamaneerut (top), *and Santhapat Periera and his wife Ratree 'Nok'* (above).

John E. King (above), managing partner in Vietnam, *and (right)* Thawat Damsa-ard, chief litigator.

in Thailand after laws for each were enacted in, respectively, 1942 and 1979, and subsequently among the first to file suits for infringement. Today, with unmatched experience and expertise, Tilleke & Gibbins handles about twenty per cent of all trademarks and patents filed in Thailand, while in the face of the growing problem of trademark and copyright infringement, it also has a large anticounterfeiting operation. In recognition, Tilleke & Gibbins was named *AsiaLaw*'s Thailand IP Firm 2004–7, and *Managing Intellectual Property*'s Thailand IP Firm of the Year in 2007, 2008 and 2009.

With more than 58 fee-earners, the IP Department is staffed by two partners: department head Mrs Darani Vachanavuttivong (formerly Ms Vipa Chuenjaipanich) and chief IP litigator Mr Srila Thongklang. Altogether it is an impressive team, with Darani identified in *AsiaLaw Leading Lawyers Survey* as one of Asia's top business lawyers specializing in the area of intellectual property. Also, in the 2005 *Guide to the World's Leading Patent Law Experts*, Darani was nominated as the top patent expert in Thailand, as well as being listed among the world's preeminent trademark lawyers in the trademarks

chapter of *Who's Who Legal*. Additionally, she is currently the president of the Intellectual Property Association of Thailand (IPAT). Aside from legal expertise, the IP Department also has a High Tech Unit comprising legal professionals with wide-ranging technical backgrounds.

What makes IP practice exceptional in Thailand is the extent of counterfeiting, something that in recent decades has swelled to pandemic proportions, the scale of the problem becoming intolerable to the international community. It is scarcely an exaggeration to say that back-street fakery was as significant a component of Thailand's economy as were the legitimate businesses and industries that contributed to the boom of the 1980s and '90s. It was not new, but it grew vastly in scale when economic growth created a greater demand for all kinds of branded products from pharmaceuticals to luxury goods and apparel, and from golf clubs to motorcycles.

Together with China, Thailand enjoys a dubious distinction of probably leading the world in terms of the volume of counterfeit goods produced and transported. That 'anything made by man can

Whisky Woes

In the 1980s, it was estimated that whisky buyers in Bangkok had a one-in-four chance of purchasing a genuine bottle of Johnnie Walker Red or Black Label whisky. The bottles were genuine, as sometimes were the labels (although these could be faked if the originals were too worn); the caps, seals and contents were not. Either the whisky was diluted with tea or some local concoction (one method of doing this without removing the cap was to heat the bottom of a bottle and insert a syringe needle), or empty bottles were refilled with a fake Thai distillation.

Miss Universe

David Lyman and his former wife 'Buk' at the 1992 Miss Universe pageant, held in Bangkok.

Miss Universe LLP, the US beauty pageant company owned by NBC Universal and Donald Trump, has for the past several years had its trademark and intellectual property rights in Thailand registered and protected by Tilleke & Gibbins. When the pageant returned to Thailand in May 2005, the firm was legal adviser to Miss Universe LLP in negotiating and closing nine separate licences and other agreements that provided the structure for the hosting of the event.

be, has been, and probably is being counterfeited' — a phrase coined by David Lyman — is well illustrated by The Tilleke & Gibbins Museum of Counterfeit Goods, which displays approximately 5,000 items in more than twenty categories (see Appendix I).

Some idea of the scale of copyright piracy and trademark counterfeiting in Thailand, and Tilleke & Gibbins' work in tackling the problem, is offered by a partial summary of cases in 2003. In that one year alone the firm secured more than 1.5 million dollars in fines, legalizations and settlements for copyright owners as a result of raids and prosecutions of retail and institutional pirates, including a record 450,000-dollar settlement for one well-known software developer. Also in 2003 trademark anticounterfeiting activities on behalf of such leading brand clients as Levi Strauss & Co., Lacoste, Timberland and Adidas resulted in the seizure of nearly a million infringing items of clothing and a near 100-per-cent conviction rate against offenders.

Among its major coups, in 2005 Tilleke & Gibbins, representing Daimler Chrysler AG and General Motors, participated in simultaneous police raids in Bangkok and Kanchanaburi province that netted tens of thousands of counterfeit auto parts and accessories valued at well in excess of fifty million baht, plus equipment valued at hundreds of millions of baht. According to a police estimate, the counterfeiting operation was one of the largest of its kind to be uncovered in Thailand.

Trademark and copyright infringement in Thailand is rather like the mythical hydra: for every head cut off another grows back, and Tilleke & Gibbins' IP practice continues to thrive. It enjoyed a gain in revenues of nearly 120 per cent between 2002 and 2004, and subsequent growth has been sustained, albeit not at quite such a spectacular level. With some 2,000 active IP criminal cases on file, Tilleke & Gibbins likely has the largest market share of the combined IP registration, litigation and enforcement market of any law firm in Thailand.

The present volume of IP business is partly indicative of the scale of work in Thailand, but it also reflects Tilleke & Gibbins' success in its recent efforts to advance its premier standing in the field. The company has put much thought into marketing and

Clockwise from top left: Ms Tiziana
Sucharitkul, comanaging partner and director
of the firm's Dispute Resolution Department;
Santhapat Periera, partner, who is an Honorary
Fellow of the Association of Fellows and Legal
Scholars of the Centre for International Legal
Studies; and Ms Darani Vachanavuttivong,
comanaging partner and managing director of
the Intellectual Property Department.

Above: *Exterior view of TG Main office on Soi Tonson.* Inset: *Portrait painting of David Lyman.* Right: *Tiziana Sucharitkul and Darani Vachanavuttivong with receptionist Panida Tongwattana at TG Main.*

staff training, positioning, itself as a one-stop shop for IP services, a strategy that has proved effective.

Taking a realistic, no-nonsense approach, Tilleke & Gibbins makes no promises to its clients that counterfeiting will end, but the firm tries to make it so difficult for counterfeiters that, in the words of former partner Edward Kelly, 'they'll go and knock off someone else'. The practice of pursuing IP cases is one of commercial value for clients, with their legal fees being effectively an investment. In a case concerning computer software, for example, it worked out that for every dollar the client paid in legal fees there was a return of ten dollars in terms of revenue gained through the successful prosecution of copyright infringement.

Tilleke & Gibbins' growth in the latter years of the twentieth century did not go unchallenged, and while the business of legal practice expanded during Thailand's boom years so did the number of law firms eager for a share in the bigger pie. New Thai practices entered the scene, as did internationally renowned firms.

Tilleke & Gibbins had not had the field entirely to itself — in 1965 Charles Kirkwood set up a practice in Bangkok, and Baker & McKenzie opened a Thailand branch in 1977 — but for as long as anyone can remember, Tilleke & Gibbins had the reputation as being the number one law firm available to foreign residents in Thailand, and to visitors, who required assistance in dealing with civil, administrative and criminal matters. By the close of the middle of the first decade of the new millennium, however, the firm faced competition from nearly sixty other foreign-business-orientated law practices.

That Tilleke & Gibbins was able to thrive and not just survive (in 2005 the firm ranked third,

Seeing Red

In March 2008 a Ferrari P4 was the centrepiece of an exhibition in Brussels. Only three of the P4 were ever made, in 1967, but this was not one of them, nor was the exhibition a motor show. In fact the 'Ferrari' was a fake and the exhibition was organized to launch an international drive against counterfeiting. According to a press report, the counterfeit P4 replicated the original in every visible detail but had in fact been made in a back-street factory in Thailand, knocked up from Japanese parts and powered by a Subaru engine. The car was about to be shipped to a European client when police confiscated it. Meanwhile lawyers continue to see red. The Bangkok Post *of 30 November 2008 reported on an independent Bangkok car manufacturer who is turning out 'replicas' of Ferraris and other top-of-the-line sports cars made from a medley of parts, none of them authentic. However, claiming to be a replica is a moot point, and simply looking like the real thing could come under the Thai Copyright Act. Tilleke & Gibbins intellectual property lawyer Mrs Hassana Chira-Aphakul says, 'In our opinion the design of a car may be eligible for protection as a copyright and, if so, a copy of such design constitutes copyright infringement'.*

Military Might

'Influential persons' influence much in Thailand, and traditionally influential is the military. In one 2004 trademark infringement case, concerning counterfeit cosmetics being sold near Bangkok International Airport, Tilleke & Gibbins coordinated with police a simultaneous raid on 25 shops in the complex. All was arranged, the day arrived, and close to 100 police in ten vans were heading down the highway. Just ten minutes away from arrival at the target, the lead police officer received a phone call. His face turned pale. 'I've just learned the shops are owned by one of the highest ranking officers in the Royal Thai Air Force,' he explained to the Tilleke & Gibbins team. 'There'll be no raid today.'

after Baker & McKenzie and Domnern, Somkiat & Boonma, in the Thai legal market's list of top-ten earners; T&G rose to second place in 2006, and continues to rank second only to Baker & McKenzie) was due in part to its timely modernization, though its very longevity is perhaps its major strength. 'We have many years of accumulated knowledge specific to Thailand and Southeast Asia,' David Lyman said in a 2003 interview. 'We can do things that international firms cannot do, or cannot do cost effectively.'

Recognition of that longevity is well illustrated by client loyalty. A total of 307 clients have been with the firm for more than thirty years, and 25 of these for more than seventy years, with the Thoresen group topping the list at 82 years, followed by GEC and Philip Morris, each clocking up 75 years as of 2009.

'We often get people calling up saying "my father used your firm before and now we would like you to . . ."' remarks Santhapat Periera. He adds, 'There is still a family feeling, a personal touch with Tilleke & Gibbins', and such would seem to account for much of the firm's ongoing success. As an issue of *Legal Management* notes, 'The key to holding client business will continue to be found in individual relationships'.

This does not imply Tilleke & Gibbins rests on past laurels — it could not and still be competitive in today's legal services marketplace — and there is a dynamism in the firm paralleling the wider social, economic and political context in which it operates.

Night Work

Product counterfeiting remains highly visible in Bangkok. A walk down any of the city's major shopping streets reveals displays of T-shirts, shoes, bags, watches and more bearing such familiar names as Lacoste, Gucci, Adidas, Levi Strauss, and others similarly famous. Only the price tags suggest the goods are not what they seem. This is especially so with night markets, which illustrate just one of the loopholes in the enforcement of intellectual property laws. The Thai courts are reluctant to permit the police to execute search warrants at night because the courts are closed at that time and there is no court or judge from whom to seek guidance.

The first years of the third millennium saw a recovery from the economic crash of 1997, and the growth and change that typified the late 1980s and early '90s continues apace, as readily witnessed in work starting up again on temporarily halted high-rise construction and major civil works. Less obvious than this physical change is radical and far-reaching social change.

'Over one generation during the last quarter of the twentieth century', write Chris Baker and Pasuk Phongpaichit in *A History of Thailand*, 'Thailand's society changed with unprecedented speed. Building on the foundations of urban capitalism laid in the American era, big-business families grew not only in wealth but also in social prominence. A new white-collar middle class embraced Western-influenced consumer tastes, and concepts of individualism. Capitalism drew into the city a much larger working class. . . . The economy became more exposed to global forces, and the society to global tastes and ideas. Equally important as globalization was the coming of mass society.'

In politics the unprecedented 2001 landslide electoral victory of Thaksin Shinawatra, the country's richest businessman, seemed to assure that big business had finally succeeded the military in taking full control of the reins of state power.

This power realignment had its parallel in a shift of emphasis in

Rojvit Periera, a valued partner for 56 years.

the teaching and practice of law. 'In the past', says Thanes Periera, 'the curriculum at Thammasat Law School focused largely on the national security and military aspects of law. Now it's different, with a much greater emphasis on business law.'

For its part, Tilleke & Gibbins grew with and adapted to the change, itself changing in the process with the creation, on 1 January 2000, of Tilleke & Gibbins International Ltd. In essence this was a reconstruction of the firm from a 1973 registered ordinary partnership (ROP) to a limited company (incidentally, the last of Thailand's law firms to do so). Most of Tilleke & Gibbins' ROP's assets and many of its personnel and professional services were transferred to the new entity, while the original partnership remains as the leaseholder of Tilleke & Gibbins' previous office site in Soi Tonson, which is owned by the Crown Property Bureau.

The principal objective of the reconstruction was to open up the firm to bring in additional partners. This bore fruit in 2002, when ten new partners were admitted, bringing the total to thirteen, the three preexisting partners being David Lyman, Rojvit Periera and Jack Hanlon. Two others, Tiziana Sucharitkul and Srila Thongklang, were made partners in 2005, the year in which

The partners as of 2009. Standing from the left: *Chinachart Vatanasuchart, Darani Vachanavuttivong, Santhapat Periera, Thawat Damsa-ard, David Lyman, Srila Thongklang, Cynthia Pornavalai and Tiziana Sucharitkul, and Chief Operating Officer Don Jones.* Insets, from the left: *John E. King , Piyanuj Ratprasatporn, Pimvimol Vipamaneerut, Anongporn Thanachaiary, Sriwan Puapondh and John R. Howard.*

John R. Howard became a partner of Tilleke & Gibbins Phuket.

On 10 September 2002, Rojvit Periera died at the age of 82. Like Albert and Freda Lyman, he had never considered retirement and worked until the end, finally succumbing to a brain haemorrhage after suffering a fall at home. He had been a law partner with two generations of the Lyman family, and as such had provided valuable continuity during his 56 years with the firm. 'Rojvit was the conscience of the firm,' comments David Lyman, 'a controlling influence that kept us all on a stable track as we developed our business rapidly.'

Ultraconservative in outlook and adhering to classic old ways, Rojvit Periera tended to view law firms as family affairs passing from one generation to the next. Today, the structure of the firm has more of a corporate look. Decision-making is in the hands of a board of directors, which presently consists of David Lyman, Darani Vachanavuttivong, Tiziana Sucharitkul and Santhapat Periera, plus two outside independent directors: Clayton Hebbard, Chairman Asia–Pacific of TMF Services Ltd, and Daniel Credazzi, an executive with the Leighton Group in Australia and

who is also David Lyman's nephew. The purpose of having outside directors is to bring fresh, objective views, as well as different disciplines into policymaking. This is an innovative concept and Tilleke & Gibbins is one of the first significant firms worldwide to initiate outside, independent nonlawyer directors.

Reporting directly to the board and acting as a kind of government whip is the chief operating officer (COO). The position was initially established by Philippe Annez, a nonlawyer previously with the World Bank, between 2003, when Jack Hanlon retired, and his

By the Book

No two witnesses ever tell quite the same story. This basic lesson that every law student learns provided the key to one of David Lyman's oddest cases. A US Army colonel, a devout Catholic, was accused of sexual abuse by his young son and elder stepdaughter and stepson. As the mother would not allow the children to testify at a court martial, the Judge Advocate-General's Office sought an administrative discharge in a 'hearing to show cause', for which David Lyman and Jack Hanlon were retained as the civilian defence counsel. (A 'show cause' proceeding shifts the burden of proof from the government to the accused, which was a sly move in this case.) The sworn testaments of the three children were presented and the case against the colonel looked clear-cut, until David queried the remarkable similarity between each of the children's stories. He was also interested in part of the stepdaughter's testament that claimed her stepfather had once given her a pornographic novel, and asked the wife of the military cocounsel, an air hostess, to try to find a copy of the book in the US. She succeeded and when David compared the plot of the novel with the incidents in the children's testaments he found them virtually identical. He was thus able to prove collusion between the witnesses. As to the children's motive, it turned out that they had fabricated their story, using the book as a guide, so as to give their mother cause for a divorce, which the Catholic colonel had refused.

untimely passing in March 2006, when he was succeeded by Don Jones.

Charged with monitoring operations, Annez described his job as 'holding up a mirror to the lawyers' in order to enforce and sharpen employee performance. This is not only akin to the more radical style of large law firms in, say, New York or London but also it is something that Annez saw as vital in the local environment. 'Here,' he said, 'lawyers are less profitable than in the US or UK. The market is harder, clients don't always like to pay and lawyers often feel bad about billing clients. It's the local culture.' Such a greater emphasis on accountability Annez recognized as

Philippe Annez, Chief Operating Officer, 2003–2006.

the biggest recent change at Tilleke & Gibbins.

In spite of its modern corporate structure, Tilleke & Gibbins arguably remains in essence a family business, or at least one with strong paternal governance and based on the cultivation of mutual respect. 'Albert and Freda Lyman imbued the firm with the culture of family,' remarked Jack Hanlon. 'David has faithfully nourished and maintained that culture. As soon as a new employee walks in the door, that employee becomes a member of the family with all the rights and privileges as well as the duties and responsibilities of every family member.'

This is not unusual for a medium-sized law firm, and David Lyman firmly holds that a benevolent dictatorship is the best management structure. It is also the code of *Lyman's Laws for Lawyers* (see Appendix III) that quintessentially underpins the professional ethos of the firm.

Accordingly, David Lyman characterizes the firm as clearly and as pervasively as William Alfred Tilleke, Samuel Brighouse and Albert Lyman. 'Such is the strength of his personality that, in the words of Philippe Annez, it 'pervades in many ways to create a

'Although you may be a hard-assed lawyer, you are a sentimental old softy. Just like your father — hard shell on the outside, whipped cream inside.' Thus did the late Father Ray Brennan, founder of the Pattaya Orphanage and long-time friend of the Lyman family, sum up the character of David Lyman.

general culture'. There is thus both a continuity with the past, as David carries on the traditions of his father and mother and retains fundamental values, and an identity that is indelibly David's.

Elements of that identity — generosity, courtesy and an old-world civility, for example — are characteristic and often commented on. Once, travelling in the wilds of Tibet, David held open the door of the tour van for a lady. 'Whoever his mother is,' said the surprised woman, 'she sure brought him up right.'

More than anything else, David combines a passion for the law, in all its political, economic and social implications, with a devotion to Thailand. These two factors, expressed through a strong, outgoing character, most clearly define his career and his stewardship of Tilleke & Gibbins. Indeed the two are inextricably bound up with each other.

'Thailand is my home,' David says. 'I have always felt that, even when I first moved here as a child

in 1949. I love the greenness of the land, while the tropical climate sets a tone. It's not a high-pressure place à la New York. Professionally, however, it's more challenging than practising law in the US. Clients are more demanding of your time, and of the time they give you to come up with a response. Also, you need to be more creative as you have to learn to put yourself in the client's position. At the same time you are able to give more. I could never have achieved personally so much in the US.'

David describes himself as a 'jack of all trades' and

sees Thailand as giving him the opportunity to be multifaceted. Indeed he is something of an advocate-at-large, possessing a keen interest and involvement in the wider community. His closely typed multipage curriculum vitae lists some seventy past and current memberships and directorships ranging from the domestic arena of, for example, the Rotary Club of Bangkok, the American Chamber of Commerce in Thailand, the Thai Board of Trade and the Community Services of Bangkok (which he

Down to Earth

David Lyman's visit to Washington in 1986 was a day to remember. In the morning he presented his testimony before the US Senate. He lunched in the Senate dining room. At 2.30 pm he was received by the Secretary of Agriculture in his office, and two hours later he met with President Reagan at the White House. He was walking on air as he went straight from the White House to the local Hertz office to rent a car for the next day. 'Sorry, sir,' said

the clerk. 'It's not possible. We can't accept a Thai-language driving licence.' David was left pondering the way of the world that allowed him to meet with the President of the United States of America and the Secretary of Agriculture — a cabinet officer — and testify before a subcommittee of the Senate, and yet be refused by a car rental clerk, all in the same day. 'It kind of brought one back to earth,' he concludes.

helped found) to the international stage of the World Economic Forum, the International Crisis Group and the International Chamber of Commerce (Paris).

No mere joiner, David has always been extremely active in these various associations, in numerous cases holding office at various times. His participation has even extended, as president (for a second term) of the American Chamber of Commerce in Thailand in 1986, to lobbying the US Senate to enact an amendment to the rice provisions of the 1986 Farm Act. His opening remarks to that august body were: 'I come before you today directly representing 400 American and associated companies, having almost four billion dollars in investment in Thailand and over 2.4 billion dollars in bilateral trade in 1985.'

The speech was widely quoted in the press, though reports omitted David's contrasting preamble. In this he apologized for his somewhat dishevelled appearance owing to the airline having lost his luggage, leaving him with only the clothes in which he had travelled from Bangkok. 'I came to Dulles [Airport] but my bags went to Dallas,' he told the senators. It broke the ice.

Twenty fishing boats were donated to a southern village as part of the firm's emergency relief after the 2004 tsunami disaster.

Recognition of David's achievements is witnessed by his listing in no fewer than four different *Who's Who* volumes, as well as in the *Dictionary of International Biography*. Given the avuncular image he projects in the office, however, it might be expected that he derives greater satisfaction from having been voted 'Boss of the Year' by the Women Secretaries' Association of Thailand in 1997.

If David has taken full advantage of the opportunities presented to him by Thailand, he has in turn reciprocated generously on the corporate and personal levels. Tilleke & Gibbins makes regular contributions to diverse Thai charitable projects, awards scholarships for law students in Thailand and Vietnam, and participates in many activities of corporate social responsibility such as, for example, providing emergency relief assistance after the 2004 tsunami disaster, when the firm donated twenty fishing boats to a southern village and a major sum to the Thai Red Cross. The firm also supports a reforestation programme that was initiated to mark Tilleke & Gibbins' centenary in 1993 and maintained ever since.

With Tilleke & Gibbins' extensive practice and the broad opportunities offered by Thailand, David's career spans an amazing spectrum of legal cases, notwithstanding that corporate

This page clockwise from top: *David Lyman, as chairman of the fund-raising committee for the US Geodesic Botanical Pavilion receiving, in 1988, a commemorative coin from HRH Princess Maha Chakri Sirindhorn; with US president Ronald Reagan at a meeting of American Chamber of Commerce regional presidents in Tokyo in 1986; and at a formal dinner with former Thai prime minister MR Kukrit Pramoj. Opposite page: HM King Bhumibol Adulyadej grants David Lyman an audience in 1986 at which the lawyer makes a donation to the Ananda Mahidol Foundation on behalf of the Albert and Freda Lyman Memorial Fund.*

work and intellectual property comprise the bulk of the firm's business. From locking horns with the Royal Thai Navy over the right of maritime treasure hunters who had salvaged priceless Chinese antiques off the coast of Thailand to proving the innocence of a court-martialled US army officer accused of paedophilia, from representing the plaintiff in a sex-change operation malpractice suit to setting a precedent for determining compensation in cases of wrongful death in plane crashes, David has been rewarded with all the intrigue and fascination a legal practice has to offer. Shrugging off death threats, resisting the temptation of a stack of currency notes placed on his desk in an attempted bribe, and similar occupational hazards further colour his career.

Asked to name just one case that he has found particularly satisfying, David replied, 'I've been rewarded in many ways, but perhaps my most fun case was for the *Far Eastern Economic Review*. Just to go through it was tremendously challenging.'

Triggering the case was a small commentary in the 10 January 2002 issue of that now defunct but then influential weekly regional news magazine, which persons in the Thai government considered bordered on defamation of the Thai monarchy (lèse majesté remains an

Local magazine cover showing Far Eastern Economic Review *journalists Rodney Tasker and Shawn Crispin, who were represented by Tilleke & Gibbins.* Inset: *congratulations after a successful settlement.*

indictable crime in Thailand). Citing 'national security', the authorities moved to revoke the visas of the two journalists responsible for the story, Rodney Tasker and Shawn Crispin. Attracting wide local and international attention, matters rapidly deteriorated into a dispute over press freedom, and the power and sensibilities of the state.

It was one of those cases where issues were so entangled and nebulous that no one could be a winner, yet there had to be a resolution. And any resolution would depend as much on a subtle understanding of Thai ways as on knowledge of the law. Representing the Hong Kong-based weekly the two reporters in Bangkok and the publisher and editor-in-chief in Hong Kong, David Lyman advised that his client submit a measured apology for 'inadvertently offending Thai sensibilities' to the then Parliament president Uthai Pimchaichon.

The apology, hand-carried from Hong Kong, was duly hand-delivered by David Lyman to Parliament, concluding four weeks of tough negotiations, deliberations, deals, backroom manoeuvrings, patience and implementations, after which the case was dropped, the battle won without ever proceeding to court. The end result, as Lyman puts it, was what everyone wanted — a 'Thai solution' that offered a compromise with no loss of face on either side. To achieve this he had drawn on a lifetime of professional experience in Thailand that allowed him to read the situation, know who to seek out for advice and assistance, know what to do and when to do it, know what the legal rights were and how to work the process to the advantage of his clients. It also required, as he readily admits, 'a good back-up team, the right contacts and a great deal of well-timed luck'.

Looking back over his career, Lyman sees little change in the services clients expect, except that because of modern forms of communication they just expect things sooner. 'They're looking for instantaneous gratification,' he says. 'That's the nature of the era in which we live. But the rules are still pretty much the same.'

As for the court system, 'it has been improved to accommodate some needs', Lyman comments, 'as Thailand is finding it to be in its own best interests to make these changes'. In particular, he notes the creation of a number of speciality courts, such as the Labour Court, Tax Court, Juvenile Court, Family Law Court, IP and International Transactions Court, Administrative Court and Constitutional Court to complement the Civil and Criminal Courts.

One area that remains lacking is the difficulty in obtaining a temporary restraining order (TRO). 'Given the speed with which money, documents and moveables can be moved these days,' Lyman explains, 'the timely

T&G 5th Reforestation Project field trip to Phrae, 17 June 2007.

relief needed to preserve the status quo simply isn't there to help. So that's an area that could stand improvement. A second process to address is the present reluctance of the courts to rule on preliminary motions, which could end a case quickly. This would shorten the life of a case in court and help clear the backlog of cases awaiting the courts' attention.'

Lyman sees the key to professional success as 'the ability to communicate, responsiveness, keeping in touch with the client — these are the most important. And, of course, you have to be right. If I had to boil it down to one word, it would be "communication". It's the ability to get your point of view across to the other person in a way that they understand. They may or may not agree with it, but at least they understand it and understand the context in which you are using it. Avoiding conflict is crucial in what we call "preventative law", just like prescribing a medicine . . . in order to catch maladies before they really get out of hand, and this is most crucial in judicial situations.'

In one major legal field, however, efforts at communication have failed. For almost two decades Lyman and the Periera brothers have striven to make environmental law another of Tilleke & Gibbins' specialist areas, but without success. As Lyman bluntly admits, 'business (i.e. corporates) is not interested'. (That is not strictly true. Some businesses have shown an interest in environmental laws — how to get around them. But that is work Tilleke & Gibbins would never accept.)

Neither effort nor initiative has been lacking. As far back as 1991, Tilleke & Gibbins organized a seminar in Bangkok on 'Environment Laws and Their Impact on the Private Sector'. The introductory remarks noted that while Thailand then had at least seventy laws on its books related to air, land and water pollution, little more could be said — the implementation and strict enforcement simply are not there. They still are not. But in spite of this bleak picture and regardless of calls to action by a number of speakers, the seminar had no practical impact on the business community.

Tilleke & Gibbins' long-established corporate social responsibility programmes continue to address environmental issues, especially reforestation, while the firm contributed the Thailand chapter to the 2002 Sweet & Maxwell publication *Environmental Law and Enforcement in the Asia–Pacific Region*.

In his personal capacity, David Lyman remains a dedicated conservationist and is, for example,

a cofounder member of the Thailand Business Council for Sustainable Development. Otherwise, environmental law for Thailand appears for the moment almost a lost cause.

Now in his early seventies, David Lyman remains extraordinarily active. In March 2007 he married his third wife, the beautiful and sweet

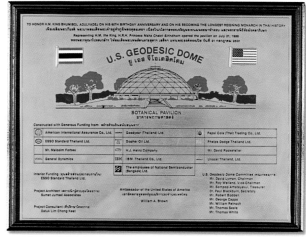

Plaque commemorating the US Geodesic Dome built at Rama IX Park in honour of His Majesty the King and for which David Lyman chaired the fund-raising committee.

Tassaneeya 'Poo' Pimpila, who he describes as his 'ideal woman'. With Poo he continues to pursue his favourite pastimes of scuba diving, photography, travel to remote places, collecting Oriental carpets and textiles, and elephants. Nonetheless his commitment to Tilleke & Gibbins remains firm, although as a realist, he has taken

steps to assure the future leadership of the firm for coming generations.

It was in 1999 that David Lyman first sought to settle the question of succession, designating one of the firm's female lawyers as heiress apparent. It very nearly proved the ruination of Tilleke & Gibbins.

For reasons that he still cannot explain, Lyman felt reluctant to confirm the succession and for two years dragged his feet over the details of putting it in place. Then, in 2001, when he and copartner Jack Hanlon were both on business trips to the US, they were alerted by senior staff in Bangkok that David's successor-to-be was attempting to walk off with the firm's IP business. After a council of war between Lyman, Hanlon and an outside party the two lawyers rushed back to Bangkok in secret to make a timely preemptive strike against the heiress designate, who was only eight days away from completing her plans. The startling discovery was also made that she was not even a qualified licensed lawyer, as she had claimed, and had essentially been living a lie for fifteen years. Given the option of resigning or being

David Lyman married his third wife, the lovely Tassaneeya 'Poo' Pimpila in 2007, and the couple share their enthusiasm for favourite pastimes that include travel to remote places, elephants, scuba diving, and collecting Oriental carpets and textiles.

Want to Buy an Elephant?

Elephants are strangely endearing animals, perhaps because of their very strangeness. Like many people, David Lyman has always had a fondness for the creatures, though he never expected to own one. It happened that in 2002, when serving as the secretary-general of the Thai Society for the Prevention of Cruelty to Animals, he met with its chief vet. The latter was interrupted in their conversation by a phone call from the owner of an elephant camp informing him that an elephant brought to him was to be put down unless someone was willing to buy it. The beast, a forest-working elephant and sadly maltreated, had killed four men and the owner felt that enough was enough. The vet looked pleadingly at David. 'Okay, how much?' David dutifully asked. And so he, along with two smaller investors, became the proud owner of Om Chakawas, a four-ton, 56-year-old pachyderm named after a famous war elephant of 400 years ago that had crossed tusks. Lyman does not take his pet for walks, though he does visit it regularly at its camp in Ayutthaya.

fired, she opted for the latter and was out of the office in thirty minutes. Even then she had the nerve to sue for unfair termination and misappropriation of her personal property.

'That taught me a lesson. It is essential to keep control of the structure of the firm and not transfer my shares,' Lyman says, and it was not until August 2006 that the question of succession was finally resolved with the appointment of Darani Vachanavuttivong and Tiziana Sucharitkul as comanaging partners. In relinquishing responsibility to the new comanaging partners David Lyman began what he calls 'phased retirement', although he remains the firm's chairman and chief values officer.

The appointment of new comanaging partners established the fifth generation of the firm's leadership since Tilleke & Gibbins was founded, and also marked the first time it has been led solely by Thais, and by women. However, it seems unlikely that the character of the firm will be altered in any radical way.

'Change will come with time', says Tiziana, 'but the core principles will remain the same. We have a unique environment and culture at

Tiziana Sucharitkul (left) *and Darani Vachanavuttivong.*

Tilleke & Gibbins, that of a family firm, and it is important to maintain that. But to compete in the modern business world we will have to adapt as necessary.'

Any immediate changes are likely to be structural, Darani points out. 'At the same time, maintaining what has always been a family firm,' she says, 'there are a lot of "loose" things internally that need tightening up. In the past these have been tacitly understood, but now we want to make them more regulated and are working closely with COO Don Jones to achieve this.'

Part of the structural change will be a focus on the firm as a whole. Previously, says Darani, there was simply too much for one managing

partner to do and, as she sees it, there was a large gap between David Lyman and the department heads. 'Each department at that time', she explains, 'was sort of run on its own. Now, both Tiziana and myself look at the firm as a whole rather than as three different departments.'

Indeed, one of the main goals of the new leadership is to try to grow and build on the strengths of the Corporate & Commercial and Dispute Resolution departments in order to enhance both recognition and performance of the two groups. 'I believe we have the people and the capability to do this, while both David [Lyman] and the board are extremely supportive,' Tiziana says.

The vision for the future, as shared by Tiziana and Darani, is 'to continue to be a top player in the legal field in Thailand and a dominant player in the region'. Achieving this will be a question of making the right decisions to go forward at the right time. As an example, Tiziana points out the recent success of the Hanoi reopening and expansion started in Ho Chi Minh City.

As for holding market share, Tilleke & Gibbins possesses valuable advantages. It undoubtedly has a strong international practice, its IP and IPD practices in particular

are known to be first rate, a fact that was reflected in August 2008 when the boutique law firm Pacific Legal Group (PLG) merged into Tilleke & Gibbins. Headed by Paul Russell, PLG is focused on the registration of pharmaceuticals, medical devices, food and cosmetics with the Thai Food and Drug Administration (FDA).

Tilleke & Gibbins further reflects solid values that are rarely seen in today's law firm environment — respect, accomplishment, integrity, celebrity and longevity are widely associated

Tilleke & Gibbins
Pacific Legal Group

Now we are one, and we have moved.

The oldest and one of the largest independent law firms in Thailand and the most experienced group of FDA/MOA registration and regulatory compliance specialists in Thailand have joined forces with effect on August 1, 2008. Our combination means we are larger and stronger, with more capability and resources to serve our clients.

David Lyman
Tilleke & Gibbins

Paul Russell
Pacific Legal Group

Together, we now operate from **our new home** at Supalai Grand Tower: 7 floors of state-of-the-art office premises from which we can serve you better.

Tilleke & Gibbins International Ltd.
Supalai Grand Tower, 26th Floor, 1011 Rama 3 Road
Chongnonsi, Yannawa, Bangkok 10120
T: 0 2653 5555 F: 0 2653 5678
E: bangkok@tillekeandgibbins.com
W: www.tillekeandgibbins.com

Notice posted on 14 September 2008 in the Bangkok Post *of the merger of T&G and Pacific Legal Group.*

with the firm — and these are combined with a desire to improve, grow and prosper. In the face of more intense competition, however, there is a need to develop a strong marketing focus. This will be the challenge of the twenty-first century and of Tilleke & Gibbins' fifth generation of partners. Efforts in this direction can be seen in a commitment to attending selected overseas law-related events.

Meanwhile, the succession of managing partners was not the only question facing Tilleke & Gibbins in 2006. The lease on the firm's main Soi Tonson offices was due to expire in November of that year and in spite of protracted negotiations with the lessor, the Crown Property Bureau, renewal was not consistent with its plans to redevelop its large holdings, of which Tilleke & Gibbins occupied a small part. Over the following eighteen months, the firm considered all options, including the commissioning of a new building by the same architects, Robert G. Boughey & Associates, who had designed TG Main in Soi Tonson. Eventually, however, when all factors had been taken into account, it was decided that the most cost-effective

solution would be to lease space in a specific existing office block.

That final choice was Supalai Grand Tower, a 34-storey building on Rama III Road in Bangkok's Yannawa district, close to the Chao Phraya River, where the firm now leases the 20th–26th floors, giving a total area of 10,000 square metres, with an option to take one more floor when needed. The move occurred on 6–7 September 2008.

In the early stages of preparation for the move, the firm's Office & Facilities Services director, Mrs Thiparat Buranaphan, was charged, among other duties, with trying to locate the artist Channarong Khongphokhar who had made the bas-reliefs of Tilleke & Gibbins' historical scenes, so prominently displayed in the Soi Tonson offices, and request his assistance in their relocation. After many weeks of fruitless searching (not helped by the fact that the artist had changed his name to Phuthipanithid Khongphokhanun), Thiparat prayed for assistance, as is the Thai custom, at the office's spirit house. Shortly afterwards, the artist appeared out of the blue, saying he had come by chance to see if he might photograph

> ## Chief Values Officer: David Lyman's Definition
>
> 'In this age of amazing technological advancements, broadband, information overload, anxiety, turmoil, extremes, diversions and hope, a chief values officer (CVO) of an organization is the guardian of that organization's values and virtues, its culture, its spirit, its integrity, its ethical principles and moral foundations, and promotes adherence thereto. A CVO keeps the engine of an organization's life running smoothly with minimal disruption to the environment and a maximum of character building and social responsibility. A CVO nurtures relationships and preserves the vital interests of all stakeholders of the organization within its immediate sphere of influence. A CVO is charged to keep the human side of an organization functioning on the course of honest, wise, responsible, legal and accountable business and professional practices, and in compliance with community standards and the organization's or accepted sectorial codes of conduct.'

his works. He, of course, then offered to help in removing the bas-reliefs to the firm's new premises.

Tilleke & Gibbins

announces the
relocation of its Bangkok office to:

Supalai Grand Tower, 26th Floor
1011 Rama 3 Road
Chongnonsi, Yannawa
Bangkok 10120, Thailand
T: +66 2653 5555
F: +66 2653 5678

E: bangkok@tillekeandgibbins.com   (map on reverse)

Tilleke & Gibbins
Grand Opening Celebration
March 31, 2009

Above: *The Supalai Grand Tower, T&G's office premises since September 2008, is based on an oval-shaped plan.* Inset: *The new office Grand Opening Celebration held on 31 March 2009. The Minister of Justice Pirapan Salirathavibhaga presenting a bouquet of flowers to David Lyman at the event.*

T&G's new offices are light and spacious, from the reception area to individual workstations. The oval floor plan provides many creative spaces throughout the offices.

IN MEMORY OF

Ralph B. H. Gibbins

Ralph Bryan Henry Gibbins
Director 1902 - 1907

Clockwise, from above, : *The new offices have a plethora of different-sized meeting rooms, all named after partners from the past to the present. The new library provides in-depth legal reference and a reading area. The T&G History Showcase provides a continual reference to T&G's colourful past. The staff lounge provides entertainment and food preparation facilities and the T&G office fitness centre is furnished with the finest excercise machines.*

A pure coincidence, sheer serendipity, or was it respect for guardian spirits and for the principles of feng shui? It may be hard to equate such ideas with down-to-earth legal practice, but the fact that the artworks that chronicle the firm's early history, especially Mr Tilleke's role in the famous Phra Yod trial, have been kept intact and are now freshly displayed in the firm's Supalai Grand Tower offices can only be seen as fortunate. It would be a distortion to try to impose a sense of symmetry on any historical account, although it is hard to escape a symbolism that bodes well for the firm.

Further examples of the firm's history and culture have also been preserved in the Supalai Grand Tower offices. The 'Hall of Fame', for example, which was formerly housed in T&G Main on Soi Tonson and displayed the many awards, trophies, plaques and other recognitions of achievement won over the years, has been recreated and expanded at Supalai Grand Tower. And now adding a more detailed chronicling of the firm's past is the 'T&G History Showcase', created on the 26th floor of the new offices. 'This new museum', says

David Lyman, 'displays historical artifacts and records of the firm to remind our staff of our heritage and their burdens, through their work, to honour the sacrifices and achievements of all their predecessors.'

Ultimately, the key to the

Tilleke & Gibbins received a plaque for winning the Managing Intellectual Property *Firm of the Year 2009 — Thailand award.*

extraordinary success of Tilleke & Gibbins lies in its rare ability to stay true to its core values while driving its practice forward in serving clients that seek professionalism and a personal touch. 'We remain a very client-orientated firm,' says Tiziana. 'Good legal advice is expected, but what makes a lawyer stand out is how he or she handles the client.'

To that end Edward Kelly, T & G's chief client relationship officer from 2006 until he left the firm in 2009, was charged with leading by example when it came to client interaction. He was well qualified for the role. 'Because of the sensitivities of being entrusted with a company's intellectual property', he remarked in a magazine interview, 'you can't help but become involved in some very deep relationships. What we realized was that clients respond well to a more personal approach and so as a firm we tried to improve how we institutionalized that.'

The effort has clearly paid dividends, as illustrated by Tilleke & Gibbins winning the *Managing Intellectual Property* Firm of the Year 2009 — Thailand award.

David Lyman sums it up with characteristic wise counsel for lawyers: 'Your clients are your income and probably what motivates you to stay in law. You're there to serve clients and solve their problems. Solving problems is a lawyer's primary job. Do it, and do it well.' Everything and nothing has changed since William Alfred Goone Tilleke first opened his practice in Thailand.

The lighter side of wise counsel: David Lyman and his office muse, a gift from his father.

The Tilleke & Gibbins Museum of Counterfeit Goods.

Appendix I

The Tilleke & Gibbins
Museum of Counterfeit Goods

From Rolex watches to Viagra pills, from Gucci bags to whole motorcycles, from bottles of Johnnie Walker whisky to golf clubs, The Tilleke & Gibbins Museum of Counterfeit Goods showcases the scope of trademark and copyright infringement in Thailand and reflects the extent of the firm's legal practice in the field.

One of only a few of its kind in the world, the museum was established at the Tilleke & Gibbins office building in 1989. At the time it housed a mere 100 items grouped in four categories: clothing, leather goods, electronics and toiletries. At present there are some 5,000 exhibits, plus countless other items that have been removed for storage in two warehouses. All have been gleaned in raids on factories and shops conducted by Tilleke & Gibbins' IP Enforcement teams on behalf of clients. To the museum's original four categories of exhibits have been added another twenty or more, including footwear, perfumes, watches, household appliances, machinery, sound systems, automotive and machinery parts, food, drugs, alcohol, stationery, musical instruments and computer software.

The IP practice of Tilleke & Gibbins does, of course, long predate the founding of the museum. It was when the fake items that had been used as evidence in court began to take up too much storage space — while serving no purpose whatsoever — that the firm sought a way by which they could be turned from being a liability into something useful.

The idea of creating a museum took root when senior partner David Lyman visited the offices of Anthony R. Gurka, principal partner of the Hong Kong investigative firm then called Commercial Trademark Services (CTS). Through Gurka's efforts, beginning in the early 1980s, CTS had built up a collection of infringing goods. On seeing the CTS collection, it occurred to Lyman that the counterfeit goods at Tilleke & Gibbins could very well prove useful as education tools if properly displayed and made accessible for public viewing. Thus the museum came into being.

Since then the museum has played a significant educational role, as well as attracting considerable public interest. Intellectual property officials of Pacific Rim countries have visited the museum as part of training courses organized by the World Intellectual Property Organization (WIPO) and the

Organization of Technical and Economic Cooperation in Thailand. Not only does the museum attract those involved in the IP field, but also it is well frequented by Thai and foreign police, Customs, Interpol officers, judges, government officials, law students, clients and other individuals from the private sector.

Feature articles on the museum have been published in numerous local and international newspapers, journals and magazines, including the front page of the US-based *Journal of Commerce*, while CNN, the BBC, Danish National Television, along with various other companies involved in broadcasting, have featured the museum in their documentaries on the counterfeit situation in Thailand. A BBC film crew were intrigued to fail a challenge made by Tilleke & Gibbins' IP staff to spot the difference between a real and a fake Newcastle United football shirt.

It is not, however, just famous and expensive brand-name items that the museum showcases, and it is surprising to discover that counterfeiters can find profit in copying such mundane items as oil filters and hydraulic brake parts, or UHU 'stic' glue and Papermate Liquid Paper correction fluid. Curiosity at counterfeiters' ingenuity turns to alarm at the sight of fake drugs, alcohol, cosmetics and foods for which it is impossible for the ordinary consumer to tell if they meet health and safety standards.

The entrance to the museum.

Most criminal infringement cases involve either copyright or trademark, but patents can also be involved, as witnessed by a 2005 addition to the museum's collection. This was a pair of jeans, netted in a police raid, which copied Levi's 'Engineered Jeans' brand in the overall pattern and in the stitch design of seams and back pocket. A successful criminal prosecution was brought against the manufacturer of the infringing product.

According to the Organization for Economic Co-operation and Development (OECD) and the World Customs Organization (WCO), counterfeiting activities account for approximately ten per cent of world trade in general. Therefore, not only do many bona fide manufacturers whose products are subjected to counterfeiting suffer direct loss of sales but also there is a considerable risk of potential loss of faith in advertised claims when customers, through no fault of their own making, unwittingly purchase and use counterfeits.

In displaying counterfeit goods alongside their genuine counterparts, the Tilleke & Gibbins Museum offers a vivid insight into the extent and consequences of the problem, and has proven to be of great educational value.

The *museum's* exhibits illustrate the fact that anything made by man can be, has been, and probably is being counterfeited.

Textiles from the Tilleke & Gibbins Textile Collection are displayed throughout the offices.

Appendix II

The Tilleke & Gibbins
Textile Collection

Visitors to the offices of Tilleke & Gibbins expecting bookcases stuffed with weighty, calf-bound law reports — as could reasonably be expected of a century-old firm — are surprised instead to see corridors and offices displaying the rich, intricate artistry of heritage textiles. Even to the untrained eye these exquisite silks and cottons are works of rare skill.

Incongruous though it may seem, Tilleke & Gibbins has one of the finest collections of mainland Southeast Asian textiles in the world. The collection was not planned as such, but what began as innovative office décor has developed to the stage where Tilleke & Gibbins is now an internationally recognized collector.

Tube skirt, Laos, 1890–1920; cotton and silk.

When the firm moved into its own building in late 1987, David Lyman wanted to decorate the offices in a way that would both give a warm feeling and be specific to the cultures of Southeast Asia. Textiles were suggested and Lyman, a collector of Oriental carpets, was intrigued and subsequently convinced of the idea when Tilleke & Gibbins was offered seventy samples of ethnic Tai weaving.

The interior design exercise was an immense success and Tilleke & Gibbins decided to collect and preserve textiles seriously, with the objective of assembling a museum-quality collection. To date, almost 1,800 pieces from different areas of Southeast Asia have been acquired and are displayed throughout the office on a rotational basis. Such is the quality of the collection that items have been loaned to exhibitions in Bangkok, New York and San Francisco, and have been photographed for illustrations in books and catalogues. Taking care of the collection is a full-time curator. A textile consultant researches and documents the vast collection.

Comprising both typical and rare fabrics, the collection focuses primarily on the traditional textiles of the Tai, an ethnolinguistic family found primarily in Thailand, Laos, northern Vietnam, southwestern China and Myanmar. Other types of textiles include examples made by Khmer and Malay ethnic groups, and by Vietnamese, Burmese and Cambodian ethnic minorities.

As described by the collection's first curator Karen Andersen Chungyampin, 'the textiles are a language. There is a meaning woven into the design.' Indeed, aside from their obvious beauty and the consummate skill of their creators, the handwoven fabrics speak in a way few other artifacts can match. There is the language of the patterns that, in floral motifs, animals, mythical creatures and other traditional designs tell of the physical

surroundings and spiritual beliefs of the weavers.

There is also the implied statement of the weaving process itself. 'These pieces have been woven without the concept of time, without any calculation of

Tube skirt, Tai people, Laos, 1890–1920; cotton and silk.

the labour required,' Karen explained. All of the fabrics, whether skirts, blankets, head cloths or swaddling clothes, were produced to serve functional and ceremonial ends, albeit made with a certain pride. As such they speak of cultures and ways of

life now mostly lost in an age when production is for profit and time of the essence.

While every piece in the Tilleke & Gibbins collection has been selected for its high quality of design and execution, many of the exhibits are exceptional examples of their kind. The *phaa phii mon* ('shaman's cloths') of the Tai produced during the early twentieth century, for example, are particularly noteworthy. Among the Cambodian textiles the *sampot hol chang kbun* (ikat 'hip wrappers') and *pidan* (ikat 'ceremonial hangings') are examples of a very high quality weft ikat that is no longer produced.

Great care is taken by the present curator of the collection Ms Wipawee Tiyawes in the preservation and display of what are extremely fragile works. The collection is kept in rolled and flat storage, and wrapped in undyed cotton muslin or acid-free archival paper. Displayed items are regularly vacuumed to prevent damage from air pollution and are protected by ultraviolet filters on the office lighting.

Whereas most people can easily come to like a painting, even without necessarily understanding it, textiles are often less readily accepted as art, primarily because to the layman they are seen as practical household objects rather than works with aesthetic value. Initially, some of the office staff did not like what they saw as old and dirty, but appreciation has come with time. Now, when a particular fabric is removed from the wall for rotation, it is not uncommon to hear a staffer remark, 'where has my piece gone?'

So what makes a textile collectable? Wipawee explains that age is not necessarily the main consideration as a very old piece might be so faded and damaged as to have lost its aesthetic value, and a contemporary weaving may require advanced skill and artistry to complete. In the Tilleke & Gibbins collection the fabrics date from the early nineteenth century up to the present day.

Generally, the difference in periods of production can be seen in the woven motifs, which tend to be enlarged in modern works, while in older pieces the patterns are smaller, tighter and with a lot more

elements to the design. Local fashions dictate changes in styles, colours and range of motifs.

Like other artworks, collector-quality textiles are not cheap. A good Tai piece can cost

Tube skirt, Tai Lue people, Laos, 1890–1920; cotton and silk.

upwards of 50,000 baht, whereas Khmer silk ikat fabric, which suddenly became popular around the turn of the millennium, commands a starting price of 80,000–120,000 baht. The finest

pieces of the Tilleke & Gibbins collection are each insured in the 100,000–350,000-baht range.

With textile collecting now in vogue, finding good pieces at source is very difficult. Many villagers have sold theirs as a practical measure or as a means of income. Often, the majority of a village's heirloom textiles has been sold. The political instability of the last two hundred years has also caused the destruction of these valuable heirlooms in their original homes.

In this light, Tilleke & Gibbins has chosen not only an unusual form of office decoration but also has succeeded in preserving superb examples of a fragile art that is now quickly changing from its traditional form into a commercial enterprise.

Having authored the *Weaving Paradise* catalogue for the 2007 exhibition of selected T&G textiles, under the sponsorship of the James H.W. Thompson Foundation, textile consultant Ms Linda S. McIntosh has been commissioned to write a definitive book on The Tilleke & Gibbins Textile Collection, with publication scheduled for 2010.

Lyman's Laws for Lawyers (and everybody else, too!), *written and first published by David Lyman in 2006.*

Appendix III

Lyman's Laws for Lawyers
*(and everybody else, too!)**

*These **LLL** are dedicated first and foremost to my parents Albert and Freda Ring Lyman, American lawyers from 1921 in Washington D.C. and then in Asia starting in 1945, who guided me to become the best lawyer they knew how to mould; and then to the US Navy for teaching me about leadership, responsibility and adventure; and to my colleagues and all the clients who taught me about professional life, business and winning; and then to all the rogues, scoundrels and scallywags who bested me sometimes but who eventually succumbed to the lessons they taught me that I learned well.*

The Beginning

The 105 *Lyman's Laws for Lawyers (LLL)* of Tilleke & Gibbins (and for everybody else, too) which follow — my substantially revised, expanded and updated 2006 edition — are nothing more than courses of good conduct clients expect of their lawyers and are what clients pay for. Some readers will conclude that you already know what is written here. So for you *LLL* can serve as a refresher course. Many readers, however, are probably slow learners like me and still have much to gain from *LLL* compiled in one place.

More often than not, these guiding principles have been learned by me the hard way, i.e. from my defeats as well as my victories, from my own mistakes, and sometimes from bitter and other times humorous but always enlightening experiences over my almost 52 years in the law and military services (US Navy). My parents, both lawyers, taught me many truisms, while some ideas were gained from other professional colleagues I admired, some from opposing parties and their counsel, and, of course, some from clients and friends.

Lyman's Laws for Lawyers does ***not*** address law firm management or business operations. It does ***not*** tell you how to make partner or where to work. Rather, its canons focus on and extol personal values, conduct, practices and attitudes.

Though my legal practice as a second-generation American lawyer in Asia (one of the very few alive today who can make that claim) has centred on Thailand, a Civil Law Code country here in tropical Southeast Asia, I have been told coincidentally that most of *Lyman's Laws for Lawyers* is timeless and applicable to many vocations in addition to the law, as well as to much of day-to-day life itself.

Redundancy within *Lyman's Laws for Lawyers* will be found. I decided that more benefit is derived from the emphasis of repetition than editing to remove repeated thoughts expressed in different ways.

Too many Lyman's Laws for Lawyers you say! Too verbose? Well, nobody promised you that the successful practice of our profession was easy or lacking in challenges. My task in giving

*Lyman's Laws for Lawyers (and everybody else, too!) was reprinted in 2009. It is reproduced here with minor amendments.

you *Lyman's Laws for Lawyers* is to teach you, to prepare you, to remind you. They reflect my philosophy, my principles and my values.

No apologies are offered for sounding like a teacher. Somebody has to tell you about the rules to follow and traps to avoid. I'm certainly far from being one of the world's greatest lawyers, but by following these principles as a starting point, Tilleke & Gibbins and I haven't fared so badly over the years. You have the freedom to abide by them or to ignore them. The choice is yours. Each option has its own consequences.

My admonition to younger lawyers and law firm staff everywhere is to follow *all* of Lyman's Laws for Lawyers simultaneously; certainly strive to. Believe in them. Be persuaded by them. Refer to them often for guidance and, I hope, inspiration. Older, more experienced successful people know that Lyman's Laws merely set out the *minimum* criteria for you to become the great lawyers that you are capable of being.

Do supplement my *LLL* with your own lessons, however learned.

I. In Practice

At all times . . .

1. Love the law. Love its practice and love serving clients. Ours is an honoured calling. To do your best, you have to truly respect and deeply care for the law, the Rule of Law, a strong, fair, and independent judiciary, our profession and for your clients. If you don't or if you are in the legal profession just for the money or for the glory or for power, do the rest of us a favour and find another occupation in which to work the way you want.

---

2. The law is about people. The practice of the law is based on personal relationships.

a. Treat all persons involved with courtesy, dignity, respect, humanity and a smile.

b. Act with honour, integrity, kindness, tolerance and compassion.

c. Be a good listener. Talk little; listen a lot. When you do talk, make sense.

d. Enjoy your career. Your enthusiasm is contagious.

e. All concerned in your practice, not just your clients, colleagues and staff but also government officials, your opponents, and their counsel and their witnesses, must trust you and respect you. Earn their trust. Earn their respect.

---

3. We have the law and the Rule of Law to keep mankind civilized, stable, free from erosion and tyranny, free of abuse by government, by the stronger, from those who wield authority, and to put boundaries of reason on our own personal conduct. As the gatekeepers, we are responsible to safeguard against being defiled, all the planet's Gaia, its creatures great and small, including man and all his dominions and diversions. This is not an airy, overreaching or pompous concept but is a never-ending task from which we of the law can neither abdicate nor shrink.

---

4. Client care, personal attention and your total reliability to them and to your partners and coworkers are your most important assignments.

5. Clearly identify exactly who your client is, and who is *not* your client. This sounds obvious but it is not always so. Correct and early identification is critical for your duties, conflicts of interest, reporting channels, billing, and knowing to whom you are responsible and who owes you your fees and reimbursables.

6. It's unpardonable to misspell a client's name. And pronounce his/her/their name as the client would.

7. Know and always use the client's full name, including the client's contact person's full name and title, plus the client's most current and complete address. Keep your databases of this information current.

8. Clients will always remember the last matter you handled for them. If you want to keep the clients, make sure that it was a positive experience for them. If it was a bad experience, you can be sure that they will never forget, and may not forgive.

9. Clients want solutions and options, not just 'No, it can't be done'. Tailor solutions which are pragmatic, fair to all concerned, and build goodwill. Help clients do the doable within the law. Exceed their expectations. Strive for a *KISS* solution: *K*eep *I*t *S*uper *S*imple.

10. Be creative and innovative in your solutions. Lawyers sell ideas. Go beyond. Seek to achieve the seemingly impossible. Don't be afraid or hesitant to challenge conventional wisdom — that's what makes change happen. And if it works in your favour, that's called brilliant judgement and good common sense. If it does not work, well, try another fresh idea.

11. Solve the right problem, and don't get sidetracked solving the wrong problem.

12. Prepare and organize thoroughly. It's inexcusable not to study and know all the known facts, and the applicable laws and regulations. Read. Study all relevant documents and other evidence before you undertake any action. They may not say what you expect them to say. Know every detail of your case inside and out, backwards and forwards. Costs of intelligence gathering are usually money well spent. Don't be caught by surprise. Know what's going on and be aware of what is happening around you. Know the lie of the land, the terrain, and your best position in relation thereto. Think ahead. Identify and shore up your weaknesses as well as buttress your strengths. Be thorough. Do not be sloppy.

13. Representing clients can lead to adversarial confrontations. Endeavour diligently to avoid battles. Peaceful solutions by way of negotiation, mediation or compromise are always preferable to war. *The best war is one that is never fought while still achieving your objectives.* But if fighting is inevitable, then pick your battles to suit your purposes, decide their objectives, gather, evaluate, and rely on intelligence, determine what is motivating the opposition, develop strategies, indulge in detailed planning and preparation, assemble all your resources, decide on timing, practise your tactics, then execute them decisively. *Make your opponents fight by your rules, not you by theirs.* You take the initiative; you set the parameters and the agenda. Make your opponents respond to your game plan. Have a Plan B, a fallback strategy, maybe even a Plan C as well. *If fight you must, then fight to win the war, not just a battle or two.* To win, you have to outwork the other side. Wars are rarely of short duration and both sides suffer casualties. Prepare yourself and your clients for protracted and hence expensive campaigns. Do not mislead or delude them, or yourself.

14. Clients want assigned tasks done right and done quickly. Maximize value added for clients. You may think about your *input* — your hours, your sweat, your brilliance, your lack of sleep but clients think only about your *output*, achieving their objectives on time while paying

you the least amount possible. But when they do say 'Thank you' whether you win or lose, then they make practising law a worthwhile and personally rewarding career choice.

15. When I would say I was overloaded and had so many things to do I didn't know where to start, my mother would respond, 'Pick one!'

16. If truth is an issue in a matter you are handling, tenaciously seek the truth irrespective of whether it helps or hurts your case. *Truth is the currency of the law.*

17. As my father taught me, clients always need the hope of achieving their legitimate objectives. It's good for their health. Don't rely on miracles to save the day. Be encouraging but honest with them, and yourself, in your assessments.

18. Identify, grasp, and accommodate the very real motivations, drivers, pressures and rewards of people in the corporate, bureaucratic, political, judicial, legislative and home environments, i.e. your arenas.

19. Reply to all incoming correspondence, including emails, faxes, short message service (SMS), letters and telephone calls within 24 hours of receipt — even if only to acknowledge receipt. Then follow up.

20. Lack of, or delays in, communications from lawyers are the major complaints of clients. Communicate with clients more than just frequently. Put it in writing. Furthermore, you are responsible to be sure you and your client are on the same wavelength of whatever it is you are communicating.

21. Make your clients full members of your legal team. Think of them. Visit them. Call them. Learn from them. Do it for free. Get to know them as people, learn about their businesses, products, services, places of work; their corporate culture, politics, policies, ownership, and dynamics. Don't charge them every time. Include them. Provide them with training and education about matters of concern to them. Clients want, and are entitled to, your personal attention. Send them newspaper and magazine clippings pertinent to them. Let them know what you are doing for them and why it is necessary for you to do so.

22. Clients, especially the Firm's existing clients, as well as your colleagues and subordinates, want and need to be courted, constantly. Courting clients is like courting women — they want to hear, repeatedly, that you care for them, you need them, you think of them, you love them, and to see that you are providing for them.

23. Lawyers live by the Rule of Law, both its letter and its spirit. Learn all that it means. Uphold this sacred principle. Do not compromise with it. Do not make exceptions or accommodations to derogation. No stretching, bending, or twisting of this principle is allowed.

24. The freedom of the individual and society to choose and to live without fear, insult, or injury is the essence of the Rule of Law. Until denied to you, you probably do not value how to cherish our freedoms, rights, duties, and hopes for contentment. **The law may not always be perfect or right, but even flawed it is far better than the vicissitudes, manipulations, and machinations of the Rule of Men who abuse or misuse their power for their own purposes or gratifications through Rule by Law.**

25. Personal and professional conflicts of interest, breaches of duties, violations of Bar Association/Law Council Rules of Professional Conduct/Ethics, dishonesty, and corruption are intolerable and forbidden. Even the appearance thereof is damaging and is to be shunned.

26. A lawyer without integrity, personal and professional honour, ethical behaviour, morality or a conscience dishonours that individual, our profession and our Firm.

27. You have a professional obligation to devote some of your time and talent to do pro bono work for those unable to afford legal services. Public service and community service should also be part of your agenda.

28. The practice of the law demands much from its adherents. As a lawyer, you must be dedicated to the law, to clients, to the Firm, to the community. While a lawyer's time is rarely his or her own, for balance you must also devote quality time to yourself, and your family; and you should engage in complementary, personally gratifying distractions.

---

29. The Blackberry, that ubiquitous fifth (perhaps Freudian) appendage, and the addictive reliance thereon by today's American legal counsellors, is justified by its adherents as giving them freedom. From my observations of the habits of its users, I find the Blackberry an intrusive slavemaster, or, alternatively, a sophisticated security blanket. It is an extremely useful state-of-the-art communications tool, but it is only a tool. Don't let it control your life. Don't let it become the tail that wags the dog.

30. Young lawyers need mentors, as did the mentors when they were young. Mentoring junior lawyers is an obligation of our profession.

---

31. You can never have enough knowledge. Read, look, listen, question. Learn as much about the law and its application to clients' needs as your brain can hold, and then learn more. Pass on such learning to clients and colleagues. Share your knowledge and experiences.

---

32. You can be selective; you do not have to take every case that walks in the door. Lawyers do not have to work for clients or persons who are impolite, rude, insulting, disrespectful, excessively demanding, who expect free service or underpay for legal work or who pursue improper, immoral, or illegal objectives. Stand up to them and say, 'No, not if that is going to be your attitude.' If they walk away, then you have saved yourself a lot of grief and aggravation.

33. No matter how driven you may be, you cannot know all the law in every field or even all the law in any one field.

---

34. Not all lawyers are effective as leaders or managers. Most of us receive no training for such tasks. Not everybody wants the job or can do the job. Fortunately, training in leadership and managing is now available to those who want it or need it. There is a place in the practice of law to suit every interest, every age, every ability, every character, every personality, every background, every ethnicity, every nationality. The pursuit of the law as a profession knows no exclusions or discriminations. Find your personal niche which presents you with the challenges you seek, which you are most comfortable with, and which provide you with the personal satisfaction of your achievements and rewards, great and small.

---

35. Absolute justice is not attainable, so substantial justice is the best you can hope for.

36. In the end, as lawyers, be thankful — it may seem distasteful but in the words of my deceased Thai law partner: **'God bless those who make problems for our clients, and for our clients who make problems for themselves!'**

II. Dealing with Legal Fees

37. Sorry, but those damnable time sheets are your lifeblood. Under all circumstances complete, clear, accurate, fully informative — and charged to the right client and matter — records must be kept for all of your time whether chargeable or not, and whatever is the fee structure agreed to with the client after an open dialogue. Without time sheets to build legal bills, both you and the Firm will starve. It is that simple.

38. Our Firm must be profitable for us all to survive. Yes, the practice of law is a profession, but it is still a business with salaries, expenses, assets, liabilities and taxes. Our only source of income is legal fees and service fees. Quality legal services are not cheap. Clients don't pay for low-quality work. But premium prices demand premium-quality work. Billing and collecting legal fees are more art than science. Bills should be transparent, justifiable, prompt, and should reflect fairness, the scope of legal services rendered, and their value to the client. Follow our current *Memorandum Concerning Legal Fee Charges and Conditions of Engagement*, which is attached to our fee letters to clients. Some clients specify their own criteria for legal fees and chargeable expenses.

39. Over the years, **our Firm's most costly mistakes have been not having written legal-fee agreements** for each client and, even better, for each matter. In some jurisdictions, they are required by law. *Be very specific as to the exact scope of work expected* of the Firm by the clients and the billing basis and arrangements — hourly, fixed, capped, contingent, value, negotiated, success kickers, premiums, hybrids or whatever. *Get deposits up front* against anticipated or agreed fees and expenses. *Don't expect the Firm to be paid for services rendered but not instructed by clients.* If the Firm does not get paid, you don't get paid.

40. Clients do not have endless patience or bottomless pockets. Be attentive to clients' objectives and time schedules. Timing is always important and may be crucial. Clients have limited resources for legal fees and expenses. *So get it right, the first time.*

41. Do not 'over lawyer' a matter to drive up legal fees and expenses. A Texas corporate client once told me in connection with limiting the number of lawyers assigned to his cases that he adopted the motto of the Texas Rangers (State Police): **'One Riot, One Ranger'.**

42. When clients say of their case you are handling, 'It's not about the money, it's about the principle', what they really mean is, 'It's about the money'. They soon realize that it costs money (legal fees and expenses) to uphold principle. Caveat: do not start or continue any activity on behalf of your client that your client is not fully supportive of and committed to complete. Recognize the signs of when the client starts calculating a cost-benefit analysis, waivers, and withholds resource and support. When they become half-hearted, it is time to reassess your and the Firm's role, the value added for the client by your work and your chances of being paid for your past and continued efforts.

43a. Law firms and lawyers are subject to unrelenting pressure to reduce their clients' legal costs. Do whatever you can to accommodate and to be more efficient, but there are limits below which you cannot go. Do a cost-benefit analysis — educate clients that *if they pay only peanuts, they get only monkeys.*

43b. If you have done your job for the client right, achieving the bulk of the client's objectives, and then the client does not pay the agreed fee, go after them tenaciously. *Attack vigorously.* Let them know they cannot cheat you and get away with doing so, that you will protect your own interests as you protected theirs.

44. Clients want premium work done by a great lawyer at low cost. Or as a Spanish lawyer colleague put it: *'They want a virgin with experience.'*

III. Golden Rules to Succeed

Remember that/to . . .

45. Never, never, never assume. Verify. Check everthing, every time. This is a postulate cast in concrete.

46. Clients and bosses don't like surprises.

47. Communicate with clients, bosses, colleagues, and subordinates —— clearly, completely, often, and honestly. Document all of your communications. Keep copies of every document you prepare and those which others produce. Back up in depth. Your matter files must be complete.

48. You have a mind — use it. All the time. Think. Be logical. Be analytical. Be thorough. Relate together all known details and facts. *Think like a lawyer!* (Another postulate cast in concrete.)

49. Keep an open and inquiring mind. Read, look, listen, touch, smell, taste, feel. Ask probing questions — Who? What? Where? When? Why? How? Get the answers, whether you like what you hear or see or not.

50. If you don't know, ask. If you do have to guess, remember it's just a guess, not fact or truth. If you need help to do the work correctly and on time — *ask for help, early.* Don't be shy or embarrassed to seek help. Don't wait.

---

51. There are facts and there are opinions and interpretations. The latter can vary; facts do not. Know which are which.

---

52. There is no such thing as a dumb question; there are only dumb mistakes. What is dumb is to keep quiet when you need to know something in order to do your job.

---

53. Errors are forgivable but carelessness is not. But don't make the same mistake twice.

---

54. Foolishness is tolerable but stupidity is not.

---

55. Keep your word.

56. Meet all deadlines, ahead of time.

---

57. Date all papers — upper right-hand corner. Date all drafts. It is advisable to precede all your computer file names by a six-digit date of creation, e.g. YYMMDD, in order to stack them up chronologically.

---

58. Teamwork usually produces better results than doing a task alone. Be a reliable and effective teammate. *It's 'We' not 'Me'.* Always give credit to those who help you; they come first, then you.

---

59. A team requires mutual trust and mutual reliance. Build internal networks. Garner support. The better the mutual understanding, respect, loyalty, cooperation, patience, and time spent working together, the more effective the team, the better the results, the fewer the mistakes.

60. Humility and modesty are in — except when what is called for is a fearsome, mad-dog litigator fighter who strikes fear into the hearts of opponents.

---

61. Never take credit for someone else's work.

---

62. Talking is easy. Actions require effort and commitment. So act and grow.

---

63. 'Murphy's Law' — 'If anything can go wrong, it usually will.' And usually at the worst possible time.' The world over, Murphy is alive and well and as disruptive as ever. (An American observation that has universal application.)

---

64. If everything is going exceptionally well, chances are you have forgotten to do something. Whatever it was, anticipate the possible consequences.

65. Avoid trouble you cannot remedy by noon the next day.

66. Never put anything in writing that you would not want to see in a newspaper the next day — one of my mother's favourite sayings. And these days, the terms 'writing' and 'newspaper' should be expanded to include emails, Internet, faxes, blogs, chatrooms, short message services, newsletters, radio, TV and phones (landline, mobile, satellite). *Nothing communicated is private these days* — from eavesdroppers to hackers, to punching the Send button by mistake, to . . .

67. Be adaptable. Maintain the capacity to respond to different situations as they arise. Have a Plan B and even a Plan C, just in case. You can't predict the future, but you can prepare and be ready for it. Never leave yourself without somewhere to go, even if it is backwards. (A lesson from my Navy days.)

68. The unexpected always happens sooner or later. Anticipate and prepare for it. Train yourself to deal with 'What if' situations, including worst-case scenarios.

69. You have capabilities and limits, strengths and weaknesses. Recognize which is which in you. You can do a lot but not everything. But don't stop trying.

70. Never, never, never belittle or disrespect another person's religion, ethnicity, culture, traditions, language, family, physical appearance, dreams, beliefs honestly held, intelligence (or lack thereof), or their choices of dress, music, art, food, drink, politics, transport or mate(s).

71. Remember who and what you are. In your day-to-day conduct, preserve your dignity and integrity. Always do yourself, the Firm and our profession proud.

72. Have personal and professional goals, and do what must be done to achieve them. Having done so, then set new goals. Have dreams, too, and work towards them. **If you give up your dreams, you die.**

73. If you don't keep up, you will be left behind. In this very competitive world in which we live and work and learn, being left behind can mean failure. Continuing Legal Education (CLE), either formal or informal, is in your best interests. It may be required by your Bar Association/Law Society, or not. How to keep up? Read; ask for and attend training courses, whether training be self-help, in-house, or outside; get colleagues and even clients to teach you. Look, see, listen, ask, use your imagination to find ways to stay ahead and not fall behind.

74. Lawyers, directly or indirectly, have power. Power itself is neutral. Power may command fear, but it does not engender respect. Respect has to be earned. Use power only for good. Do not abuse power or be swayed by its 'Dark Side.'

75. Search for wisdom. Knowledge is not wisdom. Information is not knowledge.

76. Have a sense of humour. Be able to laugh at yourself and at the humorous side of your matter. Take your tasks seriously but don't take yourself too seriously. *Laugh at least four times a day and at yourself at least twice a day.* Laughter is a marvellous stress and depression antidote.

77. Every action taken by a person is logical to him/her. I have learned from decades of working in cross-cultural environments that this is a truth, whether you think so or not. Find the starting point of that logic and then you will see the path to understanding the 'why' of their action.

78. You must have patience, imperturbability, understanding, and diplomacy to handle the delicacies of a cross-cultural challenge — and not all local citizens or expatriates are the same.

79. Eye contact is always important, though in some cultures it may be considered impolite or even hostile. Know your cultures.

80. When you play, play hard. When you work, don't play at all. It is preferable if work can be play and play can be work.

81. Everything has its place and everything belongs in its place. That way you can always find what you are looking for when you want or need it. (One of the many lessons I learned in the US Navy.)

82. To minimize disappointment, if you must do business with friends, relatives, or even loved ones, insist that the relationship be businesslike and professional. Try not to rely on trust alone.

83. Finding a good business partner is ten times more difficult than finding a good spouse. One of my law school professors at Hastings College of the Law (San Francisco, California) taught us this. I have lived to see that axiom proven many times over.

84. Know your 'enemy.' Never underestimate your adversary or overestimate or revel in your own abilities. 'Bad guys' are often smart, clever and very adept at deception and diversion. Be thoroughly prepared to face them effectively. By the way, opposing counsel, if acting professionally and ethically, is a rival. Counsel is not necessarily the enemy, though he/she may represent the enemy.

85. Know the difference between skill and luck. But know that without luck, at the right time, skill alone might not be enough to win the day. Napoleon knew this when he said, Give me lucky generals'. Coincidentally, as I alluded to earlier, don't rely on miracles to save you.

86. Control your temper. Anger must not cloud your better judgment. Besides, 'You catch more flies with sugar than you do with vinegar' — one of my mother's favourite sayings. Self-discipline is the key.

87. Life is full of risks and pains as well as ecstasies and satisfactions. *Take risks; calculated ones.* Taking no risks means no progress, no loves, no achievements, no glory, no 'Well Done.' So do surge forward but don't be foolhardy about it. And remember — sometimes you are the statue, and sometimes you are the pigeon.

88. When you decide to act, think first, if there is time, and then act rationally and calmly. Put your mind in gear before you put your mouth, or these days your fingers, in motion. This may mean, after reflection, you could decide that it is appropriate to go with your gut feeling, your instincts, your training.

89. You will have to make decisions. Some will be easy, some difficult, some will be grave, and some will be critical. Do not be reluctant to do so, even knowing that whether right or wrong, you are responsible for your decisions. Make the decision. If you make a decision which is wrong, recognize your error and make another decision to correct your course. You and the others affected thereby will have to live with those decisions, so carry that responsibility well.

90. You will make mistakes, you will have failures and setbacks. We all do. Admit them. You learn more from what you do wrong than what you do right. Get up and immediately get on with the job. Denying mistakes and your failures or hiding them leads only to consternation, and that misguided effort will come back to bite you much more viciously than the original error.

91. Never burn your bridges behind you. If you end up in hell, you will want a clear way back from whence you came.

92. Know when to back off, slow down, retrace your steps, or embark on a strategic advance in another direction. And know when to press home your advantage with vigour. (Another lesson from the US Navy.)

93. Never be boring or one-dimensional. A thorough knowledge of the law and honed skills in its practice alone do not make you an interesting, complete or well-rounded person. Get a life. Have hobbies. Read everything. Engage in a variety of activities other than the law. Be agile. Keep abreast of current events, of scientific, military, political, social, ethical, media, legal, and legislative developments. Participate in family-, cultural-, academic-, community-, spiritual-, sports-, fitness-, environmental-, conservation-, musical-, artistic-, travel-, cross-cultural-, welfare-, entrepreneurial-, and other people-and-planet-saving-orientated activities. Learn the techniques of effective negotiation, mediation, public speaking and storytelling. Learn how to protect and defend yourself and your family and to survive in dangerous or extraordinary circumstances.

94. Look after your health and fitness, mind, body and spirit. Protect your eyes — only one set per customer. Don't try to save money on footwear — use only good quality foot-supporting shoes. Many maladies have been traced to originate from neglected teeth — check yours often and replace all the metal in your mouth with modern dental resin composites. Make quality of your life a goal. Yes, exercise regularly. Do all that good stuff like cut down on caffeine, Blackberry and TV dependence; limit alcohol intake, avoid smoking and drugs. Eat your

veggies and fruits and proteins, take supplements. Meditate. Consider alternative and complementary medicine. Most important for a long, healthy and happy life is to find, give, share, and cherish love, compassion, companionship and relationships.

IV. The Firm

95. The Firm's reputation is its brand, its most important asset, as is each lawyer's own reputation. Promote, enhance and protect such reputations, such brands. They take years to build, but only seconds to damage or destroy.

96. Clients must be and must remain convinced that they have come to the right law firm to have their problems solved, and that you and your colleagues are the right lawyers to do so. Convince them by word and by deed.

97. Clients are clients of the Firm, not of any individual lawyer. This is admittedly a controversial proposition. The only possible exception is when the client is in a 'bet the company' bind and selects a specific named lawyer of known reputation to represent him/her/them.

98. Love the Firm's clients like you love the law. If you treat them right, existing clients will give you far more work more often than new clients and at far less cost to the Firm to obtain such work.

99. Our Firm has its own culture that is unique and stands us apart from our competitors. Tilleke & Gibbins is a multiservice (not a full-service) law firm with many specialities. Adopt as your own and adhere to the Firm's *Mission Statement, Creed and Rules, and Standards of Conduct* in both letter and, particularly, in spirit. Live them; breathe them. They set our Firm's business strategy and define our values, our strategic objectives, who we are and what we stand for.

To compete effectively, we must provide value added to our clients that is not provided by others.

100. Look after your subordinates and colleagues in the Firm, and have confidence in them if they have earned your trust; always treat them with sincerity, understanding, patience, humour, and humanity; be there to support them when they need help; preserve their dignity and they will reciprocate in return — except for those few self-centred malcontents who, no matter what you do, are hopeless losers or disrupters! But try.

101. As the leader of our Firm, I demand of each and every person in the Firm, or who otherwise works for me — *and they can all expect the same from me in return — total and absolute integrity, loyalty, respect, honesty and trustworthiness* to me, to the Firm, to our clients, to the courts, and to themselves. Constructive criticism courteously presented falls within the orbit of this law. Occasionally, forgiveness for lapses might be possible, perhaps, but otherwise no exceptions.

102. Anyone who deliberately hurts the Firm or our T&G family will be pursued without end. Time and expense will not be impediments to my retribution. The head of the house protects his family.

103. The Firm is a family, your family, which means you have family responsibilities and obligations in addition to benefits, protections and rewards. You can not enjoy the latter without dedication to the former. The Firm is not a charity, so perform up to standard or be prepared for the weight of the family to come down hard on you. You do not want to find yourself ostracized for letting down the family, do you?

V. The Last Law

104. When the practice of the law stops being fun, it's time to seek a new line of work.

VI. Okay, One Final Law

105. I find **lawyer jokes** (or should I say antilawyer jokes) tiresome and uncouth. My favourite rebuke to the vacuous purveyors of such tripe — best told for maximum effect in a large gathering — is the following: A good accountant might be able to save your fortune. A good doctor can save your life. A good clergyman might even be able to save your soul. But only a good lawyer (pause) can save your ass (arse)!

You are welcome to use this retort, with attribution to me of course! The impact is stupendous if you get the timing right.

Epilogue

So now you have a significant portion of my accumulated, and I hope sage, advice, my passions, and perhaps some wisdom, such as it is, about you and your practice of the law. This has been my purpose, my grand strategy, my edifice.

As I now begin to fade into a phased retirement — remember, I graduated from university in 1958, law school in 1962, and commenced full-time with Tilleke & Gibbins in 1967 — my endurance and stamina are waning and I am reaching the age of becoming venerable. That means I can preach *LLL* from the vantagepoint of experience and sincerity.

Call *Lyman's Laws for Lawyers* my legacy to the people of T&G, present and future, as well as to the legal profession, all of whom, and which, have provided me with boundless satisfaction. Not for one moment have I regretted my choices for my professional lives, civilian and military; my international upbringing; my life and long residence in Thailand; my schooling, travels, friends, diversions, avocations, hobbies, wives, loves and life experiences. May you be so fortunate!

Respectfully,

David Lyman
Chairman & Chief Values Officer
Tilleke & Gibbins
Advocates & Solicitors since 1890

Tilleke & Gibbins International Ltd
20th–26th Floors, Supalai Grand Tower
1011 Rama 3 Road, Kwaeng Chongnonsi
Khet Yannawa, Bangkok 10120, Thailand

Tel: +66 2653 5555
Fax: +66 2653 5678
Email: david.l@tillekeandgibbins.com
Website: www.tillekeandgibbins.com

Tilleke & Gibbins International's Board of Directors. Above from the left: Don Jones, Tiziana Sucharitkul, David Lyman, Clayton Hebbard and Santhapat Periera. Insets from the left: Daniel Credazzi and Darani Vachanavuttivong.

Appendix IV

Tilleke & Gibbins Staff

Trademark Section of Intellectual Property Department of Tilleke & Gibbins Bangkok.

Chief Operating Officer's Office, Finance & Accounting, Information Technology, Computer Support & Records Management and Filing Departments of Tilleke & Gibbins Bangkok.

Human Resources, Office and Facilities Services, Library, Publications, Legal Translation and Textiles Departments of Tilleke & Gibbins Bangkok.

Intellectual Property Enforcement and Patent Sections of Tilleke & Gibbins Bangkok.

Corporate & Commercial Department of Tilleke & Gibbins Bangkok.

Chairman's Office and Dispute Resolution Department of Tilleke & Gibbins Bangkok — the dogs are our Guard Assistants.

Above: *Tilleke & Gibbins Phuket.*
Left: *Tilleke & Gibbins Hanoi, Vietnam.*
Below: *Tilleke & Gibbins Ho Chi Minh, Vietnam.*

T&G Group of Companies Staff Names List

Chairman's Office

Mrs Anongporn Thanachaiary
Dr Charoen Kanthawongs
Mr Clayton Hebbard
Mr Daniel Credazzi
Mr David Lyman
Ms Khwanrutai Apaiso
Ms Phet Wongwan
Mr Pittaya Charoenpanich
Mr Rungroj Kongpermpul
Mr Suchart Kaocharoen
Mr Teeraponl Waiphip

Computer Support & Records Management

Computer Support
Mr Nuttaphong Sakathong
Mrs Pachuen Varapongsittikul
Ms Praorn Tandhavadhana
Mr Sasawin Suesat

Records Management
Mr Anucha Sawasdee
Ms Chintana Boonrawd

Corporate & Commercial

Commercial
Ms Charunun Sathitsuksomboon
Mr Chinachart Vatanasuchart
Mr Dussadee Rattanopas
Mr John Fotiadis
Ms Khanittha Khunkhamta
Mr Michael C. Yukubousky
Ms Monthaya Puenpha
Miss Nirada Tayananuphat
Ms Pimvimol Vipamaneerut
Ms Pongphan Narasin
Mrs Punvadee Roongpitakmana
Ms Rattana Thamarasri
Mr Santhapat Periera
Ms Sriwan Puapondh
Ms Waewpen Piemwichai
Mr Yingyong Karnchanapayap

Corporate
Mr Alongkorn Tongmee
Mr Anake Rattanajitbanjong
Mr Chaiwat Keratisuthisathorn
Ms Chorrat Anantachaisil
Ms Juraiwan Pattanakul
Ms Kasinee Suwannagudt
Mr Kobkit Thienpreecha
Ms Ladda Phenpol
Ms Piyanuj Ratprasatporn
Mrs Ratana Kanyaratanamongkol
Mr Roosdee Sare
Ms Thidarat Nitiamorn
Ms Ubolratana Sitakalin
Mrs Vilailuck Choenakson
Ms Wanida Sangsai
Mr Weerawat Distapinyo

General
Ms Penrurk Phetmani
Mr Pornchai Srisawang
Ms Siwaporn Saen-Glar
Ms Yupin Sangsrianantalert

Japanese Clients Development
Mrs Cynthia M. Pornavalai
Mr Pongpetch Tanomsilp
Mr Torajiro Ohashi

Dispute Resolution

Mr Buncha Suparmesit
Mr Chitchai Punsan
Mr Chusert Supasitthumrong
Ms Hathainun Prancharoen
Mr Ittirote Klinboon
Mr Kasamesunt Teerasitsathaporn
Mr Kornkieat Chunhakasikarn
Ms Marisa Maturim
Mr Michael Ramirez
Mr Noppadon Treepetchara
Ms Nuanchun Somboonvinij
Ms Panwadi Maniwat
Ms Pranee Sae-Oung
Mrs Sally V. Mouhim
Mr Sarawut Khongman
Mrs Sasirusm B. Chunhakasikarn
Mr Suthi Kaewso

Mr Thanawat Dilokvipakskul
Mr Thawat Damsa-ard
Ms Titima Boonviwat
Ms Tiziana Sucharitkul
Mr Ukrit Petpichetchian
Ms Wandee Pattrawee
Ms Wanlapa Wisutsuwan

Finance & Accounting

Accounting
Ms Atinuch Kewpaisal
Ms Chuthamas Kongnoi
Mrs Daranee Panpunya
Mrs Jantrarat Thaecharvongvanich
Mr Khomsit Katasila
Mrs Maneerat Nodthaisong
Ms Ni-orn Chinniyompanich
Mr Panawat Promcharee
Mr Patompong Treepech
Ms Phaweena Wechwimol
Ms Porntip Chuaythaisong
Ms Ratchanee Boonchay
Ms Salukjit Jantasom
Ms Suphansa Makklean
Ms Surawadee Leethaweekul
Ms Thitikan Lerttawewut
Ms Uma Jantratip
Ms Warawan Chanyangam
Mrs Watchanee Palangvitvatana

Billing
Ms Duangrat Namkainun
Ms Jeeranai Kalachukr
Ms Nittanart Chareonsuk
Mrs Orathai Saengthong
Ms Paijit Nunthaputtipong
Ms Penpaka Pimsan
Ms Somphorn Khaekhunthod
Ms Uamduan Wongkriangsakul
Ms Wichuda Jungwarawich

Credit
Ms Kulathida Pattamachit
Mr. Somkiat Nilpayak
Mr Sukprasert Trusanont
Ms Sumalee Rungsrinopakun
Ms Tatsanee Egsittishoo

Ms Vanida Kalyarat
Ms Wilawan Khaokhaen

Finance
Mrs Arisa Jiaravijit
Ms Patcharin Lertvongkornkit
Ms Sujin Jarutasanee
Mr Suttisak Vunnavittayasing

Human Resources

Mrs Arunrung Srithanuthammakul
Ms Kanodrat Pangsang
Mrs Sairoung Punthumaphol
Ms Suvimol Sae-Eaib
Ms Suwannee Likitanantachai
Mrs Wannee Pipattanachaiyapong
Ms Watcharee Wangchaisoonthorn

Information Technology

Infrastructure & Security
Ms Nualparn Srifa
Mr Patipat Sorranakhom
Mr Puttapol Pisarnmahasombut
Mr Somchit Tophun

Software Development & Database
Mr Issara Charunet
Mr Nattawut Maitreesittikorn
Mr Nawapon Patyen
Ms Nawarat Chullasang
Mr Nithi Juabsamai
Mr Sathien Sreechaisantikun
Mr Siripong Siripin
Mr Sittadej Cheaujedton
Mr Weekit Boonkhun
Mr Worapol Satirakul

Intellectual Property

Intellectual Property
Mr Alan Adcock
Ms Angkana Kanokchanya
Ms Areeya Ratanayu
Mr Christopher Anderson
Ms Clemence Gautier
Mrs Hassana Chira-Aphakul
Ms Inthupim Chokwaranun
Mr Kawin Kanchanapairoj
Ms Lukkanaporn Yampol
Mr Nandana Indananda

Mr Nuttaphol Arammuang
Mr Pakorn Dhirawaranan
Ms Panpilai Seehatrakul
Mrs Parichart Monaiyakul
Mr Pathom Wawson
Mrs Piraya Sindhusake
Ms Samonwan Srisomboon
Ms Sarannush Luangsiritanya
Ms Sineenat Treemankha
Ms Siraprapha Rungpry
Ms Sirirat Chaipanyalert
Mr Srila Thongklang
Mr Suebsiri Taweepon
Ms Sukontip Jitmongkolthong
Ms Sumana Tangtragoon
Ms Sutruedee Suwansawat
Mr Titirat Wattanachewanopakorn
Mr Vasan Sun
Ms Wanna Sukasem
Ms Wiramrudee Mokkhavesa
Ms Yuwadee Thean-ngarm

Patent
Ms Ajcharee Musiko
Mr Akarit Deemark
Ms Ampolphan Sriduangchan
Ms Aungkana Kiatkamolkul
Mr Chatchai Siricheepchaiyan
Ms Chayathorn Sandos
Ms Chirapa Kaewman
Ms Chuanpit Jindathip
Ms Duangdao Tipwangmake
Ms Dussadee Kittirotyothin
Mrs Jitluedee Siemanond
Mr Kanin Junthimathorn
Ms Kanjana Pumichatpong
Mr Nachit Vimantip
Ms Nontarom Vichaikijkul
Mr Pairat Jatuten
Ms Panarat Incheng
Ms Piriya Phoowanitlawan
Ms Pornpimol Aroonsirirat
Ms Praphatsorn Jaimun
Mr Prateep Naboriboon
Ms Radeemada Mungkarndee
Ms Saranrat Ounjit
Mrs Sirilak Imtongnuch
Ms Sonthaya Sunkapongse
Mr Surachai Sridech
Mr Surachet Tobundit
Ms Thaneeya Lalitkulthorn
Ms Titikaan Ungbhakorn

Ms Usa Dukphummarin
Mr Verasuk Sangsri
Mr Washirawit Walailaksanaporn

Trademark
Ms Ampaiwan Puttharak
Ms Benjamas Wongwanitsil
Mrs Benjawan Chunhachatrachai
Mr Burapha Langkasit
Mrs Chidchanok Nopparat
Mrs Darani Vachanavuttivong
Ms Daroonwan Siripornanan
Mr Ditthapong Kittithanutphum
Ms Hiranrat Chakartnarodom
Ms Jarima Thumkeungsuradej
Mr Jirawat Sermfang
Ms Jitnapa Bunyavan
Ms Jutharat Sukudom
Ms Kasama Sriwatanakul
Ms Ketsarin Buaroy
Ms Kevalee Akkaraviboon
Ms Khamanut Prajaktheeranon
Ms Kittiphan Khattiwiriyaphinyo
Ms Knokporn Pingmoy
Mr Kongkiat Ongsanthia
Mr Kumphon Phaladikanon
Ms Laddawan Klinsopon
Mrs Manisara Wiboonchai
Ms Natchaya Pinthanon
Ms Nawawan Intarapintuwat
Mr Niti Pattaranitiwatee
Ms Nutchaya Khongton
Ms Pannapa Rittinaphakorn
Mr Panupong Thamthavorn
Mrs Pattama Tavichai
Mr Peerapon Pantham
Ms Pimrapas Pattaraboonchaikul
Mr Pisit Kijvorasakulchai
Mr Pittaya Rattanatraivirat
Ms Porhathai Kongsut
Ms Prasipha Phatthana-Olarn
Ms Ruchiya Chuenchomrat
Mr Rungroj Kobkitwattanakul
Ms Saijai Moonthongchun
Mr Siripong Siriworanark
Ms Siriwan Phentalay
Mr Somboon Earterasarun
Ms Sunisa Trakulwongveera
Mr Sunti Sornsombut
Mrs Supatra Watanavorakitkul
Mr Thapakorn Sangkajit
Ms Thida Nopvoraprasert

Ms Thidawan Sirikul
Mr Thiwakorn Chantee
Ms Threenuch Chatmahasuwan
Mrs Varunee Pechsri
Ms Vassana Wattanapannigorn
Mr Visith Saensrikaew
Ms Wanwarang Trimanka
Mr Wiwat Nopparat
Mr Yooparach Ratangsu

Legal Translation

Ms Ame-on Budhaka
Ms Chutima Techapiroon
Ms Russirin Charoenpithaya
Mr Sakon Sookkho
Ms Sorawan Jirayusakun
Mrs Uruphan Benjarurawong
Mr Wathit Ueam-itsarayothin

Library

Ms Kirataya Suktongsa
Ms Piyanut Charoonpongsak
Mrs Supattanun Nuchanart
Mrs Yupin Srivichien

Office & Facilities Services

Ms Achara Tunsuppapol
Mr Adisak Khajonpan
Mr Apichat Arunpoolsap
Ms Chanikan Phongoen
Mr Julladit Mathuraton
Mr Kreangsak Huntrakull
Mr Narongsak Ornon
Ms Panida Tongwattana
Ms Pattranuch Likitverawong
Ms Sai Hongthong
Mrs Siriyupar Niemhom
Ms Suchada Bunsopahk
Ms Sucheera Bumrungpetch
Ms Sunisa Maneemann
Ms Surat Primanont
Mrs Thiparat Buranaphan
Mr Thongsuk Thanthong

Regulatory Affairs

Ms Naiyana Sinlapawisut
Mr Pairoj Osatapirat
Mr Paul G. Russell

Ms Pawika Chittaratana
Ms Phanwasa Boonsong
Ms Piyanant Thanasukit
Mr Somboon Wongwisuthdhikasem
Mr Tawil Juntapetch
Ms Thanyawan Looknok
Ms Thitima Rodchuey

Publications & Public Relations

Mr Andrew Stoutley
Ms Angkana Sawangroj
Ms Chayanuch Srichumsin
Ms Wanpen Puangmaha

Support Services

Mr Don Jones
Mrs Nuntawan Jaroonpipatkul

Textiles

Ms Linda S. McIntosh
Ms Wipawee Tiyawes

Partner & Director — Phuket

Mr John R. Howard

Phuket Office

Ms Chanitnan Chankhreung
Mrs Chanyavat Nuanjun
Mr Daniel Hyams
Ms Janpen Issalam
Ms Jirawan Taepongsorat
Ms Orathai Thongmee
Ms Panadda Peloha
Mr Phamorn Intra
Mr Timothy A. Taylor
Ms Walailak Phairoh

Partner & Director — Vietnam

Mr John E. King

Accounting — Vietnam

Mrs Ha Thu Truong
Ms Thuy Thi Bich Le
Ms Tra Thi Phuong Ho
Ms Yen Hai Nguyen

Commercial — Vietnam

Ms Doan Thi Minh Phuong
Mr Gocho Fumikazu
Mrs Hoang Thi Kim Tran
Mr Kien Trung Trinh
Mr Michael Kuman Lee
Ms Nhu Thi Thanh Dinh
Mr Thang Nhat Nguyen
Mr Thao H. Cung
Mrs Thom Thi Mai Nguyen
Ms Tra Thanh Nguyen
Ms Tu Ngoc Trinh

Intellectual Property — Vietnam

Mrs Dung Thi Kim Vu
Mr Dzung Duy Nguyen
Mr Hieu Trung Duong
Ms Huyen Thi Thanh Pham
Ms Jennifer Sloan
Ms Minh Thi Dieu Nguyen
Mrs Nga Thi Phi Nguyen
Mrs Ngoc Minh Le
Mr Thang Duc Nguyen
Mr Thomas Treutler
Ms Trang Thi Thu Nguyen
Mrs Tuyen Thi Hong Le

Support Services — Vietnam

Ms Binh Thi Thanh Vu
Mrs Chau Thi Minh Nguyen
Mr Dan Gia Pham
Ms Hien Thi Nguyen
Mrs Lan Thi Ngoc Pham
Ms Lien Thuy Vo
Ms Ly Thi Minh Nguyen
Ms Minh Thi Nguyen
Ms Thuy Thi Thu Ha
Mrs Tu Thien Le

Appendix V

Tilleke & Gibbins
Long-standing Clients

1926 - 1981

IN GRATEFUL APPRECIATION
TO
THE THORESEN GROUP
OF COMPANIES
FOR UTILIZING
OUR LEGAL SERVICES
FOR OVER 55 YEARS,
OUR LONGEST CONTINUOUS
ATTORNEY-CLIENT RELATIONSHIP.

TILLEKE & GIBBINS
ADVOCATES AND SOLICITORS
BANGKOK, THAILAND
DECEMBER 1981

Plaque presented to the Thoresen group of companies in recognition of being a long-standing client of Tilleke & Gibbins.

Over 70 Years

Allen & Gledhill
Asamura Patent Office, p.c.
Barker Brettell LLP
Berli Jucker & Company
British American Tobacco p.l.c.
Diethelm Travel (Thailand) Ltd.
Drew & Napier LLC
General Electric Company
Gill Jennings & Every
GlaxoSmithKline
The Goodyear Tire & Rubber Company
Hulse & Co.
Internationaal Octrooibureau B.V.
Lysaght & Co.
Mitsubishi Corporation
Muelhens GmbH & Co. KG.
Nestle Products (Thailand) Inc.
Ohshima and Company
Ohshima Patent Office
Pepsico, Inc.
Philip Morris Management Corp.
Philips Intellectual Property & Standards
Remfry & Sagar
Sugimura International Patent & Trademark Agency Bureau
Thoresen & Co., Ltd.
Trade Mark Owners Association Limited (TMOA)
Wenping & Co.
Wm. Wrigley Jr. Company
Zacco Norway AS

Over 60 Years

Abelman, Frayne & Schwab
Alcan International Limited
Asamura Patent Office
Cabinet Beau de Lomenie
Cerebos (Thailand) Limited
Donaldson & Burkinshaw
D Young & Co.
Ladas & Parry
Marks & Clerk LLP

Over 50 Years

Abbott Laboratories
AB Electrolux
American Chamber of Commerce in Thailand
Armeco Trademark Services B.V.
Australian Embassy
A.W. Metz & Co. AG
Boult, Wade & Tennant
Bugnion S.A.
Cadbury Schweppes plc
Darby & Darby P.C.
Dennemeyer & Associates S.A.
F.E. Zuellig (Bangkok) Ltd.
F. Hoffmann-La Roche Ltd.
Five Pagodas Pharmacy Co., Ltd.
f J Cleveland LLP
FMC Corporation
Fross Zelnick Lehrman & Zissu, P.C.
General Mills
The Gillette Company

Gottlieb, Rackman & Reisman, P.C.

Hale and Dorr LLP

Hanabusa Patent Office

Infosuisse Information Horlogère et Industrielle

Jacobacci & Partners

Kimberly-Clark Worldwide, Inc.

Kishimoto & Co.

Kraft Foods Global Inc.

Kyowa Patent and Law Office

Linklaters LLP

Louis, Pohlau, Lohrentz

Maersk Bangkok Branch & Related Maersk Line Companies

Mathys & Squire LLP

Matsubara, Muraki & Associates

Meldau-Strauss-Flototto Patentanwalte

Merz Group Services GmbH

Pfizer Inc.

Rechtsanwalte Dornheim und Giersch

Revlon, Inc.

Rohm GmbH & Co. KG

SANDOZ AG

Seiwa Patent & Law (the former A. Aoki, Ishida & Associates)

SKF Group Headquarters

SKF (Thailand) Limited

Soprintel, S.A.

Stevens Hewlett & Perkins

Suzuye & Suzuye

Taisho Pharmaceutical Co., Ltd.

UCB S.A.

Volkswagen AG

Von Maltitz, Derenberg, Kunin Janssen & Giordano

Weickmann & Weickmann Patentanwalte

Wella Aktiengesellschaft

Wood, Herron & Evans, L.L.P.

Wood, Phillips, Katz, Clark & Mortimer

Yoshihara & Co.

Select Bibliography

Antonio, J., *The 1904 Traveller's Guide to Bangkok and Siam* (reprint, Bangkok, 1997).

Baker, Chris and Phongpaichit, Pasuk, *A History of Thailand.* (Cambridge, 2005).

Bartlett, Norman, *Land of the Lotus-Eaters* (London, 1959).

Bock, Carl, *Temples and Elephants* (reprint, Bangkok, 1986).

Bradley, William L., *Siam Then* (New York, 1981).

Buls, Charles, *Siamese Sketches* (reprint, Bangkok, 1994).

Carter, A. Cecil, ed., *The Kingdom of Siam 1904* (Bangkok, 1988).

Chakrabongse, Prince Chula, *Lords of Life* (London, 1960).

Fournereau, Lucien, *Bangkok in 1892* (reprint, Bangkok, 1992).

Gilchrist, Andrew, *Bangkok Top Secret* (London, 1970).

Hoskin, John, *The British Club 1903–2003* (Bangkok, 2003).

Insor, D., *Thailand: A Political, Social and Economic Analysis* (London, 1963).

Jottrand, Mr and Mrs Emile, *In Siam* (reprint, Bangkok, 1996).

Kornerup, Ebbe, *Friendly Siam* (reprint, Bangkok, 1999).

Krull, Germain, *Bangkok: Siam's City of Angels* (London, 1964).

Maugham, Somerset, *The Gentleman in the Parlour* (London, 1930).

Phongpaichit, Pasuk and Baker, Chri, *Thailand's Boom and Bust* (Chiang Mai, 1998).

Reynolds, Jack, *A Sort of Beauty* (London, 1956, later reissued as *A Woman of Bangkok*).

Smithies, Michael, ed., *Descriptions of Old Siam* (Singapore, 1995).

Smithies, Michael, *Old Bangkok* (Singapore, 1986).

Smyth, H. Warington, *Five Years in Siam* (reprint, Bangkok, 1994).

Sparrow, Gerald, *Lawyer at Large* (London, 1960).

Thompson, Virginia, *Thailand: The New Siam* (New York, 1941).

Tips, Walter E.J., *Crime and Punishment in King Chulalongkorn's Kingdom* (reprint, Bangkok, 1998).

Tips, Walter E.J., *Siam's Struggle for Survival* (reprint, Bangkok, 1996).

Warren, William, *Bangkok* (London, 2002).

Warren, William, *Celebrating 100 Years: The Royal Bangkok Sports Club* (Bangkok, 2001).

Waugh, Alec, *Bangkok* (London, 1970).

Wood, W.A.R., *Consul in Paradise* (London, 1965).

Wright, Arnold and Breakspear, Oliver T., eds, *Twentieth Century Impressions of Siam* (London, 1908).

Wyatt, David K., *Thailand: A Short History* (London, 1984).

Acknowledgments

The publisher would like to thank the following people and institutions for their help and assistance in the preparation of this book. Our thanks go to Ann Sorensen; Jane Jennings; Joan Atkinson; Steve Van Beek; Pren Wiramanayake; Dilok Gunatilaka; Derek Guna-Tilaka; Thipvibha Guna-Tilaka; Richard Baker; Leon Schadeberg; Swalee Siriphol; Somsri Hansirisawasdi, The Oriental Bangkok; Veronica Isaac and Mary Eliades, Neilson Hays Library; Ian Proud, British Embassy, Bangkok; Jinda Promduang, BNH Hospital; Nunt Buranasiri, The Royal Bangkok Sports Club; Jane Puranananda, The James H.W. Thompson Foundation; Bangkok Post; The British Club; National Archives of Thailand and Fine Arts Department; Christ Church; American Chamber of Commerce; Rotary International; Prince Damrong Museum; Court Museum of Thailand; The State Attorney Museum; Father Ray Foundation and Siam Commercial Bank.

Produced for Tilleke & Gibbins International Ltd by

Mark Standen Publishing Co. Ltd
14/1 Ramkhamhaeng Soi 30/1 (Yaek 2)
Huamark, Bangkapi, Bangkok 10240, Thailand
Tel: +66 2732 9366   Fax: +66 2732 9367
Email: mark@markstandenpublishing.com
Website: www.markstandenpublishing.com

Copyright 2010, Tilleke & Gibbins International Ltd
20th–26th Floors, Supalai Grand Tower
1011 Rama 3 Road, Kwaeng Chongnonsi
Khet Yannawa, Bangkok 10120, Thailand
Tel: +66 2653 5555   Fax: +66 2653 5678
Email: bangkok@tillekeandgibbins.com
Website: www.tillekeandgibbins.com

All rights reserved. No part of this publication may be reproduced, stored in a retrieval system or transmitted in any form or by any means, electronic, mechanical, photocopying, recording or otherwise, without the prior written permission of Tilleke & Gibbins International Ltd.

ISBN 978-974-307-409-7

AUTHOR
John Hoskin

PHOTOGRAPHER
Mark Standen

DESIGNERS
Sanskrit Kritskom
Nattawan Sujarit Jaga

EDITOR
Keith Hardy

PRINTED AND BOUND IN SINGAPORE BY
Tien Wah Press PTE